Instructor's I
to accompany
Corporate Communication

Second Edition

Paul A. Argenti
Dartmouth College

Boston   Burr Ridge, IL   Dubuque, IA   Madison, WI   New York   San Francisco   St. Louis
Bangkok   Bogotá   Caracas   Lisbon   London   Madrid
Mexico City   Milan   New Delhi   Seoul   Singapore   Sydney   Taipei   Toronto

Irwin/McGraw-Hill

A Division of The McGraw-Hill Companies

Instructor's Manual to accompany
CORPORATE COMMUNICATION

Copyright ©1998 by The McGraw-Hill Companies, Inc. All rights reserved.
Previous edition 1995 by Richard D. Irwin, a Times Mirror Higher Education company.
Printed in the United States of America.
The contents of, or parts thereof, may be reproduced for use with
CORPORATE COMMUNICATION
Paul A. Argenti
provided such reproductions bear copyright notice and may be reproduced in
any form for any other purpose without permission of the publisher.

2 3 4 5 6 7 8 9 0 HAM/HAM 9 0 9

ISBN 0-07-289607-8

http://www.mhhe.com

Preface

Welcome to the second edition of Corporate Communication. For those of you who are familiar with the first edition, you will notice that I have completely revised each of the chapters and have either revised older cases or added new ones for each chapter. Overall, the book reflects changes that you have asked for after teaching the material over the last few years. For those who are teaching the material for the first time, you will find that this manual offers you several different approaches to take depending on the specific needs of your students.

This instructor's manual will help you put together a corporate communication course that will make the best use of the material currently available. My hope, however, is that all instructors will create their own materials to personalize the course for the particular needs of their students.

This manual will first present alternative syllabi for instructors teaching 10-week and 15-week terms. For those of you who are teaching this as an adjunct to a Management Communication course, I have also created a modular approach to the material that makes the best use of the book. You will also find syllabi from colleagues teaching this material at other schools.

Following the syllabi, I have written notes for each chapter and case. My purpose is to give you information you can use to put together the best possible Corporate Communication course. Each of the case discussions will include information about different approaches to the material. Where appropriate, I have also included the "B" cases to distribute to your students.

Finally, each chapter will come with possible overhead transparencies to use when you teach the material for the first time. In addition, wherever possible, I have included addresses and phone numbers for you to get more information or materials about each chapter.

If all else fails, I hope that you will feel comfortable calling me personally to clarify things that are unclear, to answer questions that I didn't even think about, or just to talk about how to approach the subject for the first time. You can reach me by fax at **603-646-1308** or e-mail at **paul.argenti@dartmouth.edu** anytime. I will do my best to get back to you as soon as possible. You can also call me at **603-646-2983**. Please leave a message if I am not at my desk when you call.

I hope that you enjoy teaching corporate communication as much as I have over the last several years. Both undergraduate and graduate students as well as executives seem to enjoy learning the subject as much as I enjoy teaching and writing about it. My hope is that you will find the same to be true.

Contents

Syllabi for Corporate Communication Courses 1
    Syllabi for Corporate Communication 3
    Module Within a Management Communication Course 6
    Tuck's Corporate Communication Syllabus 9

Other Syllabi 13

Chapter by Chapter Notes 35

Chapter 1:	The Changing Environment for Business	37
	Hooker Chemical Company (B)	42
	Appendix	65
Chapter 2:	Communicating Strategically	72
	Fletcher Electronics Teaching Note	74
Chapter 3:	An Overview of the Corporate Communication Function	78
	Bank of Boston Teaching Note	81
	Bank of Boston (B)	83
Chapter 4:	Image and Identity	99
	GE Identity Program (B)	102
	Article—The Name Game: How Corporate Name Changes Affect Stock Price	108
	Article—Managing Corporate Identity	114
Chapter 5:	The Corporation Is the Message	120
Chapter 6:	Managing Media Relations`	123
	Adolph Coors Company (B)	128
	Source Perrier S. A. Media Role Play Exercise	137
Chapter 7:	A Random Walk Down Wall Street	142
	United Technologies (B)	149
	United Technologies Teaching Note	156
Chapter 8:	Communicating Internally	161
	Brown and Sharpe	167
	Brown and Sharpe (B)	183
Chapter 9:	Managing Government Affairs	194

v

Chapter 10:	Managing Communications in a Crisis	200
	Exxon U.S.A.	203
	Exxon U.S.A. Teaching Note	211
Appendix 1:	Sample Midterm and Final Exam	215
Appendix 2:	Overhead Transparencies for Each Chapter	225
Appendix 3:	Bibliography	277

Syllabi for
Corporate Communication Courses

Syllabi for Corporate Communication

Since many of you may be unfamiliar with how to put together a course on corporate communication, I would like to offer several different approaches based on my own experience and the experience of colleagues who currently use the text.

The first section offers three different ways to teach a Corporate Communication class: as a text for a ten week or quarter-long course with twenty sessions; as a 15-week, thirty session course; or as a module within a management communication course.

For a ten-week or quarter-long course with twenty sessions:

Day 1
Introduce the course and the concept of corporate communication. Have students read chapter 1 as preparation (except for Hooker Chemical) and the introduction (especially the "Note on the Case Method"). Lecture about the changing environment for business.

Days 2-4
Have students read a business-related novel such as Upton Sinclair's *The Jungle* or Sloane Wilson's *Man in the Grey Flannel Suit*. You can also assign a more contemporary novel such as Tom Wolfe's *Bonfire of the Vanities* or Christopher Buckley's *Thank You For Smoking*. I also try to give students the opportunity to contrast contemporary business views (as in *Bonfire*) with earlier views (as in *The Jungle*). The problem with a shorter course is that novels take so much time to process.

Instead, you can show students films (either in class or as an add-on) such as Oliver Stone's *Wall Street* or Danny DeVito's *Other People's Money*. And, you can mix genres by assigning one novel to show the earlier views (like *The Jungle*) and a contemporary film (like *Wall Street* or *Barbarians at the Gate*).

The purpose of these three days is to make the notion of the changing environment for business come alive. So, use whatever you can to get that point across. Television programs from the fifties such as Rod Serling's "Patterns" are now available on video and can be contrasted with something like "Thirtysomething" (which was running at press time on Lifetime network) to show business then and now.

I usually assign a portion of the novel or novels for each day, and discuss previously viewed films at the same time. These can be exciting classes if you like to teach literature and film. But even if you have never taught material like this, you can get discussion going quite easily with students. I found this to be particularly true for *The Jungle*, which I taught for the first time last year. The goal is to get students to see a different, often negative side of business.

All of the novels are readily available and the videotapes can be rented at most video outlets.

Day 5
Assign Hooker Chemical case. See detailed analysis following notes to chapter 1 for approach to take with this case. Distribute Hooker Chemical (B) at the end of this class (also at end of chapter one analysis).

Day 6
Discuss Hooker (B).

Day 7
Assign chapter two and get students talking about the use of strategy in communication overall. You may want to read Mary Munter's chapter on strategy in her *Guide to Managerial Communication* for a more thorough understanding. This book is available in its 4th edition from Prentice-Hall.

Day 8
Assign the Fletcher case. This case is analyzed in more detail later in this manual, but the purpose of the case is to get students to think strategically about basic corporate communication problems such as a change in procedures.

Day 9
Assign chapter 3. Discuss the notion of a unified corporate communication function. This would be a good day to invite a guest from a corporation that has such a function to talk to students about what it is like from the inside. The Bank of Boston case presents an example of a corporate communication function with low credibility under fire.

Day 10
Assign chapter four. Discuss image and identity. Another good day to invite a guest from a local design firm to talk about the real world.

Day 11
Assign GE case. This case presents students with an example from a major corporation to contrast with the lecture from the day before or the visitor from a local design firm. Distribute the "B" case toward the end of class.

Midterm: this is the best place for a midterm exam. See sample tests included as appendices at the end of the book.

Day 12
Assign chapter 5 and exercise following. So many corporate ads are currently running on television right now that you can simply tape the most recent ones from any of the three nightly network newscasts to enhance the exercise. I also clip corporate ads from magazines and put them onto overhead transparencies.

Day 13
Assign chapter 6 and the Coors case. This is a very rich class on media. I like it because it presents such a positive role model for the students. The actual *60 Minutes* broadcast is available from CBS or from Coors. Distribute Coors (B) at the end of the video for students to either read in class or take home and read for discussion the next day.

Day 14
Assign a reading such as Mary Munter's, "How to Conduct a Successful Media Interview," from California Management Review (510-642-7159). Distribute Source Perrier and follow instructions I provide later in this book.

Day 15
Assign chapter 7. This is definitely a day for a visitor from the financial community or the press if you do not feel comfortable dealing with the material on investor relations by yourself. I usually invite someone dealing with investor relations from a nearby corporation. Particularly in smaller public companies, you can find managers who wear this hat in addition to many others.

Day 16
Assign United Technologies case. Especially if your students have had financial accounting and/or finance, you will want to spend a class session talking about annual reports. If you want to use something real, collect a variety of reports as discussed later along with chapter 7.

Day 17
Assign chapter 8 and the Norwich Software case. Employee communications is such a hot area right now that you should have no trouble finding more recent and geographically-relevant examples on employee communications. See discussion later for more.

Day 18
Assign chapter 9. The Dodds case offers a disguised example of a "real world" problem that one company faced.

Day 19
Assign chapter 10 and the Dow Corning case. A very rich case. See my comments later in the manual for details.

Day 20
Conclusion. You may want to assign group projects at the beginning of the class and have them present on the final day. You can also play catch-up with the extra day I have given you. I find that I have usually fallen behind after a few weeks and like having this cushion.

For information on a possible final exam, see appendix 1 at the end of this manual.

15-Week, Thirty Session Syllabus:

The fifteen-week course of thirty sessions allows the instructor to explore the most important subjects in more detail. My suggestion is to focus longer on the changing environment for business and either add another novel or more films to the curriculum. The suggestions above under days 2-4 should help. I would probably add two more sessions for a total of six on the changing environment.

Similarly, I would focus more on media and invite a reporter to speak to students about what reporters look for when interviewing executives, how they put together stories, and perhaps even ask them to demonstrate. One of the most successful classes I had with a reporter was one in which the reporter interviewed a few of the students before the class, explained what her point of view was, and then wrote a story before her visit. The students received a copy of the story before class and were able to ask questions about how the final product emerged.

I would also add another session on crisis communication. Several public relations firms now have simulations that you may be able to use for an exciting session. Contact the local office of Burson-Marstellar or Hill and Knowlton or whatever the largest public relations firm in your area is and invite them to present. Or create a simulation out of local possibilities. For example, if you are in California, create a crisis simulation about earthquake evacuation in movie theaters.

We do not cover philanthropy in the short course so you can add a session on the subject in the longer version. You can find sources on corporate philanthropy in your business school library or through a search on Nexus or Lexus.

The other three sessions can give you an opportunity to focus on your area of expertise or interest. For example, if your school puts a great deal of emphasis on finance, I would spend more time on the investor relations function. If the emphasis for most students is on marketing, focus longer on corporate advertising. If you are teaching in a school of communication, you might want to add more sessions on media and so on. Allow a few extra days for oral presentations. You might also want an in-class midterm.

I have presented an outline below as a suggestion only. Feel free to change it as necessary.

Day 1:	Chapter 1 (except for Hooker)
Day 2-7:	Changing environment through film and literature
Day 8:	Hooker
Day 9:	Hooker B (you can easily spend two days on this case)
Day 10:	Fletcher Electronics case
Day 11:	Chapter 2

Day 12: Chapter 3 with Bank of Boston case
Day 13: Chapter 4
Day 14: GE case
Day 15: Chapter 5 with exercise
Day 16: Chapter 6, general discussion of media
Day 17: Coors case
Day 18: Reporter visits
Day 19: Source Perrier
Day 20: Chapter 7, with United Technologies case
Day 21: Visit from IR professional
Day 22: Chapter 8, with Norwich Software case
Day 23: Visit from HR communication specialist or Brown & Sharpe case
Day 24: Chapter 9 with Dodds case
Day 25: Chapter 10 with Dow Corning case
Day 26: Corporate Philanthropy
Day 27: McDonalds - HBS #9-391-108; focuses on the environment*
Day 28-30: Oral presentations on company research

*Phone number for Harvard case clearing house is (617) 495-6117

Module Within a Management Communication Course

You can also use the book as an add-on for any number of days to a basic management communication course. Several of the chapters group together quite nicely. For example, chapters 6 and 10 with either Coors or Dow Corning (or both) cover the area of media and crisis at the same time. Chapters 4 and 5 group together to talk about image, identity, and how corporations use advertising to transmit image. Chapter 2 can be used as an addition to a discussion about communication strategy at the microlevel. Chapters 1 and 3 pair together to give students a brief introduction to the entire area.

Basically, it depends on what you want to emphasize, how much time you have to devote to the subject, and what other materials you are currently using. I actually teach only five classes out of 20 in the introduction to ManComm course at Tuck and use Chapters 1-4, 6, and 10 which is 6 out of 10 chapters.

Here is a Possible Six-session Module

Session 1: Communication Strategy: chapter 2 plus Fletcher case
Session 2: Changing Environment: chapter 1 plus Hooker case
Session 3: Image and Identity: chapters 4 & 5 plus GE case or advertising exercise
Session 4: Media: chapter 6 with Coors case
Session 5: Media: Source Perrier exercise
Session 6: Crisis Communication: Dow Corning case

Here is How I Use the Material in Tuck's Management Communication Course

Session 1: What is Communication Strategy?

- Read:
  1. Munter, *Guide to Managerial Communication* (GMC), chapter 1
  2. Argenti, *Corporate Communication* (CC), chapter 2

- Be prepared to discuss the following five questions in class, based on the five sections in GMC, chapter 1. You are encouraged to work in study groups; groups should air all views, not seek to gain consensus.

  1. *Communicator strategy*: What was Van Dyke's objective? What management style did he use? What management style do you think he should have used? How would you analyze his credibility in this situation? How would you have enhanced your credibility if you had been Van Dyke?

  2. *Audience strategy*: Who was Van Dyke's audience? Who would you have included as an audience? How did he try to appeal to them in his letter? What specific technique(s) would you have used?

  3. *Message strategy*: How was Van Dyke's letter structured? How would you have structured it? How would you analyze the tone? What tone would you have adopted?

  4. *Channel choice strategy*: What channel(s) of communication would you have used?

  5. *Culture strategy*: What is your analysis of the Fletcher Electronics "culture"?

Session 2: Introduction to Corporate Communication

- Due to box in Tuck 300 by 8:00 AM: Memo #2 (Individual Effort. See syllabus page 3.)

Session 3: Corporate Image and Identity

Guest speaker from a design firm.

- Read Argenti, CC, chapters 1-4 (in course packet)
- Due: Corporate identity analysis

Session 4: Strategies for Media Relations

- Read:

    1. Adolph Coors case
    2. CC, chapter 6

- Be prepared to answer the following questions:

    1. What would you advise the Coors brothers to do in terms of general communication strategy?

    2. Should Coors adopt an open-door or closed-door policy?

    3. If open, who should be the company's spokesperson?

Session 5: Strategies for Crisis Communication

- Read

    1. Dow Corning case
    2. CC, chapter 10

- Be prepared to answer the following questions:

    1. What should he do in terms of crisis communication?
    2. What should he do in terms of planning for dealing with the media?

The course includes several other sessions, but I have limited this description to the days when I cover the corporate communication material.

Tuck's Corporation Communication Syllabus

Day 1   **Topic: Course Introduction**
                Assignment: Argenti, Introduction, chapter 1
                Video: "Patterns" by Rod Serling (view in class)

Day 2   **Topic: Perceptions of Business I**
                Assignment: Argenti, chapter 2
                              Sinclair, *The Jungle* (first half)
                Video: *Barbarians at the Gate* (view in class)

Day 3   **Topic: Perceptions of Business II**
                Assignment: Sinclair, *The Jungle* (finish book)
                                Wolfe, *Bonfire* (first third)
                Video: *Other People's Money* (view in class)

Day 4   Topic: **The Corporate Communication Function**
           Assignment: Argenti, chapter 3
                       Wolfe, *Bonfire* (finish third)

Day 5   Topic: **Corporate Image and Identity**
           Assignment: Argenti, chapter 4
                       Olins, "What Corporate Identity Means"
           Case: GE Identity Program
           Guest: To be determined.

Day 6   Topic: **Corporate Design**
           Assignment: Lorenz, "More than Just a Pretty Face"
                       Olins, "Visual Style"

Day 7   Topic: **Corporate Advertising**
           Assignment: Argenti, chapter 5
                       Potter, "Institution of Abundance: Advertising"

Day 8   Topic: **Corporate Advocacy**
           Assignment: Kelley, "Critical Issues for Issue Ads"
           Case: Mobil Oil

Day 9   Topic: **Crisis Communication**
           Assignment: Argenti, chapter 10
           Case: Dow Corning

Day 10   Midterm

Day 11   Topic: **Corporate Philanthropy**
           Assignment: Gray, chapter 9
                       Nowlan & Shayon, Section V

Day 12   Topic: **Business and the Media I**
           Assignment: Argenti, chapter 6
           Guest: Reporter

Day 13   Topic: **Business and the Media II**
           Assignment: Gray, chapter 7
           Case: Bank of Boston

Day 14   Topic: **Business and the Media III**
           Assignment: Munter, "How to Conduct a Successful Media Interview"
                       Corrado, chapter 5
           Role Play: Source Perrier

Day 15   Topic: **Business and the Media IV**
         Assignment: Detwiler, "Maybe Orwell Wasn't Kidding"

Day 16   Topic: **Financial Communication**
         Assignment: Argenti, Chapter 7
         Case: United Technologies

Day 17   Topic: **The Role of the Public Relations Firm**
         Assignment: Garbett, Chapter 4
         Guest: Sally Jackson, President, Jackson & Co., Boston, MA

Day 18   Topic: **Employee Communication**
         Assignment: Argenti, chapter 8
         Case: Brown & Sharpe

Other Syllabi

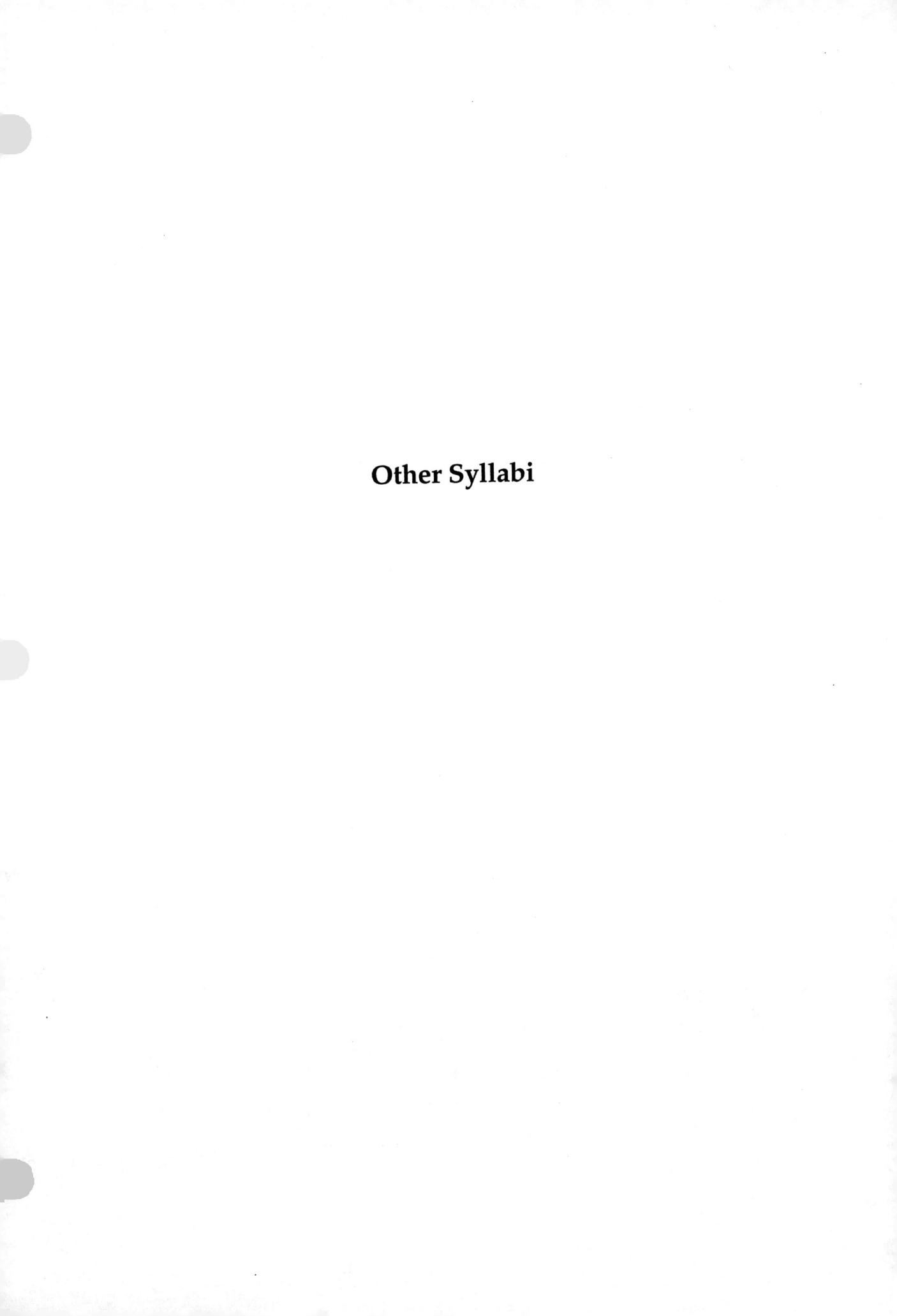

Corporate Communication
Spring 1997

Professor Argenti   Secretary
Tuck 304   Tuck 310
646-2983   646-2772

Course Objectives

This course seeks to expand and improve your understanding of corporate communication and to enhance your written and oral communication skills. To reach these goals, we will examine a variety of cases and readings that will help you understand how corporate communication relates to general management in a corporation. In addition, you will have opportunities to improve your writing and speaking.

Requirements

Class participation, written and oral assignments, and readings are equally important requirements for this course. Class participation and your knowledge of the readings and cases, will count for 25% of your grade. The final exam counts for 25% and a final group report counts for 50%.

Readings

I have chosen only a few important readings for each day. Therefore, every assignment is crucial. Required texts are: *Corporate Communication* by Paul Argenti, *The Jungle*, by Upton Sinclair and *The Bonfire of the Vanities* by Tom Wolfe. All are available at the Dartmouth Bookstore. A packet containing other readings, and cases will be available at registration.

Tuck Honor Code

I trust you to behave honorably. All assignments except those designated as "group" are meant to be individual efforts. By individual effort, I mean no one else is to read, listen to, comment on, proofread, or even type your documents or visual aids.

Attendance Policy

I also expect you to attend every class session. See page 22 of the MBA Student Handbook if a family emergency or personal illness precludes you from attending class. I will also make exceptions for important interviews and family events.

COURSE OUTLINE

Date | Class Topics and Assignments

Monday, March 24
Topic: Course Introduction
Read: Argenti, "Corporate Communication as a Discipline"
"Revised" Chapter 2 (in course packet)
Case: McDonalds and the Environment (review your final exams!)

Tuesday, March 25
Topic: The Changing Environment for Business
Read: Sinclair, *The Jungle* (first half)
Case: Food Lion (video in class)

Monday, March 31
Topic: The Changing Environment for Business
Discuss: *The Jungle*
Read: Sinclair, *The Jungle* (finish book) and Food Lion clips (in packet)

Tuesday, April 1
Topic: The Changing Environment for Business
Read: Wolfe, *Bonfire* (first third)
View: *Barbarians at the Gate* (prior to class)

Monday, April 7
Topic: The Changing Environment for Business
Discuss: *Bonfire* and *Barbarians*
Read: Wolfe, *Bonfire* (finish book)

Tuesday, April 8
Topic: Corporate Image and Identity
Read: Argenti, Chapter 4
Case: GE Identity Program (in Argenti, ch. 4)

Monday, April 14
Topic: Corporate Advertising and Advocacy
Read: Argenti, Chapter 5
Potter, "Institution of Abundance: Advertising"
Kelley, "Critical Issues for Issue Ads"
Case: Mobil Oil & Advocacy Advertising

Monday, April 21	**Topic:** Employee Communication 　　Read:　　Argenti, Chapter 8 　　View:　　*American Dream* (prior to class) Take-home midterm due
Tuesday, April 22	**Topic:** Michael Curtiz's *Female* 　　Guest:　　David Sterritt, *The Christian Science Monitor's* film critic
Monday, April 28	**Topic: Financial Communication and Corporate Philanthropy** 　　Read:　　Gray, Chapter 9 　　　　　　Argenti, Chapter 7 　　　　　　Nowlan & Shayon, Section V 　　Guest:　　Mary Flounders Greene, Bear Stearns
Tuesday, April 29	**Topic: Business and the Media II** 　　Read:　　Corrado, Chapter 5 　　Case:　　Bank of Boston
Monday, May 5	**Topic: The Media Business** 　　Read:　　Argenti, Chapter 6 　　Guest:　　Janet L. Robinson, President and General Manager, *The New York Times*
Tuesday, May 6	**Topic: Business and the Media III** 　　Read:　　Argenti & Munter, "How to Conduct a Successful Media Interview" (to be handed out in late April) 　　Video:　　"Out of Control" (viewed in class)
Wednesday, May 7	**VIDEO:** 6:00 PM - Stoneman 　　View:　　*Roger & Me*
Monday, May 12	**Topic: Business and the Media IV** 　　View:　　*Roger & Me* (prior to class) 　　Video:　　"Pets and Meat" (view in class)
Tuesday, May 13	**Topic: Crisis Communication** 　　Read:　　Argenti, Chapter 9 　　Case:　　Dow Corning 　　Guests:　Barrie Carmichael/John Byrne

Final Presentation dates to be set.

MANAGEMENT COMMUNICATION

Spring 1997

The spring semester of Management Communication expands upon the fall semester's focus on communication and the individual manager. Our aim is to expose first year MBA students to the new and evolving functions of communication in contemporary business practice. The spring semester is based on the assumption that the contemporary business environment has changed the way communication is used in organizations, particularly in the corporate context. The semester is split in focus between two fundamental developments in management communication: (1) communication issues are associated increasingly with groups, and (2) corporate communication is emerging as a business function. On the practical level, class exercises and assignments will prepare students for their summer internships and second-year course work.

Module III

Group Communication

The Group Communication module provides the opportunity for student groups to experience intensively the challenges of integrating and synthesizing research and of collaborating on and producing a convincing business concept. Through preparing and presenting the business plan project, students can put their group communication skills into practice.

Module IV

Corporate Communication

This module introduces students to the burgeoning field of Corporate Communication. As organizations flatten and decentralize, many find that a coordinated and centralized communication function improves communication on the level of the corporation as a whole. Moreover, for the individual manager to be an effective member of a team or an organization increasingly requires knowing and understanding how a company tells its story. Readings, cases, and guest speakers will expose students to the corporate communication issues related to four topics: (1) corporate image and identity, (2) internal relations, (3) investor relations, and (4) media and crisis communication.

Graduate School of Business Administration
University of Virginia
PO Box 6550
Charlottesville, Virginia 22906-6550

Management Communication
Module Four: Corporate Communication

4/8   Topic: Investor Relations: Corporate Repositioning
       Case: "Investor Relations at United Technologies"
       Read: Argenti, Chapter 7

4/9   Topic: Introduction to Corporate Communication Strategy
       Read: Argenti, Chapters 1 & 2

4/15   Topic: Investor Relations: The Annual Report
       Case: "Coca-Cola Company 1996 Annual Report"
       Read: Argenti, Chapter 3

4/17   Topic: Image and Identity: Corporate Design
       Case: "GE Identity Program," pp. 81-85 in Argenti text
       Read: Argenti, Chapters 4 & 5

4/22   Topic: Business and the Media
       Cases: "Adolph Coors Company," pp. 128-136 in Argenti text
              "Communicating a Difficult Message: AT&T's Restructuring and Downsizing"
       Read: Argenti, Chapters 5 & 6

       Cases: "How Normal is Normal: The Mitsubishi Motors Sexual Harassment Case"
              "Texaco: The Secret Tapes"
       Read: Argenti, Chapters 8 & 9

4/29   Topic: Communicating Corporate Strategy
       Case: "Intel's Floating Point Division Bug"

5/2   Individual Corporate Communication Papers Due
       Conclusion

Assignments:

Group Presentation Option (GPO): Beginning 4/15, each class will begin with a group presentation by two self-selected teams. Each student is responsible for roughly five minutes of "air-time" to help begin class discussion. Think of these presentations more in terms of opening interesting questions or pointing to potential courses of action rather than wrapping up the topic at hand. Groups may present on the case assigned for the day or use the topic of the day as a springboard to explore related issues, companies, and industries.

Individual Corporate Communication Paper: Due at 5:00 p.m. on the last day of class, this 5 page double-spaced paper should analyze and take a position on one of the issues raised in class, or alternatively, take the form of a caselette dealing with an aspect of corporate communication.

The text, *Corporate Communication* by Paul Argenti, is available at Courts and Commerce and on reserve in the Camp Library

Corporate Communication

From Intel's costly Pentium problems and Disney's high-profile history theme park debacle to the vexing issues of communicating corporate identity in an era of downsizing, corporate communication plays an increasingly visible role in today's business world. As companies de-centralize, does a centralized communication function become more important to maintain corporate image and identity, reputation and brand equity? Building on the first-year spring module in MC, this course provides a more specific look at the corporate communication function. Where the first year introduces some of the broad themes of this field in the context of "communication for managers" this course explores the strategies for "managing communication." We will emphasize the connections among the multiple constituencies of the contemporary corporation by examining employee and labor relations, advertising and media relations, investor relations, communicating to suppliers and customers, and crisis communication. As these topics suggest, there will be ample opportunity to integrate students' knowledge in the core functional areas and to address the intersections between communication and IT, re-engineering, and the learning organization. Students' critical thinking as demonstrated in writing and presentations will receive particular attention, and students should see this as an opportunity to further their development in written and oral communication while exploring an exciting field.

Course materials will draw on Darden cases being developed for this course, an ample literature of recent Harvard and Western Ontario cases, case research underway by colleagues at Stern and Tuck, as well as articles, and films. Classes will include guests with functional expertise, case discussions, role plays and videotape analysis.

Graduate School of Business Administration
University of Virginia
PO Box 6550
Charlottesville, Virginia 22906-6550

Corporate Communication, Spring 1996

The Purpose of this course is to explore three questions:

1. What are effective ways to communicate change in changing organizations?

2. How is communication changing in organizations?

3. In what way will the answers to the first two questions alter the corporate communication function?

We begin with these hypotheses:

1. Almost every organization will change as a result of the end of the cold war, innovations in technology, and shifts in mature and emerging markets.

2. Communication technology will change the ways corporations communicate to external and internal constituencies; changing technologies will alter the architectures of corporate structures and genres of communication creating new opportunities for competitive advantage.

3. Managers at almost every level will increasingly need to be familiar with how to communicate in crisis situations.

4. Corporations and managers will be communicating in increasingly crowded and sophisticated media environments.

Course Themes

Module One: Shifting perceptions of business in media; historical background of corporate structure/ advocacy advertising (JR).

Module Two: Corporate Image and Identity--Communicating Change

Module Three: Communicating change to Internal Constituencies

Module Four: Technology--The Net/ Software

Module Five: Investor Relations

Module Six: Crisis Communication

MANAGEMENT COMMUNICATION 633
Prof: Frank Jaster, Ph.D.

(Summary: This course is built around <u>Corporate Communication</u>, by Paul A. Argenti. It uses <u>Corpcom</u>'s text and cases as the bases for individual reports and briefings and for team presentations. In addition, the course requires students to apply <u>Corpcom's</u> principles to current business cases such as ValuJet, Denny's, Texaco, and Dow Corning in written and oral reports.)

I. <u>Course Description and Objectives:</u>

    A. To function effectively in today's complex business environment, managers must understand and be able to use many different communication skills and behaviors to accomplish their own objectives as well as those of the organization This course attempts to impart both the underlying concepts and the skill-building exercises necessary for managers to communicate effectively

        1) within their own work groups,

        2) horizontally and vertically within their organizations,

        3) with clients outside their organizations, and

        4) with people from cultures and backgrounds other than their own.

    B. Equally important are the premises that students

        1. understand some basic management communication concepts leading to effective decision-making,

        2. analyze each audience to create messages which meet their audiences' needs and expectations and which accomplish their own objectives,

        3. use a problem-solution approach to analysis of business issues and articulate the steps to problem-solving orally and in writing,

        4. understand the different ways to persuade others and to gain commitment to the organization's objectives,

5. become familiar with the language of business and use that language clearly, concisely, and correctly,

6. select, organize, and present data in appropriate oral and written forms for a variety of business settings,

7. become more familiar with their own strengths, biases, and weaknesses in working effectively with others in teams and be able to articulate their attitudes orally and in writing,

8. become familiar with different tools available for surveying individuals and teams to determine the best mix of individual styles and organizational needs to accomplish team objectives,

9. become familiar with the corporate communication function as it operates in large organizations and as it affects the organization's relationships with its constituents, and

10. review and evaluate several corporate image/identity/advocacy campaigns as part of the corporate communication function.

C. To accomplish these and other objectives this course requires each student to prepare and present three oral briefings or presentations, one of which is based on a written report. The presentations and all writing assignments will follow certain general guidelines, but they will also require thought, imagination, flexibility, and maturity of judgment in their execution.

II. Course Requirements

A. Reading Material

1. a. The Business Writer's Handbook. Charles T. Brusaw, Gerald J. Alred, Walter E. Oliu, 4th edition. New York: St. Martin's Press, 1993

b. Corporate Communication. Paul Argenti. Irwin, 1994

c. Management Communication. Frank Jaster & Jim Marvel. Packet (Purchase at the Tulane Copy Center)

d. Other materials as they become available during the semester

B. Required Papers

1. A report to management based on a case

2. An executive summary of a report

3. A team report on a new venture, either asking for funds or, in the case of an internal audience, making recommendations to top management. This report becomes the information base for the third oral presentation

C. Required Oral Presentations

1. A one-point presentation

2. A briefing based on a new product or service or the modification of an existing product or service

3. A team business presentation to funding specialists or to top management

4. If time permits, a hostile press briefing or a combination management/press briefing

III. Policies:

A. We have an inflexible approach to flexibility in this course, but some things are "engraved in stone": all written work must be typed or printed if it is to be turned in for grade. Papers must be submitted in class on the date due.

1. Our adjunct writing instructor provides you with tutorial help during the writing process. Please observe the following policies when using this service:

a. When you seek help from the tutors or graders, please have your outlines or manuscripts typed.

b. Sign up on the bulletin board outside the Management Communications Center (MCC) at Room 200.

c. If you have questions concerning papers, make an

appointment with your writing instructor for clarification.

    2. All of your written reports must be done on WordPerfect or some other wordprocessing package.

    3. The first oral presentation must include visual aids or props or both. Part of the second oral presentation must include a PowerPoint or some other computer projected segment. The third (team) presentation must be done entirely in PowerPoint or some other computer projected program.

B. All oral presentations must be completed as scheduled.

    1. You may negotiate among yourselves any switching of speaking dates or times. Please let me or the teaching assistant know at least 24 hours in advance.

    2. You will receive written evaluation comments from me on the oral presentations. Videotapes of individual presentations should be viewed in the Media Services Center in Room 261.

    3. Also, you will be asked to evaluate peers much the same way a supervisor counsels subordinates in industry.

    4. On days when you are NOT presenting, you must attend class. Professional courtesy demands it, your classmates need your support, and I need you to be there and help in the peer evaluations.

C. If you must miss a class for any reason please arrange for your team leader to pick up any handouts and to give you the assignment. Let me or the teaching assistant know beforehand if you are going to miss a class.

D. Parts of this course resemble training seminars of many companies. Assume throughout the course that you are a member of management and you and your colleagues are involved in the decision-making process and responsible for those decisions.

E. General house rules: to be discussed in class; however, I ask that you

1. come to class fully clothed [men: shoes, shirts (no tank tops), pants or shorts; women: shoes, shirts (no tank tops), shorts or slacks or skirts]; please do not wear hats or caps in class.

2. <u>Bring No food to class.</u> Coffee or cokes are OK, but you must clean up the cups before you leave.

3. Please wear business attire for your individual and team new venture presentations.

4. Please do not put your feet on the furniture.

F. Grading: Written work

Diagnostic case analysis	50 points
Case analysis	100 points
Executive Summary	100 points
Group Management Report	200 points

Oral presentations

One-Point Presentation	50 points
Briefing	100 points
Group Presentation (group grade)	100 points
(individual grade)	100 points

Quizzes

Midterm	100 points
Final (may be optional)	100 points
Total Possible	1000 points

Somewhere along the line, I may do some "cold-calling." The subject may be on any relevant or irrelevant topic. I give extra credit to people who are well-prepared for relevant questions and to those who can respond "off the tops of their heads."

I think the key to success in this course and in life is to be open-minded, flexible, and committed to success. Critical attributes would include a sense of humor, a healthy skepticism toward dogma in all its forms, a disdain for the mean, median, and mode (sorry Russ), a desire to do one's best, and a refusal to fall back on those tired old excuses from undergraduate days: If I had more time, I could have done a better job, etc. I could go on, but you get the idea.

Enjoy the ride.

IV. Professor for the course:
Dr. Frank Jaster
Goldring-Woldenberg Hall 654
Office phone: 865-5489
Home phone: 504-893-4713
Office hours: by appointment or by ambush

Teaching Assistants: Johanna May and Laura McAdams
Phones:

MEDIA AND MANAGEMENT
B45.2302, Fall 1997, Professor Schenkler
Monday/Wednesday, 5:30 p.m., 5-90 MEC

Office and Mailing Address:
Management Communication Program
Stern School of Business
40 W. 4th Street, Suite 202
New York, NY 10012

Office Hours:
Monday/Wednesday
4:00-5:00pm and by appointment

phone: 212/998-0093
fax: 212/995-4213
e-mail: ischenkl@stern.nyu.edu
www: http://www.stern.nyu.edu/mc

Readings:

Argenti, Paul Corporate Communication, Irwin, 1994.

Barton, Laurence Crisis In Organizations: Managing and Communicating in the Heat of Chaos, South-Western, 1993.

Supplementary material will be distributed during the semester.

BROAD FOCUS OF THE COURSE

This course examines the relationship between business and the media. Starting with an overview of corporate communication, we look at how companies can use public relations as a vehicle for disseminating their various messages. From there we will consider how the media acts as a catalyst as well as intermediary in this process. Some of the questions that will arise will be: Is the relationship inherently antagonistic? Should it be? What would be the optimum relationship? How would the public best be served?

In order to examine these and other aspects of the relationship, students will be exposed to multiple points of view in the next fifteen weeks, including my own, and a host of media and business representatives.

COURSE PROCEDURES AND REQUIREMENTS

1. Regular attendance and intelligent participation in class discussion. Since many sessions will feature guests from the media and business sectors, I hope you will actively contribute to their presentations with your questions and comments. At times students will be selected to lead discussion sections based upon guest speaker's presentations.

2. A term paper (7-10 pages) will be due December 10. The topic, to be chosen in consultation with the instructor, should concern either 1) a company that has faced or

currently faces a serious problem or challenge in public relations/affairs or 2) an overview of corporate communication at your company addressing issues of credibility, image, identity, and constituencies. Please submit two copies of the paper. Complete instructions will be forthcoming.

An oral presentation based on your paper topic will be required during weeks 14 and 15 of the course. This presentation will be graded. Further details will be provided.

By October 22, you must submit your choice of topics in short written form (paragraph outlining the subject and your intention). This statement may be submitted via e-mail. The instructor will help you choose the best one. (This assignment can be done in small groups).

3. Midterm exam. This will be given on October 20 and will consist of a case to be analyzed in class.

4. Final exam. This will be given December 17 and consist of short answers and essay questions.

GRADING:
- 15% midterm exam
- 30% term paper
- 15% oral presentation on research paper
- 10% class participation
- 30% Final Exam (short answer and essay)

NOTE: READINGS ARE LISTED FOR THE DATE ON WHICH THEY WILL BE DISCUSSED

Week 1 **Introduction to the Course**
(9/3) Course procedures. In-class exercise.

Week 2 **Public Relations: An Overview**
(9/8) The development of public relations in historical perspective.

    Reading: Argenti, Chapter 1 (excluding case). Barton, Intro and Chapters 1 & 3. J. Horton, "Describing Corporate Communication," excerpted from Integrating Corporate Communication (hand-out) For Wednesday's session

(9/10) **Perception and Persuasion: How Companies Use Public Relations**

    Speaker: James L. Horton, Senior Vice President, Robert Marsden Associates. How communication and economic transactions relate. Why corporate activities are dependent upon communication. Corporate messages and media as tools to achieve economic transactions and build wealth: a theoretical model for corporate communication.

Week 3 **What is Corporate Communication?**
(9/15) Corporate communication: what it is, how it has evolved, and how it integrates with the other primary organizational functions. Communications management and stakeholder relations. How external public relations counsel supplements the in-house staff. How to decide when outside firms are necessary.

    Reading: Fombrun, "Enlightened Self Interest" (handout), Argenti, Chapter 3 (excluding case),

(9/17) **Corporate Communication: The Changing Scene**
Speaker: Chris Atkins, Executive Vice President, Ketchum Public Relations
How communication strategy links with corporate strategy. Changes in the nature of media relations during the past decade.

Week 4   **The Media and Business**
(9/22)   The Media and Business. Challenges and Opportunities. In-class viewing of "Eye on the Media", roundtable discussion focusing on business and media distrust.

        Reading: Argenti, Chapter 6 (excluding case).

(9/24)   **How the Media Views Business**
Guest Speaker: Claudia Deutsch, Business Reporter, <u>New York Times</u>.
Media and the public: inherent versus perceived conflicts

Week 5   **Issues and Insulation: Why Companies Get in Trouble**
(9/29)

        How companies identify and adjust to contemporary issues that may shape the future of the organization. Changes in corporate communications strategies; how the press has covered business; the challenges for the next decade. Focus on Walmart and its grass roots opposition during the past five years.

        Reading: Barton, Chapter 3; "Issues Interception" (handout).

(10/1)   **Issues and Insulation, continued**
Student teams will present strategies on the Walmart scenario discussed in the previous sessions. Selected teams will assume the perspective of management, others that of the opposition groups.

        Reading: Prepare Coors Case for discussion next week (Argenti, p. 128 ff)

Week 6   **The Coors Company Case**
(10/6
10/8)   Assessing strategic choices in the face of media inquiry. In class discussion of the Coors case, and viewing of CBS 60 Minutes profile of the Coors company. Group exercise.

Week 7   **Communicating with the Media: A Hands On Approach**
(10/13)   Guest: Jeff Bloch, Media Trainer. How to adapt to different kinds of journalistic inquiry. Getting your message across under pressure.

        Reading: "Media Training" (handout).

(10/15) **Corporate Image and Identity**
Speaker: David Boorstin, Senior Vice President, Diefenbach Elkins.
Corporate image and identity. How organizations distinguish themselves through image, symbol, and graphic design. Using media to convey identity.

Reading: Argenti Chapters 4 & 5 (excluding cases); Fombrun, "Shaping Consistent Images" (handout).

Week 8
(10/20) **Mid Term Exam**

(10/22) **Financial Public Relations**
Investor relations: communicating with shareholders, analysts, and the media. The global dimension of investor relations.

Reading: United Technologies Case (to be distributed); Argenti Chapter 7 (excluding case).

Week 9
(10/27) **Introduction to Crisis Communication**
Internal and External Communication in a Crisis: A Theoretical Model
A review of notable organizational crises, 1979-1997

Reading: Barton, Chapters 4 & 6. Argenti, Chapter 9

(10/29) **Introduction to Crisis Communication, continued**
Focus on rumors, hoaxes, contamination fears and consumer products companies

Reading:. P. Turner, "Consumer/Corporate Conflict", excerpted from I Heard It Through the Grapevine

Week 10
(11/3) **The Corporation Fights Back: Food Lion and ABC**
An in-depth look at the Food Lion crisis. Students will review newspaper and televised accounts of the controversy and in teams will prepare analyses of the principals' strategies (materials will be distributed in class).

(11/5) **Crisis Communication: Strategy and Tactics**
Speaker: Robert Mead, President, Bozell, Sawyer Miller Group

Student teams will present their analysis of the Food Lion case to the guest speaker and receive feedback. Other topics to be raised: environmental scanning and issues management. Strategies for crisis planning. The components of a plan.

Week 11 **Crisis in Your Organization**
(11/10
11/12) Role-plays focusing on potential crises that could affect your company. Students will write short scenarios which will be exchanged and discussed. Instructions will be provided.

Reading: Barton Chapters 7 & 8.

Week 12 **An Incident at Riverton: Workshop in Crisis Communication**
(11/17
11/19) Speaker: Richard Hyde, Managing Director, Hill and Knowlton
Hands-on role-play simulating a crisis situation. Working in teams, students will determine their approaches to handling the event, especially how they plan to deal with the news media.

Reading: Prepare Hooker Chemical Case (pp. 13-26, Argenti text) for discussion next session.

Week 13
(11/24)
The Hooker Chemical Company: A Crossroads in Crisis Communication
In depth discussion of the communication issues facing this company. We will develop a strategy in class that addresses primary and secondary stakeholders. We will also view several videotapes from the era. Students will engage in role-play exercises.

(11/26) **The Professional Presentation: Tips for the Final Oral Project**
Structuring your ideas; using visual aids effectively; enhancing delivery techniques.

Week 14 **Student Presentations Based on Research Projects**
Week 15
(12/1
12/10)

Chapter by Chapter Notes

Chapter 1: The Changing Environment for Business

This chapter gives you an opportunity to go over several different things with students. First and most important is the information about changing attitudes toward business in the United States. I have included some graphic representations of the data that you can use to make these points come alive in the classroom (see Appendix 2 for possible overhead transparencies).

I usually also show the annual meeting scenes from both Oliver Stone's *Wall Street* and Danny DeVito's *Other People's Money*. Both are available throughout the United States and in many other parts of the world as well. The scene from *Wall Street* is in the second half of the film. It includes an introduction by Richard Dysart followed by the famous "greed is good" speech by Michael Douglas's character. The characterization of older management is that they are a bunch of lazy, overweight, overpaid bureaucrats shuffling paper back and forth. Gordon Gekko looks quite appealing by contrast, but you must point out to students that Gekko is actually a very negative figure in the film as well.

Thus the depiction of business is a choice between bloated/bureaucratic versus charming/corrupt; neither is acceptable. You will want to point out that the Gekko character is representative of a typical outsider—a very appealing characterization in both literature and film. Also people like entrepreneurs rather than corporate types.

The clip from *Other People's Money* is toward the end of the movie. Danny DeVito comes to speak at Gregory Peck's annual meeting in this case. Here, the older manager is not a bloated bureaucrat, but clearly out of touch with the times. DeVito is unlikeable but ultimately correct.

<u>A Note About Use of Literature and Film</u>

Many of us involved in this area have some background in literature or at the very least, the liberal arts. What I have found is that exposing business students to this material, particularly MBAs, can be a very rewarding experience in that at least some of them have just never had the opportunity to read something as gruesome as *The Jungle*.

The problem is, they are also not very adept at picking up on major themes nor analyzing characters in novels or even in films. You have to do a lot of work before these sessions and have lots of notes written to yourself about how you want to cover this material.

Use whatever is currently on the bestseller lists to point out examples of negative impressions of business in literature. You can also find lots of good examples on television and in magazines and newspapers. Again, the more you can tailor the information to your own needs the more relevant it will be to you and your students.

For those of you who have an international bent, you will want to spend more time on the section about the borderless world. I have had the opportunity to teach extensively in Japan, Finland, and Vietnam so I usually try to broaden students' perspectives about how much more internationally-oriented companies and managers need to be today based on personal experience. But, you don't need to have personal experience to talk about the international business environment. Everyone takes this idea for granted today. Just try to come with some of your own examples.

Conclude the session with an overhead transparency that lists my five ways to compete (see Appendix 2). These give you the chance to wrap-up the session and to end with some positive information after what can be a very gloomy discussion.

Hooker (part one)

This is a real case, and all of the things that you read really happened. If you are interested in learning more about Hooker, please refer to Michael Brown's book, *Laying Waste*, listed in the bibliography. It will tell you everything you could ever possibly want to know about the Love Canal crisis and more.

You should also explain to students that this was the first major environmental crisis. Today, such occurrences are more commonplace. Nevertheless, the main idea of this case is to demonstrate how out-of-touch managers, such as those at Hooker and Occidental, can fall prey to the gnat theory described in the first chapter of the book.

Make sure that students have read the "Note on the Case Method" from my introduction. Then get them to focus on the major problems for this company. Here are some of the things that students typically come up with:

Problems for Hooker

1. Sandie Kroeger is ill-equipped to deal with a problem of this magnitude. She was hired to do internal communications and finds herself in the middle of one of the all-time worst environmental crises managing public relations.

2. Hooker management is out of touch with contemporary attitudes about business particularly as they relate to the environment. The notion that it will all go away on the part of Hooker and Oxy leads the general public to see them as arrogant.

3. The history of the canal including who owned what, when, and where is much too complicated to fit into sound bites. Rational arguments will never work against the potential pictures of oozing sludge and sick mothers and children.

4. Hooker is not technically or perhaps even legally responsible for the current problems, but because of the negative views that people hold of business they will be held accountable in the court of public opinion.

5. Hooker has a technical-engineering-production bent and is used to dealing with other technicians through its industrial, rather than consumer, relations. They are simply unused to handling things related to the general public. In addition, Occidental and Hooker seem to be influenced by lawyers.

6. The unfriendly Mead takeover attempt has unfortunately allowed the company to become extremely vulnerable to attack since all of its documents are now public. Students will point to Exhibit 1-5 as an example of what the company now must realize is public information. See especially #2 under probability (low) and amount held in reserve (only 5 million dollars), and recovery options (totally legal). They could have decided to buy up the homes before, but the lawyers held them back.

7. Students who like to crunch numbers should be able to pick out some interesting things from the financial statements. For instance, the company seems to be doing very well financially which makes them vulnerable to the kinds of attacks they are likely to get from the community.

8. The company has just faced a major reorganization that has centralized staff of different businesses. This put Hooker's top management thousands of miles away from Niagara Falls in Texas and the parent company in Los Angeles!

9. Hooker is under pressure to produce for the Russian Project, a pet project of the Oxy chairman. This makes matters worse for them.

10. They have no overall corporate communication strategy nor do they have any plans for dealing with media.

11. The case presents the situation as a choice between proactive and reactive. This is not really a choice since we already know that they are totally reactive.

12. A state of emergency has been declared.

Possible Solutions to Hooker:

1. *Do nothing.*
   This is basically what they did. Unfortunately for them, a reactive approach in this case was the worst thing that they could have done. Doing nothing leaves you vulnerable to public demonstrations, etc. But, it gives you less potential liabilities down the road.

2. *Get going!*
   Clearly they need to realize that the good old days of business as usual are over. They need to get all of their facts straight, present information before rather than after it is asked for, and start trying to get the media on their side.

Some students may suggest that they try to coopt the community. Others will suggest buying up homes, etc. But, these are difficult choices for them given the orientation of this company.

Try to get students going in both directions at first, but then lead them to the right solution.

Hooker B (see end of this chapter for a copy of the case)

In this case, we see the problem from the perspective of the local management. We also see more about the main protagonists in this situation like Lois Gibbs, Michael Brown, etc.

The good news is that the government is now involved and some of the blame is likely to go their way. Particularly with the way the chromosome study was handled, you can see that if Hooker starts cooperating fully and being more active in local affairs, the government is going to look a lot worse.

You need to think about how you want to use the B case. It can almost be used as a stand-alone document. And there is enough richness here to keep another class session going.

If you give it to them as an additional case to analyze, you will inevitably see that students almost never pick up on the government as scapegoat angle, which is, of course, what really happened.

CBS had a *60 Minutes* episode on about Love Canal. Virtually everyone covered this event. Shop around beginning with CBS and keep looking for more in your library and video store on Love Canal. You will find a film about Lois Gibbs, starring Ellen Burstyn, tons of footage, and a whole lot more.

Hooker is one of the richest cases in the book. You might want to get students focused on the first part just to get them into analyzing communication cases and to see how managers fail to be proactive. Then come back to it when you cover media and/or crisis. Or you could assign the "B" case as a final exam, which creates some excellent symmetry in the course.

Overall, I strongly suggest further reading about Love Canal before teaching this case and make sure you analyze it thoroughly yourself. I'm still seeing different sides to this problem after teaching it sporadically for almost 15 years. One last note. Although the case was written in the early 1980s, it is still timely. Do not let students tell you it's "out of date." As an historical event it's worth reading, but more importantly, students don't remember it, which makes it easier for them to analyze the case as a business problem rather than a current event.

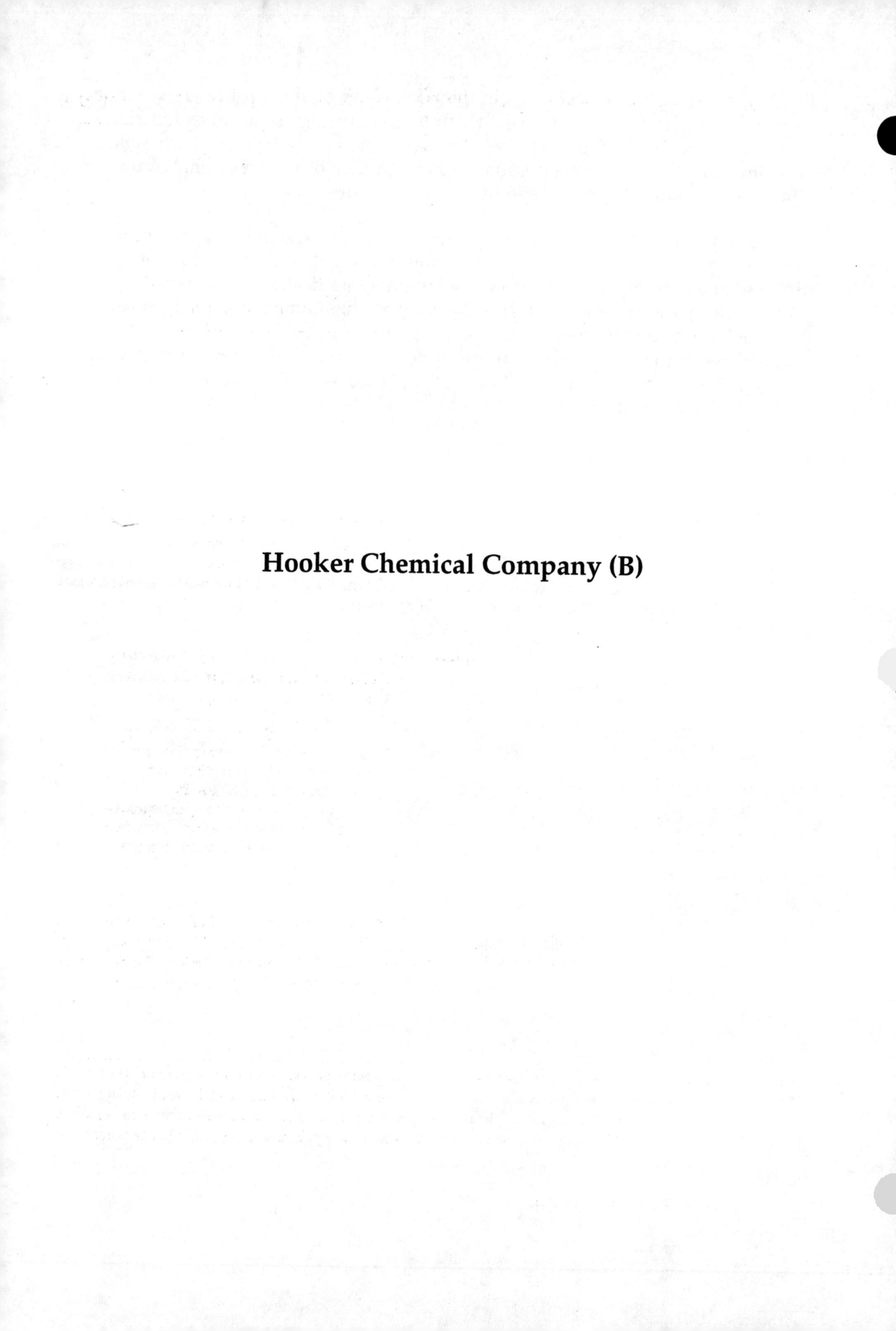

Hooker Chemical Company (B)

HOOKER CHEMICAL COMPANY (B)*

Jim Green, manager of public relations, started working for Hooker at its Niagara headquarters in 1968, right before Occidental Petroleum acquired the company. He saw seven new presidents in the first seven years he worked for Hooker. Green was "on the front lines" when the Love Canal story hit national news headlines. He describes some of the complexities of dealing with corporate parents thousands of miles away as well as persistent local reporters:

> We were often hamstrung by cumbersome clearance procedures. In the early days of the crisis, we, at Niagara HCC, were restricted in talking with national media; all press releases had to be cleared with Oxy headquarters in Los Angeles. We spent our time screening calls, dealing with the day-to-day problems, and preparing Bruce Davis, Hooker V.P. in Niagara Falls, to be able to answer questions. He went out of his way to be accessible, but often we simply did not have the answers. It really took a year until we were comfortable with a base of historical background information. We needed data we could stand by. HCC was very careful and very defensive in developing information. Eventually Davis promoted Frank Neruda, one of his up-and-coming business managers, to be the vice-president of environmental affairs. Neruda spent all his time on litigation and remedial programs to give Davis some time to run the company.

Just as the Niagara office began responding to the Love Canal crisis in the summer of 1978, other Hooker pollution violations were fast becoming hot news items. Not just the plant at Montague, Michigan, but also those at Taft, Louisiana, and White Springs, Florida, plus four other Hooker dump sites within the Niagara city limits. All were fodder for local and national news.

---

* This case was prepared by Professor Paul A. Argenti of The Amos Tuck School, Dartmouth College, and Evelind Schecter of the Columbia University Graduate School of Business. Research Assistant: Marian White, The Amos Tuck School. The case is intended for class discussion rather than to reflect either effective or ineffective handling of a management situation.

All rights reserved. © 1983

LOVE CANAL: A PR SUMMARY AS TOLD BY JIM GREEN

Love Canal is a story that never really broke in the usual blockbuster style of a catastrophic news story. It simply grew, and grew, and grew. On August 2, 1978 -- the day that the commissioner of health of New York State, Robert Whalen, declared a medical emergency at Love Canal -- we at Hooker were totally engulfed.

The story had been festering for some time: As far back as January 1970, the Niagara County Health Department records list some nine complaints related to odors in the air and in the basements of homes in the area, as well as the appearance of pungent liquids and exposed drums. Our Niagara plant had already been the subject of adverse national publicity stemming from a state decision to prohibit the consumption of game fish from Lake Ontario, the site of a burgeoning new sport fishing industry related to the stocking of fresh-water Chinook and salmon. The fact that Canadian authorities looked at the same data and limited their action to a mere cautionary warning against eating excessive amounts of fish from this same lake did little to appease the anger and concern of fishermen and citizens on this side of the border. The problem was blamed on discharges from our plant associated with the former production of a fire ant control, Mirex. The state never has proven its case, but in the public eye the damage had been done.

So when the Love Canal problem hit the national press, the public had already been conditioned to associate the Hooker name with environmental disasters.

Love Canal is, and was, a disaster. It contains all the elements that could go into one of the longest running soap operas in history. For openers, it has that wonderfully sexy name: Love Canal. Then there is the magic appeal of a Niagara Falls dateline. Mix in mothers and fathers frightened into emotional peaks of hysteria by the hype of media reporting, both print and electronic.

Add a laundry list of real, imagined, or suspected diseases and illnesses, miscarriages, and birth defects. Throw in a daily barrage of questions to which no responsible medical or regulatory authorities had the answers. And blame it all on indifferent-appearing local authorities and the alleged misdeeds of a corporate giant that was not positioned, nor staffed, nor able -- despite its best efforts -- to quickly develop the type of technical data needed to stem the tide of unanswered questions, and you have a potentially explosive situation.

MICHAEL BROWN

The man generally credited with bringing Love Canal into the national media is Michael Brown. Born in Niagara Falls, Brown joined the *Niagara Gazette* as a reporter in 1977. He became interested in the old Love Canal dump site through research on other environmental stories in the *Gazette* files. His early stories (see Exhibit 1) precipitated complaints of sensationalism. Undaunted, Brown contacted residents of the area. Their stories of unusually high rates of cancer, nervous disorders, respiratory ailments, and skin rashes caused Brown to look at the health issues rather than the environmental ones. Although his editor pulled him off this story to work on others, Brown continued in his spare time.

Through an agent, he was able to place a detailed account of Love Canal in the Sunday *New York Times Magazine*. The story was supposed to appear in print in June 1978, but a strike at the *Times* delayed publication until January of the following year. Donald McNeil got wind of Brown's story before it was printed and ended up bringing the tale to the front page of the *Times* later that summer (see Exhibit 2). Brown gave McNeil many of his sources, and together they hashed out the August 2 piece (according to Brown).

Through coincidence, McNeil's story appeared the same day an evacuating order came down from the Health Department in Albany. The national news media showed up in force on the following day. Suddenly Love Canal became associated with toxic waste.

JIM GREEN CONTINUES HIS STORY

Late in 1976, the first newspaper accounts appeared in the local press (See Exhibit 3). The Niagara Gazette approached Hooker in October of that year for information about past landfills, such as Love Canal. An engineering firm reported finding hydrocarbons in studies of leachate in November, and in December the city of Niagara Falls was asked to take some action. All of these steps were duly reported by the local paper.

Hooker participated in the study program which included our partial underwriting of a remedial action proposal. The site was the subject of a number of follow-up articles in the local press during 1977 (see Exhibit 4). The story dragged all through 1977, with the city, the county, and finally the state all involved at various times at various levels. Our position during this period was up-front participation in the local study committee and open offers of technical assistance. The Niagara Gazette was relentless in its coverage. Not a day went by without a Love Canal or other company-oriented environmental story. In fact, our records show that the Gazette carried its crusade on a daily basis to the extent that a thirteen-month period went by before they published an issue that did not contain at least one Hooker-oriented environmental story.

In March 1978 another engineering firm, Conestoga-Rovers, was commis-sioned by the city to study the situation and recommend a plan of action. This report was issued in June, the same month the New York State Health Department began a house-to-house health survey in the area. The state legislature authorized up to $500,000 for a health study, and the city and Hooker agreed to share an $11,000 engineering study bill for a leachate collection system.

In July things started to boil over. The state tried to hold a public meeting to explain its program. The Health Department officials were booed, cursed, and humiliated; they couldn't get out of town fast enough. The TV and press reports of this meeting were devastating in their graphic portrayals of the depths of fear and concern among the Love Canal residents. The Love Canal Homeowners' Association took form and its president, Lois Gibbs, firmly took the reins. Things haven't been the same since.

LOIS GIBBS

Lois Gibbs moved into Love Canal in 1973. She and her husband purchased a three bedroom ranch on a small lot for $17,900. For them it was a dream house; they knew nothing about the old chemical dump site.

In 1978 their five-year-old son, Michael, developed a urinary tract infection and he began having epileptic seizures during his first year at the 99th Street School -- the one constructed near the original canal site.

That same year, Lois Gibbs read Michael Brown's *Gazette* pieces. His explanation of the chemical buried in Love Canal and of the diseases it could cause frightened her. Lois Gibbs began to see her son's illness in a dangerous light. She soon organized her neighbors into a cohesive group, and, as a result, she was elected president of the Love Canal Homeowners Association. Gibbs claims that the state and federal governments also wanted her to be a spokesperson because she had taken the responsibility for her neighbors with the petition she circulated.

In her mind, ". . . the media was a tool to show the world what was going on. If we could have worked with the government, we would have avoided the media more than we did. Instead, the media allowed us to get the support we needed from outside Niagara Falls."

JIM GREEN CONTINUES

And so, on August 2, Commissioner Robert Whalen declared a health emergency and recommended the evacuation of children under two and pregnant women living in homes in the first two rings. Twenty families were affected. He also recommended the temporary closing of the 99th Street School.

A few days later Love Canal became a centerpiece of Governor Carey's local re-election bid when he visited the site and said the state would buy <u>all</u> homes affected by chemicals.

It was at this point that Hooker offered funds up to $280,000 or one-third of the $850,000 total cost estimated by Conestoga-Rovers to install a remedial correction program in the southern end of the canal.

While all this was going on and being reported -- and, indeed, for many more months -- a special Hooker task force was working on a crash basis to develop information -- data that we could stand by -- to deal with the countless questions we were being asked day after day by the media.

One of the earliest decisions made by HCC and Oxy management was to designate Bruce Davis as the only local Hooker official authorized to speak for the company on this issue. He had to appear before committees of Congress in Washington and in the New York State Legislature in Albany and here (Niagara Falls) in traveling road shows to deal with some, or all, of these issues. The unflattering internal documents released to the public as the result of the Mead affair meant Bruce Davis was very busy and a very active local press spokesman.

The media interest in the subject was, and to some extent still seems to be, insatiable. The coverage was relentless and unending. The pressures, the demands for instant answers to complex questions, were with us on a daily basis. Crisis seemed to pile on top of crisis.

The day-to-day management of the media's interest in the company's affairs was pretty much left up to Hooker-Niagara, while the long-term strategic planning, policy-making and overall management of our response remained in Houston. For many months, we had all we could do here just to sort out the inquiries and help position Bruce Davis to deal with them.

Complicating our ability to respond was a clearance policy and procedure that was cumbersome at best and intolerable and unbending at its worst. It is better -- much better -- now, but there were numerous opportunities lost to Hooker and Oxy to get our side of the story on the record because our internal system just was not able to cope with rapidly moving developments.

During this period we issued very few formal press releases. Practically all of these efforts were geared to defensive explanations. This did not, of course, deter the hordes of newsmen from all over the nation -- indeed, from as far away as London and Stockholm -- from visiting Love Canal and Hooker's local headquarters. Davis took them all on; he returned all their calls, which were screened and handled through the Niagara public relations office, and he granted countless interviews. At more than one point, (our) conference room looked like your typical Washington scene: a battery of microphones, lights, cameras, and a clutter of pushing, ill-mannered newspeople.

The message Davis delivered was simple and plain; however, it rarely seemed to get the same news play given to those clamoring for relief. And it wasn't until March 1979 that we felt we were in a position to go public, to go on the offensive. We held a full-scale press conference in Buffalo on March 15 of last year (1979) and followed it up the next day with the first of a series of full-page ads (see Exhibit 5), four of them environmentally oriented -- featuring local employees talking about the company -- and three of them describing our new Energy-from-Waste plan project which is just now getting ready to come on stream. In addition, we published internal communications.

Bruce Davis also held a series of special briefings for local officials, community leaders, and the administration of Niagara University (see Exhibit 6), plus FactFile was all developed in cooperation with Houston.

That, in brief, tells something of how we got where we are today. During this period, we have attempted to maintain a policy of open communication with our people, the community, and the media. Obviously this task has been compounded by the simple fact that not we, nor the state, nor anyone in any position of responsibility that we know of, has all the answers to all the questions that are still being asked. And now that the matter is in the courts, our public discussions of these matters are necessarily constrained.

I believe we all recognize that, although the Love Canal story is not playing to the massive audience that it once commanded, it is a story that is destined to go on playing for some time, and that it is a story that we will have to live with for longer than I really care to contemplate.

THE CHROMOSOME STUDY

In late 1979, the Environmental Protection Agency hired a Texas firm to study the effects of chemicals buried in the canal on the chromosomes of residents. This was to be a pilot study.

To justify a more intensive effort, the hired firm asked Dr. Beverly Paigan, a local cancer researcher who was very concerned about the residents of the Love Canal area, to get forty people from the most contaminated area in Love Canal -- people who clearly had medical problems. Due to limited funds, a study on a control group (which should have coincided with the chromosome study of the Love Canal residents) was never performed.

On May 16, 1980, at 11:00 p.m. a local news broadcast in Niagara Falls announced that blood tests taken from residents in December 1979 showed a high incidence of chromosome breakage. Some say the report was leaked from the EPA to the media. It claimed that eleven of the thirty-six tested had damaged chromosomes. The thirty-six residents had not been given the results of the test yet, and the news put most of them into a panic.

The next day, the EPA flew a team of doctors to Niagara Falls to meet privately with the thirty-six families involved in the test. Each family was allowed one-half hour to ask questions about test results and to talk with the physicians. At the end of the allotted time, the family was asked to leave -- even if they were still unclear about test results -- so the doctors from the EPA could stay on schedule. Residents with chromosome breakage were told that they had an increasing chance of developing cancer, reproductive disorders, and of producing children with birth defects.

At noon that same day, the EPA held simultaneous press conferences in Niagara Falls and Washington. They officially announced that eleven of the thirty-six residents tested in the Love Canal area had evidence of chromosome breakage: ". . . a very rare observation in any population." An EPA official described the aberration as the inclusion of extra chromosomal fragments and attributed their existence to some environmental agent.

Residents were told they would be moved temporarily until the report went through a peer review process. With that, the press conference ended. The residents were infuriated, and the mayor of Niagara Falls said, "It's like they dropped a bomb on this city, then left us here to pick up the pieces."

Lois Gibbs sent a telegram to President Carter demanding the relocation of all families. "Please act immediately and let my people go!" she wrote.

On May 19, a local newspaper headline read: "White House Blocked Canal Pullout." The article went on to say that the EPA wanted to evacuate residents on the 17th, but the White House ruled against it. Residents began to gather in front of the Love Canal Homeowners Association office after seeing the headlines. Within a short time, hundreds of angry residents were gathered in the streets. They began to stop cars entering the community, turning away non-residents. They cried, "Find another route, this area is unsafe. If the government won't protect you, we will."

As the hours passed more people gathered around the Association office and some started fires in the grass, burning the letters E-P-A into the soil.

At the same time, two EPA representatives arrived to answer questions. Once inside the Association office, they were not allowed to leave. Residents encircled the office and told the officials they could not leave until the federal government provided the necessary assistance for canal families to move.

Sandie Kroeger and other members of the Communications Department watched the news on television at Hooker headquarters in Houston that night.

They wondered what effect this recent development would have on the company's already tarnished image. A call came in from a national network news team demanding an interview with Don Baeder.

EXHIBIT 1

NIAGARA GAZETTE

Monday, May 15, 1978 — Page 2-B

Local

Vapors from Love Canal pose 'serious threat'

By MIKE BROWN
Gazette Staff Writer

Chemical vapors have been found present in the basements of homes near the old Love Canal dumpsite at levels that suggest a serious health threat, according to a federal study released today.

The U.S. Environmental Protection Agency reached its conclusion after a February sampling of the air in basements and the contents of sump pumps.

Although a verification test has not yet been conducted, the Region II office of the EPA said levels of halogenated organic vapors and benzene "suggest a serious threat to health and welfare."

Regional Administrator Eckardt C. Beck, in a letter to Rep. John J. LaFalce, D-Tonawanda, said his staff will provide additional assistance to local authorities in developing a remedial plan.

According to Beck, it was the EPA's basement test results that precipitated a mandate from state Health Commissioner Dr. Robert Whalen directing the county to make sure a site clean-up was implemented immediately.

Dr. Whalen last month told the Niagara County Health Department the surface of the old dumpsite, between 97th and 99th streets and Colvin Boulevard and Frontier Avenue, must be covered with clay, and homes adjacent to the area "properly vented" for removal of toxic vapors.

It is not yet known exactly what homes were most affected in the area nor how many were above EPA levels of acceptance.

Beck said steps being taken by the county should reduce immediate health hazards. But he said a final solution "will not come easily."

"A reasonable remedial plan of action must first be developed and then funds must be secured for its implementation," Beck said. "We have hired an EPA contractor who will conduct a limited field investigation and analysis to suggest a best course of action."

A spokesman for the state Health Department today said the state "is in complete agreement" with the warnings from the EPA.

Chemicals were buried in the area during the late 1940s and early 1950s by the Hooker Chemical Corp. Chemical drums are now surfacing in the neighborhood and leaching underground.

Last week the city began spreading clay on the site to temporarily stop chemicals from gurgling up from the ground. The clay was donated by Chem-Trol Pollution Services Inc. in the Town of Porter.

In some instances rainwater mixed with a red liquid had formed pools behind 460 99th Street. A tanker sucked up the surface effluents.

So unstable is the ground in the area that a loader and dump truck sank into a black sludge and had to be yanked out by a bulldozer.

Officials have not yet determined how to solve the problem permanently. Completely removing the chemicals is the only sure solution, but the cost of doing that would be astronomical.

Pending is a federal decision on revolving funds that would go toward a stoppage of leaks from the area, but Beck said before these funds are made available it must be shown there has been migration of chemicals since June 12, 1973, the date a provision of the Clean Water Act that would dispense such money was took effect.

Meanwhile, the state has demanded that a fence limiting access to the site be constructed and surface chemicals removed while experts search for an answer.

EXHIBIT 2
Reprinted courtesy of The New York Times

UPSTATE WASTE SITE MAY ENDANGER LIVES

Abandoned Dump in Niagara Falls Leaks Possible Carcinogens

By DONALD G. McNEIL Jr.
Special to The New York Times

NIAGARA FALLS, N.Y., Aug. 1 — Twenty-five years after the Hooker Chemical Company stopped using the Love Canal here as an industrial dump, 82 different compounds, 11 of them suspected carcinogens, have begun percolating upward through the soil, their drum containers rotting and leaching their contents into the backyards and basements of 100 homes and a public school built on the banks of the canal.

Children and dogs have received chemical burns playing on the canal site, and large numbers of miscarriages and birth defects have been found among residents of the homes along the site.

Tomorrow, the State Health Department is scheduled to recommend whether the Governor should declare a health emergency and evacuate the area's families with small children.

The canal, dug in the 1890's to provide power and water for a model-city scheme, was used as a toxic-waste dump by the Hooker Chemical Company from 1947 to 1952. Thousands of drums were dropped directly into the receding water or buried in its banks.

In 1953, Hooker sold the land to the

Continued on Page B9, Column 1

Abandoned Upstate Waste Site May Endanger Lives

Continued From Page A1

city's Board of Education for $1.

The school was built on it, and lots were sold to developers of "raised ranch" and box houses, which sold for $20,000 to $30,000 a few years ago.

In 1976, after six years of abnormally heavy rains, the canal "overflowed its underground banks," residents say, and the stuff began surfacing — an incredible mixture of 82 industrial chemicals so far, 11 of them suspected carcinogens, according to the Federal Environmental Protection Agency.

Children and dogs have been burned playing in the fields, visitors have had the soles of their shoes corroded through, and some backyard trees have been completely gnawed away by chemical action.

It has also begun seeping through basement walls, and air monitors placed by the Federal agency have counted levels of from 250 to 5,000 times as high as is safe for some chemicals in some homes.

The State Health Department ran blood test and epidemiological histories on residents of 97th and 99th Street between Frontier Avenue and Colvin Boulevard — about 100 families.

Preliminary figures counted four children with birth defects among 24 in the southern block of the stretch, all of them mentally retarded, one mother said. It also showed a miscarriage rate of 29.4 percent. Thus far the department has refused to draw conclusions from these figures because the statistical sample is very small.

A Case in Point

Residents say many in the neighborhood have died of rectal, breast and blood cancers, and the Health Department has said it plans to make a study going as far back as 20 years to test the truth of this. Many residents said their dogs had died of tumors or distemper before they reached the age of 3.

Karen Schroeder, one of whose four children was born with a cleft palate, an extra row of teeth and slight retardation, grew up at 476 39th Street, and now lives at 460. Her protest to The Niagara Falls Gazette and Representative John LaFalce, Democrat of Tonawanda, first raised official concern for the neighborhood.

Her backyard seems to be the lowest draining point for the waters leeching out of the fill. Her swimming pool was popped out of the ground by the rising water table, her whole garden killed. The redwood posts of her backyard fence eaten away, and local authorities pumped 17,500 gallons of chemical filled water out of her yard in two days this year, water that even Chemtrol, the county's biggest waste disposal company, refused to handle, she said. So it was trucked to Ohio and poured down a deepwell disposal site.

Her dog died young and now her husband, Timothy, jokes that their daughter's Easter rabbit has become their miner's canary. "If it dies, we'll know to move away."

Asked to Repeat Tests

She and 40 other neighbors have been asked to repeat their state blood tests because of "abnormalities" that were found. A State Health Department spokesman identified them as liver abnormalities, but said it might be a laboratory problem.

Mrs. Schroeder said she had heard they found a high white blood count in her and in her mother, Aileen Voorhees, who is the neighborhood record-holder for chemicals detected in basement air: 12,835 micrograms per cubic meter.

"Do you want to see the paper of what's coming through my wall?" Mrs. Voorhees asked yesterday, handing over a sheet sent her by the E.P.A. to translate blips that had come over on the air monitoring machine installed on a big basement workbench. The elements included chloroform, benzene, trichloroethene, toluene, petrachloroethene, 1,3,5,-trichlorobenzene — high amounts of nine of the 11 it could test for — at least two of them carcinogenic.

The homeowners who bought land next to the canal did so because they had been told it would be turned into a park and be near the school, Mrs. Voorhees said.

'Ticking Time Bomb'

"They didn't let anybody know it was dangerous," she said. "They didn't know how far the stupid chemicals were going to run."

The Love Canal site is one of 38 known industrial waste landfills in Niagara County, and probably the most serious health hazard of the thousands in the nation, Eckhardt C. Beck, regional director for the E.P.A. said.

"We've been burying these things like ticking time bombs — they'll all leech out in 100 or 100,000 years," he said. "We're mortgaging our future if we don't control them more carefully. And the bottom line is who's going to pay to clean this thing up?"

The Hooker Company, which has offered to share the cleanup costs of a tentative city plan to dig tiled drainage ditches along the sides of the canal, has had no comment throughout the controversy.

A spokesman at the company's Houston headquarters, Sandie Kroeger, said the president, Donald Baeder, could not be reached yesterday.

No lawsuits have yet been filed by any party to the dispute, and no culpability has been acknowledged by anyone.

The city appears to have been uncooperative with neighborhood requests for help and with state and Federal agencies. sioner, Robert P. Whalen, ordered the county to fence off and decontaminate the area, cover or remove all the exposed pesticides, and ventilate the homes.

Tax Abatements Denied

The County Health Commissioner, Francis J. Clay, installed $15 supermarket fans in two homes, and put up a fence children still walk through without knocking down.

The city's Tax Assessor has refused to grant any tax abatement on the homes, even though banks now refuse to mortgage them, or lawyers to title them, Mrs. Schroeder said. And she must still pay $1,200 taxes on a home whose market value she says has fallen to zero.

The City Council voted last Thursday to acquiesce to the opinion of its bond counsel they ought not spend any public money on the land since some of the canal site is owned privately, by a school teacher in Pennsylvania who, according to a local reporter, has stopped paying his taxes.

Federal involvement and liability is also an issue.

Representative LaFalce's office is investigating whether the Army dumped chemical warfare material into the canal. A retired city bulldozer operator, Frank Ventry, said that he had helped backfill about 18 barrels the Army trucked to the area from what he called a chemical warfare site. The Army has denied any files on such dumping, but told Mr. LaFalce's assistants it was still checking.

"If the Army dumped, we should get Federal aid, damn it," Mrs. Schroeder said. "If they dumped, let them get their fanny in here and clean it up, too."

A young man who asked not to be identified who used to swim in the canal as a child, said he had seen the Army dump maerial there three times. Over the years, as dumping continued, the canal's water began to sting like battery acid and boils appeared "the size of silver dollars, he said." Every kid I knew had them. The Army has talked to lots of them."

He is 34, and totally disabled with Hodgkin's disease, a lymph cancer. "Two of my friends from then has the same thing — but not the bleeding so much, he said. "My brother has nerve disease. But I got Social Security. I don't want trouble. I don't want help. I don't want nothing from the Army, from Hooker, from the city, from nobody."

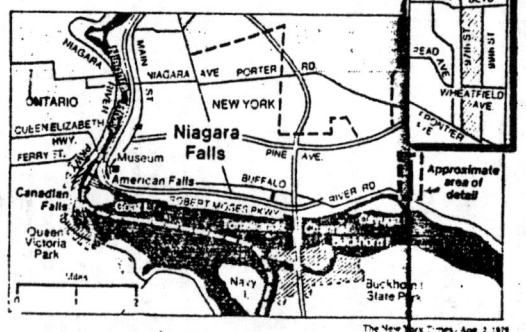

Detailed map in upper right shows neigborhood in Niagara Falls where 82 different chemical compounds have been percolating upward through the soil.

EXHIBIT 3

Reprinted courtesy of the Niagara Gazette, from October 3, 1976

Hooker dump troubles neighbors in LaSalle

Closeup | By DAVID POLLAK
Gazette Staff Writer

NIAGARA FALLS — Civilization has crept to the doorstep of a former Hooker Chemicals and Plastics Corp. waste deposit site, and the combination contains the elements of an industrial horror story.

The chemical landfill located on a 224-foot wide strip between rows of single-family homes along 97th and 99th streets has not been used for more than 20 years, but its contents still make their presence felt:

— Neighbors tell of the time a boy ran barefoot in the unmarked, open field and came home with minor burns on both feet.

— The Peter Bukla family has gone through three sump pumps in the past year, the machinery unable to contend with a black, oily substance leaking through their cellar walls some 100 feet from the deposit area.

— Four years ago some children discovered raw phosphorous chips in an adjacent chemical dumping grounds alongside the Niagara River, then watched the rocks explode as they were hurled against concrete.

— Ninety-ninth Street School principal Rudy Marion, whose building partially extends over the chemical dumpsite, recalls the time two years ago when a two-foot diameter hole suddenly appeared on the ballfield behind the school. One of the metal barrels containing the chemical wastes had rotted through, and the land above it collapsed. No substances were noticed and the hole was simply refilled.

The greatest mystery about the chemical dump area, where the smell of chlorine is particularly sharp after heavy rains, is exactly what lies buried beneath the surface.

City and county health department records do not go back to the period from 1947 to the mid-1950s when the dumping grounds were in use.

Repeated inquiries to Hooker itself drew only a "no comment" from Niagara plant officials, and even the State Department of Environmental Conservation was told to put all requests in writing regarding any of three dump areas located within city limits.

The DEC, which spent the last week checking Hooker sites for Mirex discharges, is not giving up, however, and may look further into the old waste facilities once the Mirex probe is complete.

While several sources discounted the likelihood that any complex chlorinated hydrocarbons like Mirex or other harsh insecticides were dumped at the 99th Street site, three chemicals cited in a confidential DEC memo published by the Albany Times-Union as potentially hazardous were being produced at Hooker by 1958.

The three chemicals listed are benzotrichloride, a colorless liquid strongly irritating to the eyes and skin and used in the preparation of dyes; benzoyl chloride, a colorless liquid with a sharp, characteristic odor used in the manufacturing of synthetic perfumes and dyes as a highly reactive acid chloride; and monochlorotoluene, a clear liquid with an almond-like odor used as a solvent for rubber and other synthetic resins.

While specific answers are unavailable as to the exact materials in the dump, those knowledgeable with the Hooker operation between 1947 and the mid-1950s indicate a combination of caustics, alkalis, fatty acids and simple chlorinated hydrocarbons are probably buried both as a limestone sludge and in metal barrels.

The chemical waste area between the Niagara River and Colvin Avenue in the LaSalle area of the city was known as the Love Canal for decades before Hooker acquired the property.

In 1894 the Niagara Power and Development Corp. broke ground at the site with the dream of constructing a ship canal from the Niagara River to Lake Ontario allowing for passage around the cataracts.

The canal was to have connected at Model City in the Town of Lewiston, then veered westward to the lower river area beneath the falls.

Construction ended about one mile north at Colvin Boulevard, leaving the neighborhood with a swimming hole until another use could be found for the hollowed-out ground.

Hooker purchased the land in 1947, and according to the DEC, used it as the company's first solid waste disposal location. In 1953 the Board of Education expressed an interest in acquiring the land as elementary enrollment boomed in the LaSalle area. The chemical company agreed to transfer the property north of Frontier Avenue and south of Colvin to the board, but disclaimed any responsibility for future injuries related to chemicals stored underground.

The July, 1953, deed reads in part:

"...As a part of the consideration of this conveyance and as a consideration thereof, no claim, suit, action or demand...shall ever be made by (the board) against (Hooker)...for injury to a person or persons including death" caused by the presence of industrial wastes.

Even after the property was deeded to the school board, Hooker retained the right to continue dumping in areas not directly connected with the 99th Street School grounds until a new dumping site could be found.

Hooker then began sharing a chemical waste site south of Buffalo Avenue along the Niagara River between Griffon Park and the city limits with Oldbury Electrochemical and Niagara Alkali.

Continued on 3A

EXHIBIT 3 continued

LaSalle residents troubled by neighbor Hooker dump

Continued from 1A

Those firms were later purchased by Hooker as it expanded in the 1950s.

The Love Canal property is now divided between three owners. The city owns the land between Colvin Boulevard and Read Avenue since 1960 when the board deeded the property, the school board retains the land from Read to Wheatfield avenues, and in 1974 a Kane, Pa., man purchased the land between Wheatfield and Frontier avenues.

(Contacted at his Pennsylvania home, Lee Armstrong said he purchased the land from a private individual two years ago for "speculation." He said he was not aware of its former use.)

For the most part, the existence of the chemical dump in the area of 99th Street school has gone mostly unnoticed except by those families living in the immediate vicinity.

"This really hasn't been a problem area for us," said Ernest Gedeon, Niagara County assistant commissioner for environmental health.

SECOND DUMPING SITE — Once the waste deposit site between 97th and 99th streets was closed in the mid-1950s, Hooker and other chemical companies used an area immediately south, alongside the Niagara River just east of Griffon Park. Shown above, the area has become overgrown with weeds and bushes. Gazette Photo by Dan Shubsda.

"We used to get a number of odor complaints," he added. "While residents still point to the definite chlorine smell as a problem, Gedeon said additional land cover has helped.

Six weeks ago county officials were asked to investigate a report of a black substance oozing at the bottom of a two-foot hole dug by boys playing in the field. "Hooker identified it for us. It was nothing caustic, some sort of a fatty acid I think," Gedeon said.

A black, oily substance has been troubling the 97th Street home of city police office Peter Bulka since the family moved in 11 years ago.

"You oughta smell the cellar here," Mrs. Bulka said. "We've always had a problem with it, but it seems to have gotten worse in the last year."

After eight futile years, Mrs. Bukla said grass finally started to grow in her backyard three years ago. "We couldn't even get weeds until we kept putting compost and topsoil back there."

"When we moved here, we knew it was the old Love Canal behind us, but we didn't realize chemicals were in there," she added.

City records indicate the last series of complaints about the chemical dumpsite came in 1969 when the building inspection office was dispatched to the area south of Wheatfield Avenue. The inspectors saw rusted-out barrels which had come to the surface, holes formed by collapsed underground barrels and a yellow tint to puddles which caused a discoloration of a granite curb.

The contents of the dumpsite were dangerous enough to reportedly cause Hooker officials to warn the Board of Education not to dig on the property and the only subterranean section of the school is a boilerroom on the corner of the lot farthest away from the actual dumping grounds.

Whether the contents remain dangerous more than two decades later is something undetermined as of yet.

With the public less conscious of the potential dangers in improper chemical disposal back in the 1950s, neutralizing techniques available today possibly might not have been used.

"It wasn't realized there could be potential problems, so therefore little or no precautions may have been taken," one DEC sanitary engineer said.

If the DEC goes ahead with its plan to determine what chemicals lie below the surface, property-owners whose backyards abut the old Love Canal will at least have the uncertainty ended.

EXHIBIT 4

Reprinted courtesy of the Niagara Gazette, from June 5, 1977

ZETTE

Niagara Falls, N.Y. 14302 — 11 Sections

NIAGARA GAZETTE — PAGE 1 — 6/5/77

Family recalls fires at Hooker dump

By DAVID POLLAK
Gazette Staff Writer

NIAGARA FALLS — Karen Schroeder was only seven years old in 1952, but her memories are clear.

She recalls how the chemical landfill behind her family's 99th Street home would frequently catch fire.

She remembers how workers would run screaming into her yard when some of the toxic chemicals they were dumping would spill on their skin or clothes. She remembers her mother washing them down with a garden hose until first aid could arrive.

Now 32, Karen Schroeder watches closely as the state and city work together in an attempt to learn exactly what lies buried at the former Hooker Chemicals & Plastics Corp. waste site and what can be done to minimize its contact with the environment.

The backyard where she and her husband Timothy live at 460 99th Street offers plenty of evidence that a problem exists.

"We had a a fiberglass swimming pool back there," Mrs. Schroeder said, "but water began collecting underneath it and forced the pool up."

Two years ago the pool was taken out of the ground. According to Mrs. Schroeder, the hole filled up immediately with an acrid-smelling water which has posed a recurring problem.

The land where the water receded has turned a rusty brown and now all the Schroeders can do is complete plans to level off their property with a bulldozer.

The recent attention focused on the chemical waste site where homeowners report toxics seeping into basements, fouling up sump pumps and noticeable odors throughout the house creates an additional obvious problem.

"We know this is going to knock property values down, but I guess we're not planning on going anywhere for awhile," Mrs. Schroeder said.

Mrs. Schroeder's parents, Ed and Aileen Voorhees, still live up the same street where they have resided for the past 27 years. The family has seen the once-sparsely populated neighborhood grow to the point where houses now line the length of the old Love Canal.

Whatever health hazard may be connected in the future to the proximity to toxic chemicals, Voorhees can joke about it now.

"Whatever it may be, we've probably grown immune to it," he cracked.

His wife provides details of what life was like living next door to a chemical landfill.

"They had holes big enough for houses to fit in," Mrs. Voorhees said, describing the pits where the chemicals were dumped.

"If a drum containing a certain material would break, the air would hit it and it would catch on fire. It seemed Hooker was always out here putting out fires," she added.

"We always had Hooker's telephone number right out. We used to call them and they would come out with a bulldozer and put fires out."

A Hooker spokesman said this week the company is unable to locate any records of incidents 25 years ago at the landfill, but is in the process of evaluating its work at the site.

Hooker has acknowledged to the state Department of Environmental Conservation that fly ash was dumped at the site. The Voorhees remember how it blew all over their house.

"If they had the ecology standards then that they do now, the company would never have gotten away with it," Voorhees said.

Their house at 476 99th St. retains an industrial smell.

State environmentalists concur that Hooker was not violating any contemporary dumping regulations, but only following standard industry procedures for the 1940s and 1950s.

What makes the 99th Street situation stand out is the fact society has encroached on what was once a relatively deserted strawberry farm.

Farming or even gardening now faces restrictions.

"You can hardly get anything to grow," one resident said. "And you can't plant potatos or carrots or anything that grows in the ground. It just picks up the taste of the chemical."

CHEMICAL SMELL OOZES FROM BACKYARD OF THE SCHROEDER FAMILY AT 460 99TH ST.

EXHIBIT 4 continued

6-B Niagara Gazette Tuesday, June 28, 1977

A TELLING SIGN — This sign one of several placed around the perimeter of the former Hooker Chemicals & Plastics Corp. dumping site between 97th and 99th Streets, bears a blunt message. Dr. Joseph McDougall, engineer at the Waste Water Treatment Plant, said the signs have been placed around the old Love Canal site as a precautionary measure. He said the signs were installed in the public interest until tests by the Calspan Corp., to determine the nature and scope of waste buried there, are completed and analyzed. Gazette Photo.

EXHIBIT 4 continued

Public now vigilant in environmental matters

NIAGARA '77 Year in Review

By MIKE BROWN
Gazette Staff Writer

The heightening of ecological consciousness that was born in the 1960s still continues in Niagara County. And although improvements have not come overnight, the attention paid to the environment has certainly brought some significant changes for the better.

Naturally, there are still some serious problems. The Niagara River is still dirty, air pollution levels throughout the area are still not in compliance with federal regulations, and residents in the area of the old Love Canal still have to contend with chemical run-offs from an old Hooker Chemicals and Plastics Corp. dumping site.

But officials are working on those problems and the public is aware of what is going on. A decade ago many of the conditions now considered abhorrent would have passed by ignored, rationalized away as a necessary result of progress.

The year 1977 saw more public pressure on government officials to watch the environment than just about any other previous 12-month period.

In the news most was Chem-Trol Pollution Services Inc., a plant that landfills and treats toxic wastes derived from industry.

For years, Chem-Trol had existed off Balmer Road in the Town of Porter nearly unnoticed by local residents. During that time the company created a number of potentially hazardous situations through sloppy housekeeping and questionable practices.

About 11 months ago, that unawareness came to a quick halt. Elected officials from Lewiston, Porter and Youngstown banded together in a persistent attempt to get the company in shape. They feared that if action weren't taken quickly, Lake Ontario and neighboring soil would be contaminated for good.

So strong was public reaction, Chem-Trol became a constant subject of conversation among regional Department of Environmental Conservation officials who felt were letting a serious hazard pass in the night.

The DEC has backed Chem-Trol's right to existence as a deterrent to surreptitious chemical dumping by industry, but at the same time the company knows it can't get by with practices that will endanger the rural community. Right now, Porter has Chem-Trol in court, trying to restrict and possibly even eliminate operations there.

All along, there have been complaints the DEC and Niagara County Health Department were not adequately looking out for public health. If there is any neglect on the part of those agencies, concerned citizens have made up for it. They have watched the plant with magnifying glasses and each potentially unsafe practice has been just about immediately spotted.

For a while, private airplanes glided over the facility several times a week to see what was happening and on Dec. 19 when an oil spill occurred near the plant, representatives from a local citizens group were right there taking samples for laboratory analysis.

Perhaps the most blatant environmental problem was that of the Love Canal dumpsite, an area bounded by 97th and 99th streets.

Back in the late 1940s and early 1950s, Hooker used the site to discard drums containing a number of toxic chemicals. Now, those drums are leaking and causing all kinds of problems for those who live nearby.

Neighbors report caustic substances gurgling from the ground onto backyards and seeping into cellars. Frighteningly enough, experts are not even sure exactly what was buried there. Last July some scary chemicals were found — polychlorinated biphenyls (PCBs), suspected carcinogens.

Today, a situation like that of the Love Canal would be far less likely to happen. New rules necessitate thorough recording of wastes disposal and a company would not be allowed to bury drums in such an unsophisticated way. Besides, ecology-minded citizens would scream up a storm over any such landfilling.

One interesting point is that the Love Canal trauma may have been avoided had there been a facility like Chem-Trol around back then. Chem-Trol's landfilling techniques are not guaranteed for total safety, but they're certainly better than techniques used in the past.

Right now, city and environmental officials are still working on a plan to remedy the chemical seepage. As soon as the ground freezes enough, a clay and topsoil cover will be bull-dozed over the 224-foot wide site to stop rain from penetrating down to the leaky drums.

In the future, a system of drain tiles may be installed to collect substances leaching from the area underground. The cost of such a project is still unknown and no one is quite sure who will pick up most of the tab.

How many similar trouble spots will be discovered in the future is something only time will tell. All that's predictable is that more will sprout up because across the country chemical companies have always been in a quandary over how to rid themselves of residues and there is no doubt that many of them have disposed of their garbage the same way Hooker has.

Hooker is also involved in another major, ongoing environmental problem, this involving the level of Mirex in Lake Ontario. Mirex is the trade name for a chlorinated hydrocarbon manufactured by Hooker at its Niagara Falls plant from 1959 to 1967 and ground and packaged there until April 1975.

More than a year ago, DEC officials banned fishing in the lake because the pesticide had accumulated in certain species. At the time, experts analyzing Ontario fish said the level of accumulation was above that accepted by federal law.

Whether lake fish are acceptable is now the subject of a major scientific controversy. Hooker hired an independent scientist, Dr. John Laseter of the University of New Orleans, to check over lake levels. Dr. Laseter concluded there wasn't all that much to worry about, that Mirex had not contaminated the lake beyond what is acceptable under U.S. Environmental Protection Agency standards.

Whether fishing will soon be allowed is something that won't be settled at least until January, when a team of scientists employed by the state reevaluates Dr. Laseter's findings.

EXHIBIT 5
Tonawanda News, from May 22, 1979

LET'S SET THE RECORD STRAIGHT.

There have been charges and allegations that Hooker Chemicals "covered up" knowledge of health hazards at the Love Canal site 20 years ago. These charges are not true.

Here are the facts. In the late 1950's, there was road construction over the Love Canal site, and some of the buried chemicals were disturbed. Children playing in the construction area were burned by some of the chemicals and were treated accordingly.

We looked into the problem and advised the School Board, who owned the property, to take precautionary measures so that there would not be further accidents.

Did we know the chemicals were hazardous? We knew they could cause burns and that some of what was buried in the Love Canal site could be poisonous. But we did not have—nobody had—the knowledge of toxicity then that we have now.

One more thing. The main problem with the Love Canal site was chemicals seeping into the basements of homes bordering the Canal area. There was no evidence of this happening back in the 50's; Hooker management had no evidence of this until 1976.

There was no cover-up in the 50's. There isn't one now. But there is a problem at the Love Canal and Hooker is very much concerned about it and wants to see it solved. Sensationalism and false accusations won't do that.

HOOKER CHEMICAL
Ask the people who know.

EXHIBIT 6

FACTLINE

Number 11
June 1980

LOVE CANAL: THE FACTS (1892–1980)

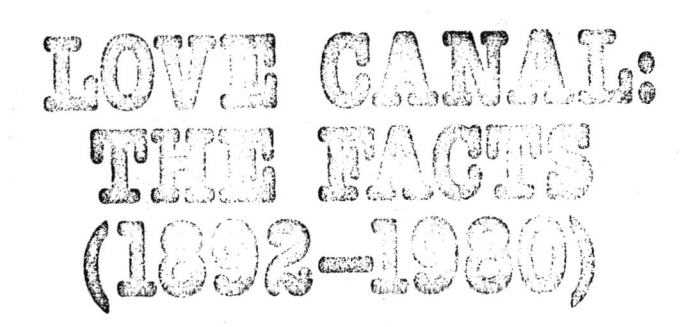

Hooker Chemical
Public Affairs Department
(713) 840-2801
P.O. Box 4289
Houston, Texas 77210

HOOKER CHEMICAL

What started out as the utopian dream of the 19th century industrialist, William T. Love, has become one of the most emotionally charged environmental issues of our time. The magnitude of the situation and the continuing distorted reports regarding what happened at Love Canal require a dispassionate presentation of the relevant facts.

EXHIBIT 6 continued

FACTS VS MISPERCEPTIONS

Since the fall of 1976 when the information first became available that chemicals had migrated from the Love Canal, misperceptions and misinformation rather than facts have been widely repeated. The following are the facts:

FACT: Hooker did not use the Love Canal property for waste disposal until 1942. It continued using it for disposal until it was deeded in 1953 to the Niagara Falls Board of Education. (Please see—1942 to 1953 and 1957)

FACT: The nature and use of the Love Canal property as a chemical waste disposal location was better than many methods of disposal used by industry at the time. The site would conform to pending Federal RCRA regulations. (Please see—March 15, 1979 and June 30, 1980).

FACT: The Niagara Falls Board of Education and the Administrative Officers were informed of the prior use of the Love Canal property and Hooker had repeatedly warned that subsoil conditions made any excavation undesirable and possibly dangerous. (Please see—1952, 1953 and 1957)

FACT: Hooker warned the Board of Education that chemical wastes had been buried in the Love Canal. It documented the warnings to the Board in the transfer deed, and in letters to and appearances before the Board. Hooker warned that the area was not suitable for construction. The public was informed of Hooker's warnings through articles appearing in local and area newspapers. (Please see—1952 to 1958)

FACT: The original understanding provided to Hooker by the Board of Education was that the Love Canal property would be used only for a school and a park. (Please see—1952 and 1957)

FACT: What went wrong at the Love Canal was not the way Hooker had disposed of the waste material but what happened to the property during the following 25 years when Hooker no longer had any control over the property. (Please see—March 15, 1979)

FACT: The clay covering the materials was disturbed by city and state road construction, and thousands of cubic yards of the cover were removed, at direct order of the Board of Education. This allowed water to seep into the Canal and it gradually filled up with a mixture of water and chemicals just like a bathtub and overflowed. (Please see—1953 to 1955 and 1958)

FACT: Hooker does not now own, nor has it owned, nor had management responsibility for the Love Canal property for 27 years. Hooker sold the property in 1953 to the Niagara Falls Board of Education under threat of condemnation. (Please see—November 21, 1957)

EXHIBIT 6 continued

Elon Huntington Hooker was a visionary who saw in Niagara Falls, N.Y., what William T. Love had seen before him—a source of unlimited energy. In 1903, Hooker founded The Development and Funding Company in Brooklyn, N.Y., which moved to Niagara Falls in 1905. The name was changed to the Hooker Electrochemical Company in 1909.

A knowledge of the events and facts regarding the Love Canal is critical for a clear analysis and understanding of the present situation. All of the relevant facts have not been communicated by the news media to the public. This FACTLINE outlines, in chronological order, the significant events between 1892 and mid-1980 that explain and place in historical perspective what actually transpired regarding the Love Canal.

1892: William T. Love arrived in Niagara Falls, N.Y. to bring about a long-held dream of building a planned model community with easy access to nearby markets, via canal, and an abundance of inexpensive power. He believed this combination would make his Model City a mecca for industrialists looking for suitable plant sites. This was especially true in an age when electricity was generated as direct current, making it essential that industry locate close to the source of electrical power.

1893: In January, Love formally announced his plans for a new city which would house approximately 600,000 people. Within a few months, he purchased or obtained options on 20,000 acres of land and began laying out the site. That same year, Love's dynamism and charisma were brought to bear on the New York legislature. He became the second private citizen to address a joint session of the State Senate and Assembly. They granted him a charter for his new company, the Niagara Power and Development Company (other companies that later merged with it were the Niagara County Irrigation and Water Company and the Modeltown Company). In October, he opened the first factory on the townsite.

1894: Work began on excavation for the canal, but Love's dream began to fade when the country found itself in the grip of a full-scale economic recession. Money and backing began to slip away from Love and his Model City. To compound the situation, Louis Tesla discovered a way to transmit electricity economically over long distances by means of alternate current. Tesla's discovery eliminated one of Love's prime selling points.

1896: Love left his project and several others attempted to fulfill his concept until 1910.

1903: Elon Huntington Hooker founded The Development and Funding Company in Brooklyn, N.Y.

1905: Hooker moved The Development and Funding Company to Niagara Falls, N.Y.

1909: Hooker changed the company name to Hooker Electrochemical Company. The basis of the company's initial success was a process to turn brine inexpensively into chlorine and caustic soda. This technology became the cornerstone for Hooker Chemical, a company that today manufactures and sells chemicals worldwide with more than 70 operations in the U.S. and around the world.

1910: Love's dream finally died. For the next 30 years, the excavated portion of Love's canal, located in an undeveloped area several miles from downtown Niagara Falls, lay fallow.

1939: On August 14, a Certificate of Dissolution was filed by Niagara Power and Development Company. Under the laws of New York, the company was allowed to dispose of assets at a later date.

1941: In September, Hooker initiated feasibility studies to determine the suitability of using the unfinished canal because its bottom and sides were of impermeable clay. It was determined that the canal was suitable as a disposal site for wastes from its Niagara Falls manufacturing operation. Since the canal had been dug out of clay it assured that the chemical wastes would remain in place indefinitely. Although the company anticipated that the sale of the canal property would close the following month (October) defects in the chain of title prevented the consummation of the sale until 1947.

EXHIBIT 6 continued

1942: Hooker entered into an agreement with the Niagara Power and Development Company to purchase the area known as part of Lot 60 of the Mile Reserve (Love Canal property). On April 15 a letter was received by Hooker from Niagara Power and Development Company granting permission to use the property for waste disposal until the sale could be completed. Aerial photographs taken of the property at the time show only six houses adjacent to the canal property.

Hooker began using the property under a license for the disposal of waste material from its Niagara operations. Its use was better than many methods of disposal used by industry at the time. As Hooker disposed of wastes, that portion of the canal area was covered with a layer of the same material which lined the bottom and sides of the canal. The use of clay to contain chemical wastes even meets pending Federal Resource Conservation and Recovery Act (RCRA) standards.

1947: On April 29, Hooker acquired legal title to the Love Canal property.

1951: The area around the canal was zoned "General Residential." This zoning permitted the continued use of the canal as a location for waste disposal.

1952: The Niagara Falls Board of Education (Board), realizing that the general area around the Love Canal was going to continue to develop, announced it wished to build a school in that neighborhood. The Board indicated that the canal property was the only area it felt suitable for the school.

In March, Hooker Executive Vice President B. J. Klaussen visited the site with the Niagara Falls School Board Superintendent and President. Klaussen had a map prepared showing where wastes were deposited, how they were covered and the results of testing that had recently been completed. On the map provided to the Board he stated,

> "No evidence of chemicals anyplace digging down 10' right up to within 1' of the excavations. In places where we have dumped chemicals the chemicals are almost unchanged in form and found 4' below top surface."

On October 16, B. J. Klaussen sent a letter to the Board confirming the company's understanding from the Board that the Love Canal property was to be used for a school "and the balance of the property to be maintained as a park." He also again reminded the Board,

> "As explained to you at our conferences, in view of the nature of the property and the purposes for which it has been used, it will be necessary for us to have special provisions incorporated into the deed with respect to the use of the property and other pertinent matters."

On October 17, the Board responded to Hooker that the letter had been read at the Board's meeting the prior night, that the proposal had been accepted and the Board stated:

> "It is understood that as you explained to the Superintendent of Schools, it will be necessary for you to have special provisions incorporated into the deed with respect to the use of this property."

The deeding was done by Hooker so future members of the Board and others who might take possession of the Love Canal property would be warned that it was not suitable for construction since chemical wastes had been disposed of in the canal.

The deed from Hooker to the Board states, in part:

> "Prior to the delivery of this instrument of conveyance (deed), the grantee (Niagara Falls Board of Education) herein has been advised by the grantor (Hooker Electrochemical Company) that the premises above described have been filled, in whole or in part, to the present grade level thereof with waste products resulting from the manufacturing of chemicals by the grantor at its plant in the City of Niagara Falls, New York, and the grantee assumes all risk and liability incident to the use thereof. It is, therefore, understood and agreed that, as a part of the consideration for this conveyance and as a condition thereof, no claim, suit, action or demand of any nature whatsoever shall ever be made by the grantee, its successors or assigns, against the grantor, its successors or assigns, for injury to a person or persons, including death resulting therefrom, or loss of or damage to property caused by, in connection with or reason of the presence of said industrial waste

EXHIBIT 6 continued

:t is further agreed as a condition hereof that each subsequent conveyance of the aforesaid lands shall be made subject to the foregoing provisions and conditions."

1953: On May 7, Ralph A. Boniello, the school district Deputy Corporation Counsel, told the Board that the deed

"provides specifically that the Board of Education has been advised by the Hooker Electrochemical Company that the above premises have been filled, in whole or in part, to the present grade level thereof with waste products resulting from the manufacturing of chemicals by the Hooker Company, and that the Board assumes all risk and liability incident to the use thereof."

He also said that,

"In the event that the Board shall accept this deed, it is my opinion that there is placed upon the Board the risk and possible liability to persons and/or property injured or damaged as a result thereof arising out of the presence and existence of the waste products and chemicals upon the said lands referred to in the said deed."

The Board voted that the deed and conveyance be accepted. The deed transferring the Love Canal property from Hooker to the Board was recorded on July 6. On August 6 the Board approved removal of 4,000 cubic yards of soil from the Love Canal for "grading at the Ninety-third Street School."

1954: On January 21, the Board approved removal of up to 3,000 cubic yards of fill from the canal site.

1955: A set of architectural plans dated August 18 indicate the intention of removing various amounts of soil from the top of the canal to grade the site. The amount to be removed ranged from 1 to 2.88 feet or approximately 10,000 cubic yards.

1957: Because of a pending transfer of unused sections of the canal property to private developers, A. W. Chambers of Hooker appeared before the Board's regular meeting on November 7 to remind them of the possible dangers of using the Love Canal for construction because of the chemicals buried there. The following is an excerpt from the Board's minutes:

"He (A. W. Chambers) reminded the Board that, due to chemical waste having been dumped in that area, the land was not suitable for construction where underground facilities would be necessary. He stated that his company (Hooker) could not prevent the Board from selling the land or from doing anything they wanted to with it but, however, it was their intent that this property be used for a school and for parking. He further stated that they feel the property should not be divided for the purpose of building homes and hoped that no one will be injured."

That same night the Board approved

"that a letter be forwarded to the Hooker Electrochemical Company expressing appreciation for sending their representative here tonight to explain the conditions of the soil near the Ninety-ninth Street School when there was no legal obligation on their part to do so."

On November 8, the *Niagara Gazette* newspaper reported on Hooker's presentation before the Board. The story said Hooker used

"a section of the old Love Canal to bury chemical waste. He (A. W. Chambers) said this use made the land unsuitable for construction..."

On November 21, A. W. Chambers again appeared before the Board and presented a communication from Ansley Wilcox 2nd, Vice President and General Counsel of Hooker, opposing the sale of the property and amplifying the remarks made by Chambers at the Board's November 7 meeting.

The following are excerpts from Wilcox's letter:

"At the time it (the Love Canal property) was acquired it was a sparsely settled section and our purpose in acquiring the same was to obtain an area for burying industrial wastes.

"The area was used for this purpose for a number of years, and, in fact, was still being used when we were approached by Dr. Small (Superintendent—Board of Education) and other representatives of the Board of Education who stated that the Board of Education would like to acquire at least a portion of the property for the creation of a new school. We explained in detail to Dr. Small the use which we were making of

EXHIBIT 6 continued

the property and stated that we were very reluctant to sell the same, feeling that it should not be used for the erection of any structures. However, after several discussions with Dr. Small and others it was pointed out to us that the School Board felt that this was the only property available in the location in which a new school had to be constructed and that they were so desirous of acquiring the same that condemnation proceedings might be resorted to. "As a result, our management considered the matter very carefully and came to the conclusion that if the property was so important to the Board of Education we would make a gift of the same to the Board with the understanding that it should be used only for the construction of a new school and the maintenance of a park. We were thoroughly convinced that should the property ultimately be used for any other purpose the residues which had been buried thereon might well have a serious deleterious affect on foundations, water lines and sewer lines, and, in addition, we felt it quite possible that personal injuries could result from contact therewith...

"...since the Board of Education itself had no facilities for maintaining a park it was reluctant to accept a conveyance containing an affirmative agreement to do so. It was pointed out that actual maintenance of a park could probably only be carried out by the City and some agreement would have to be made with the City to do this. Therefore, at the request of the Board's representatives this provision was not included in the deed. However, its omission in no sense indicated that we felt it would be safe or proper to use the property for any other purpose."

The following excerpt is from the minutes of the Board's November 21 meeting:

"It was pointed out that, although it was not so stated in the deed, there was a mutual understanding that the property would be used only for the construction of a new school and the maintenance of a park... A copy of a communication from the Hooker Electrochemical Company to the Superintendent of Schools, stated the Administrative Officers and the members of the Board of Education knew of this restriction. (Please see—October 16-17, 1952). Mr. Wilcox stated they (Hooker) feel very strongly that subsoil conditions make any excavation undesirable and possibly hazardous; he urged that arrangements be made to use the property for the purpose intended since additional park or recreation facilities in this area are desirable."

On November 22, the *Niagara Gazette* reported that A. W. Chambers had said that

"there had been an unwritten understanding at the time of the gift that the board would not dispose of the land in any way that might lead to digging or construction work." The report continued," 'There are dangerous chemicals buried there in drums, in loose form, in solids and liquids. It was understood the land would be used for a park or some surface activity if it was developed,' he said."

In conjunction with the planned construction of Read and Wheatfield Avenues, the City in 1957, and again in 1960, constructed storm sewers across the landfill site, cutting both the clay covering and walls of the disposal area.

1958: The City of Niagara Falls began construction of Read and Wheatfield Avenues and installation of utilities through the property, disturbing the cover of the canal, and causing some chemical waste to become exposed. Children playing in the area received minor skin irritations after coming in contact with the exposed chemicals. They received medical treatment. Hooker told the Board to cover the area to protect others from possible injury.

1960: On June 2 the Board deeded 6.6 acres of the Love Canal property to the City for a park which was never built. The deed incorporated by reference the restrictions in the 1953 deed.

1961: Read Avenue across the canal was paved by the City.

1962: Wheatfield Avenue across the canal was paved by the City.

On January 25, the Board sold six acres of the

EXHIBIT 6 continued

Love Canal property to Ralph Capone of Niagara Falls for $1,200. The special provisions in the deed from Hooker to the Board were included in the deed. Capone deeded the property with references to these deed provisions to L. C. Armstrong of Kane, Pa., on June 13, 1974.

1968: The State of New York's construction of the LaSalle Expressway resulted in the relocation of Frontier Avenue through the southern portion of Love Canal, requiring the removal of some buried chemical wastes and soil.

1976: On October 3, reports stated that chemicals had seeped into basements of some homes on the periphery of the Love Canal property. Although there are now some allegations that there were earlier instances, this was the first confirmed indication that chemicals had migrated from the canal into adjacent property.

1977: A task force, comprised of the City of Niagara Falls, the Niagara County Health Department and Hooker, began to study the situation. The City, acting as lead, commissioned Calspan Corporation of Cheektowaga, N.Y., to prepare an abatement plan. The Calspan report was presented to the City in August.

1978: In March, the City commissioned Conestoga-Rovers of Waterloo, Ontario, Canada, to design a remedial program. In June, Conestoga-Rovers presented its recommendations for a system to contain wastes migrating from the canal. Hooker also participated in this study and offered to pay one-third of the then-expected cost of remedial work for the southern section of the canal, which was estimated at $840,000.

On August 2, the New York State Health Commissioner ordered the temporary closing of the 99th Street school and recommended the temporary evacuation of pregnant women and children under two living in the first two rings of homes around the canal property during the completion of the remedial program. Approximately twenty families could have been affected. On August 9, Governor Carey visited the area and announced that all 236 families living on both sides of 97th and 99th Streets would be evacuated and their homes purchased. In November, remedial work began on the canal property.

1979: In February, Beverly Paigen, a biologist with Roswell Park Memorial Institute in Buffalo, urged the evacuation of more families in light of her study suggesting a high rate of birth defects and miscarriages among Love Canal residents. The New York State Department of Health did not concur with her findings. Dr. David Axelrod, N.Y. Commissioner of Health stated,

> "We cannot say with certainty that the higher rates found in each of the categories are directly related to chemical exposure but the data do suggest a small but significant increase in the risk of miscarriages and birth defects. Although the magnitude of the additional risk to this population is indeed small, prudence dictates that we take a most conservative posture to minimize even that small additional risk."

Based on this, he recommended temporary relocation of all pregnant women and as a further precaution, temporary relocation of children under the age of two.

On March 15, representatives from the American Institute of Chemical Engineers (AIChE) Task Force on RCRA (Federal Resource Conservation and Recovery Act) met with staff members from the Senate Environment Subcommittees on Natural Resource Protection and Environmental Pollution. The Task Force provided input to both the Congressional staff members and to Environmental Protection Agency (EPA) officials. The Task Force reported that,

> "The Senate staff members were impressed with the statement that the design of the Love Canal site was well within the standards of RCRA. What went wrong with Love Canal can be attributed in large part to lack of monitoring, invasion of the site itself, and lack of remedial work."

On December 20, the U.S. Justice Department filed a lawsuit against Hooker Chemical Company relating to the company's earlier use of the Love Canal.

The first of what has now become hundreds of personal injury suits was filed in 1979 against

EXHIBIT 6 continued

Hooker and various other parties associated with the Love Canal sought damages for alleged personal injury, property damage and other losses.

Among the personal injury suits are five purported "class actions" which seek recovery of millions of dollars on behalf of various groups of persons who claim to have been injured by the chemicals at Love Canal. The court ruled that these purported "class actions" failed to satisfy any of the prerequisites of the New York class action statute and ordered that the cases could only be considered on behalf of the individually named plaintiffs.

Hooker asserts that the three-year statute of limitations applies to the plaintiffs' claims in the Love Canal actions in which Hooker is a party. The rule in New York is that the statute of limitations, with respect to personal injury claims, starts to run when the invasion of the body occurs and not when the injured party claims to have discovered his or her injury.

1980: In January, the City issued $6.5 million in bonds to pay for remedial work in the south section of the Love Canal.

In April, the State of New York filed a $635 million lawsuit against Occidental Petroleum, Hooker Chemical Company and Hooker Chemicals & Plastics Corp., accusing them of responsibility for the Love Canal problems. During the month the Atmospheric Science Center published a paper by H. B. Singh, et al., entitled *Atmospheric Measurements of Selected Toxic Organic Chemicals: Halogenated Alkanes; Chlorinated Ethylenes, Chlorinated Aromatics, Aromatic Hydrocarbons, and Secondary Organics*. Information from that study and from studies by the Research Triangle Institute by E. D. Pellizzari, entitled *Formulation of a Preliminary Assessment of Halogenated Organic Compounds in Man and Environmental Media (July 1977)* and *Ambient Air Carcinogenic Vapors: Improved Sampling and Analytical Techniques and Field Studies (May 1979)* indicate that the outdoor air in the Love Canal area compares favorably with outdoor air in Los Angeles, Oakland, Phoenix, and a number of cities in Texas and New Jersey. These studies, prepared for the EPA, also show that the air inside homes at Love Canal, including homes adjacent to the canal, is even cleaner than the outdoor air.

Appendix

Source: *Niagara Gazette*

THE LOVE CANAL:
Chronology

1894

William T. Love begins the manmade canal that he envisions linking the Niagara River to Lake Ontario, providing water and hydroelectric power for a model industrial city.

1942 to 1952

Hooker Chemicals and Plastic Corp. takes over the fifteen-acre site and by 1952 has buried thousands of tons of toxic chemicals there.

1953 to 1958

Hooker sells the canal for $1 to the Niagara Board of Education and writes into the deed a disclaimer of responsibility for future damages due to the presence of buried chemicals. The board subsequently builds a school there and sells off land that is developed with residences.

October 3, 1976

The *Niagara Gazette* reports that materials from a chemical landfill between 97th and 99th Streets have been seeping into basements of homes in the area. Reports of illness and injuries to human, animal, and plant life.

November 2, 1976

The *Gazette* reports chemical analyses of residues near the old Love Canal dump site indicated the presence of fifteen organic chemicals including three toxic chlorinated hydrocarbons.

November 4, 1976

The *Gazette* reports that toxic chemicals seeping into the cellars of homes are being carried through city storm sewers and improperly discharged into the Niagara River.

September 1977

Rep. John J. LaFalce, D-Tonewanda, and federal Environmental Protection Agency representatives begin looking into problems at Love Canal. *Gazette* continues investigations on its own and urges governmental action.

April 1978

The state health commissioner orders county health department to restrict access to the area and begin health studies.

Source: *Niagara Gazette*

Chronology: Page Two

May 1978
Federal Environmental Protection Agency (EPA) concludes from air samplings in basements at Love Canal that toxic vapors are a serious health threat. State health department reveals plan for medical studies of residents.

June 1978
State continues studies and does some house-to-house sampling and collecting of blood samples for analysis. Pentagon officials deny any knowledge of records pertaining to possible disposal of U.S. Army wastes at Love Canal.

July 1978
Gov. Carey signs legislation granting additional emergency powers to state health commissioner to deal with Love Canal problems and appropriates $500,000 for long-range health studies.

August 2, 1978
Acting under wider powers, the health commissioner declares a state of emergency exists at Love Canal and orders closing of 99th Street School and evacuation of children under 2 and pregnant women.

August 7, 1978
President Carter approves emergency financial aid for the area so state can start buying homes of 236 families; eventually relocated at a cost of $10 million.

November 10, 1978
Two hundred tons of dioxin, a lethal chemical, are reported buried in the canal. Residents' fears heighten.

November 22, 1978
Over two hundred chemical compounds are identified as being buried in the canal.

December 8, 1978
Reports of findings of dioxin and other chemicals and state's refusal to relocate another fifty-four families on the outskirts of the contaminated area bring vehement protests from residents. One protest leads to the arrest of seven Love Canal homeowners. Charges are later dropped.

Source: *Niagara Gazette*

Chronology: Page Three

January 23, 1978
Dr. Beverly Paigan, a cancer researcher for Roswell Park Memorial Institute, Buffalo, urges evacuation of more families in light of her study revealing a high rate of birth defects and miscarriages among Love Canal families.

January 29, 1979
The federal Disaster Assistance Administration rejects a state appeal to reimburse it for $22 million spent on the Love Canal relocating residents and cleaning up the site.

February 8, 1979
State announces it will pay temporary relocation costs for about thirty families with either children under age two or pregnant women between 97th and 103rd Streets after documenting claims of birth deformities and pregnancy-related problems outside the first ring of Love Canal.

March 21, 1979
A House subcommittee begins hearings into Love Canal problems. Hears residents and others argue that the state underestimated the scope of health problems and failed to respond in an efficient and timely manner.

March 29, 1979
Bruce Davis, executive vice-president of Hooker's industrial chemicals group, tells the Senate subcommittee it has no legal liability for last summer's Love Canal environmental disaster. The state legislature grants a property tax rebate for Love Canal residents for five years, retroactive to 1978.

April 1979
Michael Bayliss, a former Hooker employee, releases Operation Bootstrap, a 1975 company management study of the Niagara plant documenting obsolete equipment, substandard environmental conditions, and massive discharging of wastes into sewers leading to the Niagara River.

April 11, 1979
Rep. Albert Gore, D-Tenn., charges Love Canal was avoidable had Hooker paid attention to danger signals. He cites an internal Hooker memorandum dated June 18, 1958, that described three to four children burned by materials at Love Canal.

Source: *Niagara Gazette*

Chronology: Page Four

April 14, 1979
Reports that dioxin levels at Love Canal are one hundred times higher than previously reported. Reports that contaminant is also found at Bloody Run Creek near Niagara University.

April 24, 1979
EPA approves $4 million for remedial work at Love Canal. City receives $1 million in federal Disaster Assistance Administration funds to help pay debts incurred at Love Canal.

May 4, 1979
State finds traces of highly toxic chemicals around 93rd Street School and orders more tests to determine extent of contamination.

May 26, 1979
Fifteen bids are received for abandoned Love Canal homes. Future of sales and relocation of houses in doubt as former residents protest action.

June 14, 1979
State legislature extends property tax exemptions to another three hundred families in area of Love Canal. Carter administration reveals plans for a $1.63 billion superfund for hazardous waste clean-ups across the country. Fate of that plan still hasn't been resolved although funds were proposed in the 1981 budget.

July 12, 1979
EPA announces creation of a special task force to aid in identification and cleanup of toxic waste sites, including thirty-six on the Niagara frontier.

August 30, 1979
The Board of Education closes 93rd Street School pending the outcome of further studies of chemical contaminants. Students transferred to various schools throughout the city.

September 4, 1979
Over two hundred canal residents take up residence at Stella Niagara Education Park over the Labor Day weekend after being moved out of hotels and motels in the area. They had left the canal area after complaining of noxious odors from the remedial work.

Source: *Niagara Gazette*

Chronology: Page Five

September 13, 1979
State Supreme Court orders extension of state-funded relocation of residents for a few days to allow the residents time to submit statements signed by physicians that they are unable to live in their homes due to the remedial work.

September 26, 1979
The first Love Canal lawsuits naming Hooker and three public agencies are initiated.

October 3, 1979
State Supreme Court rejects a $2.5 billion lawsuit filed on behalf of nine hundred Love Canal residents.

October 5, 1979
Actress Jane Fonda and activist husband Tom Heyden visit Love Canal.

October 14, 1979
House subcommittee recommends relocation of another 140 families after reviewing research by Dr. Paigan that chemicals from the Love Canal are migrating.

October 31, 1979
Over eight hundred lawsuits totaling $11 billion have been filed naming Hooker, the city, the county, and the Board of Education.

November 1979
A federal report indicates the odds of Love Canal residents contracting cancer is as high as one in ten.

November 6, 1979
Remedial work on canal is said to be completed and state says 110 families temporarily relocated can return.

December 20, 1979
Federal Justice Department initiates a $124 million lawsuit against Hooker in connection with chemicals buried at four sites in the city.

December 23, 1979
Albert Elia Construction Co. awarded a contract to operate an on-site treatment facility at Love Canal for one year.

Source: *Niagara Gazette*

Chronology: Page Six

January 1980
    The city sells $6.5 million in bonds to pay for remedial work in the south portion of Love Canal.

February 1980
    EPA announces it has found four chemicals suspected of causing cancer in air samplings at Love Canal.

March 1980
    State declines participation in a Love Canal revitalization program initiated by the city.

April 1980
    State files a $635 million lawsuit against Occidental Petroleum and two of its subsidiaries, Hooker Chemical Corp. and Hooker Chemicals and Plastics Corp., claiming they are responsible for Love Canal disaster.

May 13, 1980
    Niagara Falls City Council creates the Love Canal Revitalization Authority, a nonprofit corporation. Town of Wheatfield later joins.

May 17, 1980
    EPA announces chromosome damage has been found in eleven of thirty-six residents tested in the Love Canal.

Chapter 2: Communicating Strategically

This chapter is an excellent bridge from the traditional material that most management communication courses cover on communication strategy. I would strongly urge you to read chapter 1 in Mary Munter's *Guide to Managerial Communication*, 4th edition, Prentice-Hall, as a companion piece to this chapter.

For those of you using Corporate Communication as a module in a larger survey course on communication, you should probably start with this chapter rather than the first chapter in the book. You will find that the comparisons to what goes on at the individual (or micro level) and what goes on at the macro (or corporate level) in terms of communication strategy are not really that different.

Faculty trained in rhetoric can make much more of my very short treatise on this. Much has been written about this. In fact, this might be an area to spend an extra day on if you are so inclined.

The most important ideas, from my perspective, in this chapter are the notions of credibility and constituency analysis. You can give students lots of interesting exercises in association with these concepts. For example, have them determine the credibility of a group of local companies by surveying people in the community. Or use published information about a larger corporation to determine which would be the most important constituencies.

Another possibility for the material in this chapter is to work with the faculty who teach business policy or strategy in your school to discuss the connection between corporate communication and the corporate mission. You could organize group projects where students need to think about how mission and overall strategy are connected to communication in specific companies. These sorts of strategic alliances with other faculty help to strengthen the overall curriculum at your school while giving this new subject credibility by association with more established fields like business policy.

Just getting students to focus on the notion of communication as something strategic, which you really have to think about and plan for rather than something that you do by the seat of your pants, is a huge step in the right direction.

The overhead transparencies I have created for this chapter come out of both Munter's model and my own. Although this chapter comes second in the book, it is the core of the book in terms of importance. I debated about putting this chapter or chapter 3 first, but decided to go back to the original structure. My thinking is that you need to understand why corporate communication is important first then how to approach it strategically before getting an overview of the function.

Fletcher Electronics Teaching Note

This is a new case based on many others you may be familiar with. I think it is deceptive in that students tend to think it is easy because it is so short. Instead, the case can be an excellent focus of discussion for classes ranging from 30 to 90 minutes.

The way I teach the case is to start by getting students to discuss the first case question: "What problems does Fletcher Electronics have that will affect its communications?" Once you have listed these, get them to focus on how it all relates back to the Munter model (see Figure 2-1, p. 32) and the Argenti model (see Figure 2-3, p. 43). I end with a discussion of possible solutions.

<u>Fletcher Problems/Van Dyke's Problems</u>

Here are the kinds of problems you are likely to get from students:

1. Bad timing—busy season.

2. Weak credibility for Van Dyke.

3. Wrote to wrong audience.

4. Hid his true objective (to centralize).

5. Didn't listen to Wilks—visiting would have helped.

6. No motivation for managers to respond.

7. Materials managers were not positive about doing what Van Dyke asks.

8. Communication is one-way.

9. Board of directors irrelevant to materials managers.

10. Van Dyke didn't have enough information.

11. Van Dyke and his position not announced/handled correctly.

12. Van Dyke is attacking managers' perks (relations with suppliers include lunches, gifts, golf, etc.).

13. Return letter implied Van Dyke's request was a "suggestion."

14. Tone of Van Dyke's memo is pompous.

15. Tone of response is too informal.

16. Possibility that many orders coming in under $100,000.

17. Wilks is trying to undermine him (see her response to his memo).

Relate Back to Strategy

When you analyze the case in terms of Munter's model (see p. 32), put the model up on an overhead transparency or on a PowerPoint slide and write in students comments about all four parts of the model:

1. Objectives (see p. 33 of text)

    "As a result of reading Van Dyke's memo, the materials managers would notify him of contracts over $100,000." If this were his objective, he has failed miserably since the case states: "... headquarters heard nothing from plants about contracts being negotiated with suppliers."

    Students may point out that what he is really after is to centralize procurement. If so, he never states this explicitly in the memo, but it's definitely implied. Again, he fails to meet this objective.

    Finally he could just be trying to assert himself (credibility building by association with the board of directors, etc.). Again, the response from managers suggests he has gained little credibility in this interaction (see how they demote him to Procurement Coordinator, for example).

2. Credibility (see p. 36 of text)

    Students will typically point out that Van Dyke has "rank" credibility in that he is a vice president. But, in fact, his rank is useless in this organization because of its decentralized focus.

    In addition, headquarters itself (and staff managers like Van Dyke in particular) lacks credibility in a decentralized company like Fletcher. He operates under the false assumption that materials managers will be moved by his mention of the board of directors, his title, and his authoritarian style. All fail to move his audience to act on his objective.

    Finally, at the personal level, he should have tried to gain credibility through Wilks, who obviously has rapport with managers in the plants. Instead, he dismisses her advice to go visit, and doesn't ask her to help him build relationships with plant managers and materials managers.

3. <u>Constituency analysis</u> (see p. 37 of text)

   As students will eventually point out, Van Dyke picked the wrong constituency in this case. He should have communicated with plant managers and/or their boss (who is probably a fellow staff VP of Operations). This is one of the keys to the case, and for reasons I still can't figure out, it's not obvious to students.

   You can get into a good discussion of who is a part of the audience for his message. For example, the suppliers will be interested in his message, but he doesn't address them directly.

   The constituencies will not likely be happy about what he has to say because he challenges them in the memo to materials managers: "... when we are finding it more difficult to secure good deals at the local level." In addition, he is taking authority from them with his plan.

   Finally, in terms of constituency analysis, Mr. Van Dyke is really an unknown quantity, but his hidden agenda is quite clear. So, from their perspective, someone they don't know wants to take away their authority. They are unlikely to be positively disposed.

4. <u>Delivering messages appropriately</u>

   Obviously, Van Dyke picked the wrong channel for his message. The one-way nature of a written memo left little room for consultation with the materials managers. He should have followed Wilks advice and met with them face-to-face.

   He structured the message directly in terms of the $100,000 contract notification, but the hidden message was that he is trying to centralize procurement. So, in a sense, he was direct about the contract negotiations but indirect about his real objective.

5. <u>Response</u>

   The response is meant to be a contrast in tone with Van Dyke's memo. Notice again that they demote him, point out that he's an outsider ("Welcome to Fletcher!") and end with a smiley-faced emoticon (:-)). In all, however, he didn't get the desired response so his communication is a failure.

Solutions

Ask students to brainstorm solutions given the problems and their strategic analysis. Here is what you are likely to get:

1. <u>Go out and meet the materials managers.</u>

    This would have been a great idea if he had done it when Wilks told him to do so, but it's hard to imagine him meeting them without talking also to the VP of Operations and the plant managers.

2. <u>Call them all in for a meeting.</u>

    This is probably not a good idea because there is strength in numbers. The materials managers have probably communicated with each other already. They could be a very hostile audience. And, he would also have to work through plant managers to arrange such a meeting.

3. <u>Call them on the phone.</u>

    I like to role play this when students suggest a phone call. This is an example of using a bad communication channel to solve his problems. They don't know him, which makes this less than optimal. A bit of humor works well here.

4. <u>Meet with the VP of Operations.</u>

    This is probably the best place to start. You can also role play this interaction. I play the smug VP of Operations to their Van Dyke. You can show how hostile the VP of Operations is likely to be and how he or she now has the upper hand.

I usually end by pointing out that none of these solutions are great and that he would have been much better off if he had thought about communications strategically <u>before</u> writing and sending the memo.

In the end, I go back to my discussion in Chapter 2 about time (see text p.35). Correcting mistakes like Van Dyke's takes more time rather than less. Wouldn't he have actually <u>saved</u> time by meeting with the materials managers first? You cannot cut corners in communications.

Chapter 3: An Overview of the Corporate Communication Function

This is the heart of the *Corporate Communication* text. The chapter has so much meat, that you will probably need two days to cover the text and the Bank of Boston case. Read *PR! A Social History of Spin* by Stuart Ewen (Basic Books, 1996) for more on the roots of this field.

To start off a discussion of this chapter, begin by talking about how the need for such a function grows logically out of what you covered in the first two chapters and cases. How else can companies deal with a changing environment and these sorts of problems unless they first realize the need to deal with communications strategically (as we discussed in the last chapter) and then try to create a functional area to work through all of the different aspects of corporate communication?

You should also spend time explaining the difference betwwen a simple "flak" operation that reacts to everything and a proactive corporate communication department that deals with issues strategically before they happen. Most companies would never dream of letting their financial affairs proceed by letting others set the agenda for them, why should they do so for corporate communication?

Unfortunately, you will therefore have to get into a discussion about the inherent lack of respect for this field. Why else would companies over and over again put peole in charge of communications who have no experience at all in the field? And, why would they also put managers in charge who could never make the grade in what many companies consider to be the core functions of finance and production?

You will also have to get into a discussion about public relations firms. You may want to do a bit of reading about the profession as it existed in the old days by picking up virtually any textbook on public relations from your business school library (e.g., *Effective Public Communications*, Cutlip and Center, Prentice-Hall). This will give you a sense of the nice cozy relationships that the firms built up and how it was in their interest to keep the companies coming back for more rather than becoming independent through the development of a new functional area.

Centralization of the Function

The discussion of a centralized function for corporate communication gives you an opportunity to broaden the discussion beyond this subject and get into areas like organization design. You might want to discuss these issues with your colleagues in organizational behavior or read some of the materials that I suggest in the bibliography to this chapter.

Reporting Relationships

Again, where the function reports grows out of the same discussion (see also OHT in Appendix 2). In my view, the function must report to the top, but in the real world, it often does not, with predictable results.

The key takeaways for students is that the function needs to be at the same level as other functional areas (like Marketing, Production, and Finance) and it needs to be centralized.

The Subfunctions

I would spend the bulk of my time discussing and demonstrating the power of each of the subfunctions outlined in the chapter. Start with the OHT in Appendix 2 on the subfunctions and work your way through each of these subgroups.

For the discussion on image use Wally Olins' 1989 book, *Corporate Identity*, available from Harvard Business School Press. It covers the field in lots of detail and provides endless minicases for you to use in going over this area. You should also show some good examples of logos and identities, which are always available through advertisements, and from the companies themselves. Use color transparencies to show these logos; they can really make your lecture come alive.

Thomas Garbett's 1981, *Corporate Advertising*, published by McGraw-Hill is the most comprehensive on this subject. It is an elaboration of what I cover in chapter 5. Show a couple of current campaigns available from any magazine as examples. You will want to get lots more for your discussion of chapter 5.

There is so much written about media relations, that you should have no trouble finding something that you can use to introduce this subject into the general lecture on the function. If you have an example from the school itself, that would be better. For example, an article about the school from the local paper might serve as a good example, if you can find out how it came about, etc.

For product publicity, turn to Phil Kotler or some other textbook writer in marketing. This will give you a little more background than I have, but you don't really need to say very much about this. You could also mention the importance of grand openings, special events marketing, and public relations activities in this segment.

Financial communications can be dealt with by showing one of the more unusual annual reports from the crop available. This year, I used the McDonald's annual report, because it came in a box that opens like a Big Mac, it has a poster in it, and it also comes with a videotape. The Marvel annual report looked like a comic book in 1991, so it was visually striking enough to use in front of a large group of students as well.

Try to get hold of some employee relations literature to deal with this area in the lecture. You can also refer to a current event such as a crisis to make a point about this subfunction. For example, how should Pepsi have dealt with its production crew that makes cans when they were more or less being accused of putting needles in the cans?

Philanthropy may only come up in this class, so you may want to say a bit more than I have in the book. What is the philanthropic nature of the companies in your local community? Do they follow any kind of discernible strategy? If not, get students thinking about what they would suggest.

Government relations is tangential to this area, but one that you can find out more about by looking at a book called *Leveraging the Impact of Public Affairs*. It will give you lots of examples. Discuss whatever industry PAC you can find out about as well, such as the Edison Electric Institute for the power companies. You will cover this in more detail in chapter 9.

Crises are always occurring for you to throw in an example here or there. In today's news, NASA was trying to figure out what happened to its space probe to Mars. That would make for a rich introductory discussion about crisis in general. Read the paper for a few days, and you will find lots of fuel for this.

Integrating the Function

Trying to integrate the function runs into some of the same problems as trying to decide where it reports and whether to centralize or not. See the corporate design experts in your organizational behavior area or look into the literature to figure out the ins and outs of this material.

If you are using this book for executive education classes, the first three chapters can be combined to form a great lecture on the emerging functional area. I start with clips from the films I mentioned earlier, then show some of the statistics in graphic form (see overheads in Appendix 2), then show the overview slide on the function, and pick up on a few ads, some logos, etc. It makes for a very rich class.

Bank of Boston Teaching Note

Bank of Boston presents a classic example of a company that failed to focus on corporate communications and the function itself to the extent described in chapter 3. You will find that it is more accessible than Hooker Chemical and more meaty than Fletcher Electronics.

The Problem

1. How to communicate in the press conference.

2. Allen reports ultimately to legal.

3. Chairman Brown is a weak communicator uninterested in corporate communication.

4. Allen has been kept in the dark—little for him to do about the problem now; he's out of the loop.

5. Brown not involved in development of the strategy.

6. The corporate communication function is relatively small and focused primarily on image and reactive approaches to media.

7. Bank of Boston has just gone through a restructuring.

8. The banking industry itself is changing.

9. No outside counsel has been hired to help advise management.

10. Allen is not in charge of developing the strategy.

11. Lots of politics involved here; William Weld is looking to build his career.

12. Press release reads like a legal document.

13. The fine is the biggest ever, which makes it a more interesting story.

14. Conservative image, long history of the bank at odds with this incident.

15. Taking reactive, "wait-and-see" approach to this problem.

Solutions

Once you have brainstormed with students about the problems, you might want to take them through the communication strategy model (Figure 2-3) on page 43 of the text.

Who are they trying to communicate with? What objectives do they have for each constituency? What credibility do they have as an organization? Who should speak at the press conference? Should they pursue other channels besides the press conference? A close look at the strategy will help students develop the best solutions.

You can also get them to focus on answers to the case questions on p. 72 depending upon what came up during the discussion of problems. Here are some quick answers to the questions:

1. The corporate communication function is on the right track with its focus on image, but too reactive with media.

2. The structure causes them to have a legal approach to all problems. Corporate communications executives are usually at odds with lawyers, who are much more conservative. Allen reports to the lawyers, which limits his ability to influence the court of public opinion.

3. Allen needs to explain why he cannot solve problems easily if he remains out of the loop.

4. Brown should be as honest as possible and try to build confidence in himself and the bank.

5. Bank of Boston's actions and statements will heavily influence how people perceive its reputation going forward.

Overall, the Bank of Boston needs to communicate clearly what it knows and how this situation developed. Brown should be the spokesman, but he will need media training within 24 hours. The objective should be to show management in control and the image on the mend.

Allen personally needs to build rapport by providing information to key reports about what's really going on.

Once you have had students develop solutions, have them read the "B" case, which I have attached here for you to use.

B case next

Bank of Boston (B)*

On Monday morning, February 11, just hours before Bank of Boston Chairman William Brown would go before a full media audience to explain recent federal charges against the bank, the Wall Street Journal hit the streets with a story revealing a direct link between the bank and a reputed organized crime family. (See Exhibit 1.) The story cited a 1983 affidavit filed in federal court in Boston that said the Angiulo family used the Bank of Boston to "dispose of cash." The story confirmed what had been earlier alluded to in The Boston Globe, when an anonymous source said the federal investigation into violations of currency reporting laws indicated organized crime links to the bank.

Bank officials, who had spent the previous 36 hours preparing for that day's news conference, were stunned. Despite the barrage of critical reaction that would inevitably follow the Journal report, bank officials knew the delicacy of the Angiulo trial, scheduled for the next month, would prevent the bank's officers from offering any comment in explanation of the organized crime connections.

Brown, accompanied by bank executive vice-presidents Richard Wiley and Eugene Tangney, entered the noon press conference prepared to answer only questions about the felony charge against the bank. Their hope was to explain to the public the details of the bank's violation of federal currency reporting laws, and the legitimacy of the bank's foreign exchange activities.

MEDIA CONFERENCE

"This statement is intended to clarify the background surrounding our guilty plea and to address several questions raised over the last several days," stated Bank of Boston Chairman William Brown. The media conference was the first communication from the bank's officials since the previous Thursday, when Bank of Boston issued a press release announcing its plea of guilty to a felony charge. Following an emergency strategy-planning session on Saturday, February 9, the bank's senior officials had spent the weekend scrambling for information to compose formal statements from Brown, Tangney, and Wiley (See Exhibit 2), and to prepare Brown for the inundation of questions that would inevitably follow.

---

*This case was prepared by Professor Paul A. Argenti, Amos Tuck School of Business Administration, Dartmouth College, and Karen Garnett (D'86) with research assistance from John Fontana (T'86). Copyright by the Trustees of Dartmouth College, 1985. All rights reserved. Do not reproduce without written permission.

A few hours before the press conference, Brown had issued his first direct communication with the bank's employees regarding the crisis. In a one-page memorandum (See Exhibit 3), Brown informed the staff of the impending press conference, enclosing copies of the prepared statements that would be made by the three senior officials. Brown's memo offered reassurance that the Bank of Boston had not and would not compromise the "high ethical standards which have always governed the affairs of this institution."

In his opening remarks to the media, Brown offered the general public the same reassurance. Brown's formal address insisted that the bank's reporting error had occurred because of a "systems failure" rather than any intentional wrong-doing. Further, Bank of Boston had simply not known about the 1980 change in the Federal Currency and Transactions Reporting Act, which required banks to report to the IRS international cash transactions exceeding $10,000. Brown pointed out that by pleading guilty to "knowingly and willfully" violating the law, Bank of Boston had simply admitted that it *should* have known about the 1980 regulation, but had not complied with that law.

In response to numerous rumors and the Journal article from that morning, Brown firmly stated that Bank of Boston was not involved in any illegal activity. Brown declined to comment specifically on the Journal report, but insisted the shipments of currency that had occurred were part of the bank's routine international networking and the $1.22 billion figure was not unusually large, especially when compared with the bank's monthly domestic correspondent banking volume of $1.4 billion.

Executive Vice President Tangney followed-up Brown's defense by describing in greater detail the nature of international banking to justify the large sums of cash that had been shipped by Bank of Boston to various European banks. In a dramatic demonstration, Tangney held up a two-foot long "brick" of four-thousand $100 bills to illustrate how Bank of Boston typically transported cash to foreign countries (See Exhibit 4).

Executive Vice President Wiley's remarks also reiterated Brown's statement emphasizing that the bank had taken all the necessary steps to come into compliance with the currency reporting law, once the reporting error had been detected. Wiley further stated Bank of Boston's support for federal investigations into any type of illegal activities, and the bank's willingness to fully cooperate with the government.

The following day, Brown sent a letter to the bank's shareholders, offering the same defense of the bank's actions and reassurance of the bank's integrity. (See Exhibit 5.)

MEDIA RESPONSE

By refusing to comment on the Journal article and the Angiulo connections, it seemed as though the worst of the bank's problems were only beginning. Although news reports of the press conference reflected Brown's strong defense of the bank, and described his handling of the media as "cool and firm," the new angle on links to organized crime would quickly overshadow management's explanation of the bank's actions.

The Boston Globe reports on Tuesday, however, did not explicitly explore the Angiulo link, but reported the proceedings of the press conference. The headline reading "Bank of Boston: We did nothing illegal" played up Brown's defense, but made clear bank officials' reluctance to approach the issue of an organized crime connection.

By Wednesday, the Globe came forward with its own investigation into Bank of Boston's link with the Angiulo family. Two former employees of the bank's North End branch revealed that two real estate businesses run by Gennaro Angiulo had been placed on a special list, exempting any of their transactions from the usual federal reporting procedures.

According to the Globe report, the North End branch of Bank of Boston had regularly sold cashiers checks in amounts above $10,000 to Angiulo's businesses without reporting those transactions. The Angiulo accounts had been placed on the exemptions list that allowed, under the currency reporting laws, for banks not to report single transactions of businesses that legitimately had large sums of cash on a regular basis, such as supermarkets or restaurants. The provision was intended as a way to reduce paperwork for banks. The bank employee responsible for adding the Angiulo real estate businesses to the list reportedly thought she was "doing the right thing."

The Globe story still did not definitely link the Angiulo exemptions and the bank's conviction on failing to report international cash transactions. However, it did quote one source close to he federal investigation as saying the conviction on international cash transactions was discovered when federal officials began investigating a connection between the Angiulos and the bank. News reports implied that Brown's firm remarks denying Bank of Boston's association with any illegal activities had possibly been a cover-up.

A NEW STRATEGY

Senior officials would have to make another major decision about managing media and public relations—the second in less than a week—and Allen knew the bank's future would rest on how successfully the bank could defend itself. Monday's media conference had ultimately been overcome by the news of the Angiulo businesses. Allen knew the bank's credibility would be in grave danger in a second news conference if the same type of "circus" atmosphere was present.

Regardless of whether officials would go before the media a second time, permission from the Justice Department to disclose more details of the Angiulo case was imperative; further "no comment" statements would do nothing to restore the public's faith in the bank. To close its doors to media inquiry, at a moment when the bank's integrity was most severely under scrutiny, could result in irreparable damage to the bank's image and a permanent loss of public confidence.

EXHIBIT 1

Bank of Boston Unit Currency Transfers Found in Probe of Alleged Crime Family

By Rob Davis
Staff Reporter of The Wall Street Journal.

BOSTON — Federal prosecutors were first alerted to overseas currency transaction problems at First National Bank of Boston in connection with a criminal probe into cashier's checks by members of a reputed organized crime family.

According to an affidavit filed in federal court in Boston in September 1983 in connection with a racketeering and loan-sharking indictment filed against five members of the Angiulo family of Boston, the Angiulos used the Bank of Boston unit frequently to dispose of cash.

Edward M. Quinn, special agent with a Justice Department organized-crime strike force, said in the affidavit that during 1982, the Angiulos purchased more than $1,765,000 in cashier's checks from the bank. Of that amount, he said more than $250,000 in cashier's checks was purchased with "new cash," that is "cash that was not withdrawn from any existing account."

Mr. Quinn said that the cashier's checks were used for various purposes, including paying more than $270,000 to Cowen & Co., a Boston investment company.

The Justice Department earlier said that the investigation into First National started as a money-laundering probe, during which investigators discovered currency-law violations.

As previously reported, First National pleaded guilty to a felony charge of "knowingly and willfully" failing to report $1.22 billion in cash transactions with nine foreign banks.

Investigating Tool

The currency-transaction law was designed to give federal authorities a tool to investigate cases involving drug deals, corruption and organized crime, where large amounts of cash change hands.

Separately, a spokesman said the bank plans to hold a news conference today to deny that the bank was engaged in a money-laundering operation or any organized-crime activity.

Jeremiah T. O'Sullivan, chief prosecutor of the New England Organized Crime Strike Force, headed the investigation of the Angiulos. He also oversees the investigation into First National. But he declined to answer questions about any connection between the two investigations.

The First National spokesman said the bank "won't discuss specific inquiries by the Justice Department."

In his affidavit, Mr. Quinn also said that the five Angiulo brothers—Gennaro, Vittore, Donato, Francesco and Michele—had a "current total balance" at an institution identified only as the "Provident," of about $340,000. Between Sept. 29, 1981, and July 1, 1983, the Angiulos purchased more than $250,000 in cashier's checks from the Provident which were then made payable to Cowen, Mr. Quinn said.

Indictment Names Angiulo Brothers

The indictment names the five Angiulo brothers as "members and associates of the Patriarca family of La Cosa Nostra." The indictment also named Raymond L.S. Patriarca, who died last year, as the organized crime boss of "Massachusetts, Rhode Island and elsewhere." Gennaro Angiulo was described as the "underboss," or second in command.

Officials at Cowen weren't at work on Sunday, when calls were made asking for comment.

THE WALL STREET JOURNAL MONDAY, FEBRUARY 11, 1985

Much of Mr. Quinn's affidavit, along with at least three affidavits made by other parties, weren't made public because of objections by attorneys for the defendants that the information on which they were based was obtained through illegal wiretaps. Federal Judge David Nelson has yet to rule if the wiretaps were legal. The Angiulo case is scheduled to come to trial next month.

A spokesman for First National said that the bank was first subpoenaed in May 1983 but that the information requested related to "information on shipments of currency primarily between domestic banks."

U.S. Attorney William Weld said that the investigation originally focused on domestic cash transactions, but not between banks. He said the cash transactions were between banks and either individuals or companies. Mr. Weld and the bank agree that later on, the investigation shifted to foreign inter-bank transactions.

Mr. Weld also said that he is continuing to investigate First National as well as other banks, but wouldn't provide details. But he said he is "unlikely to bring other charges in the near future."

The First National spokesman, Barry Allen, first vice president for corporate communications, denied that the bank's overseas currency transactions had anything to do with organized crime. He said it was a routine part of the bank's business for about 10 years.

"We are like a warehouse where people send in currency," he said, adding that he didn't know who the source of the money was.

Mr. Weld has charged that 73% of the $528.5 million in foreign deposits made at the bank between July 1, 1980, and Sept. 30, 1984, was in small bills of $50 or less. Of the $690.1 million in withdrawals, 79% was in bills of $100 or more. First National didn't issue reports on this money, most of which came from Swiss banks.

Mr. Allen said all transactions are done at the behest of the foreign banks. First National derives income from the transactions through handling fees, he said, and by using the money as assets on which to make loans.

EXHIBIT 2

```
          OPENING REMARKS BY
          WILLIAM L. BROWN
              CHAIRMAN
           BANK OF BOSTON
          FEBRUARY 11, 1985
```

On Thursday last week the Bank pleaded guilty to a charge filed by the U.S. Attorney's office in Boston that we had failed to file reports with the Internal Revenue Service concerning currency transactions between us and foreign banks. Under the Currency and Foreign Transactions Reporting Act (Title 31 of the U.S. Code), banks are required to report to the IRS cash transactions with foreign banks of amounts in excess of $10,000.

As charged by the government, we did not file the required currency transaction reports during the period from July 1980 to September 1984. This statement is intended to clarify the background surrounding our guilty plea and to address several questions raised over the last several days.

There are two fundamental issues here. One is the violation of Title 31, which we admit: There was a failure in our reporting system. Second, is the suggestion that there is somehow a link between this "systems failure" and organized crime, which is being investigated by the Justice Department. To the best of our knowledge, this is absolutely untrue.

It has been suggested that large movements of currency in small denominations in and out of this country involves illegal activity. There is no evidence whatsoever in this case to support that suggestion.

There are, however, several points which have been reported in the media which need to be clarified or corrected. First, the shipments of currency whether from Bank of Boston to foreign banks or vice versa are strictly at the initiation of foreign banks and are either for deposit or withdrawal at each foreign bank's own account at Bank of Boston. Second, only banks are involved in any way with these transactions on either the shipping or receiving end; no individual or other non-bank customer is involved. Third, the large shipments of cash in small denominations have been from foreign banks to Boston, and not the reverse. Fourth, Bank of Boston has nothing to do with the decision of how much or in what form those shipments are made. In 99% of our shipments overseas, we are requested to and do ship in the form of "bricks" or bundles of new, sequentially numbered and recorded bills.

There is a related issue here. Somehow the impression has been left that a bank sending or receiving currency to or from another bank -- in this instance a foreign bank -- is somehow illegal or unsavory at the very least. Nothing could be further from the truth. We have been in this business for many, many years. Shipping currency is a business that is basic to banking and is highly competitive. There is nothing illegal or unsavory about this business whatsoever. We are continuing in this business. If any government official, any member of the media, or any member of the public knows any reason why this business or any aspect of it is illegal or unethical, we trust and hope any such person will bring it to our attention.

There also has been the suggestion that individuals carrying "bags" or "satchels" brimming with cash have managed to use this bank-to-bank cash transfer business for allegedly illegal ends. First, it is impossible for any individual to transfer cash overseas by utilizing this correspondent bank service; this service is strictly between banks. Second, I repeat that all of these transactions have been initiated by the foreign banks for their own accounts.

It has been reported in The New York Times in a statement attributed to Mr. John Walker of the Treasury Department that there is a large and growing market for American currency overseas, partly spurred by the rising strength of the dollar. He is reported to have said, however, that this is generally a legal market, where the banks involved in transferring the cash complied with the government's reporting requirement. He also is reported to have said that the $1.22 billion the bank transferred "is a much higher figure than is normal for one bank." Some might infer from these remarks that our transactions could be interpreted as illegal. Bank of Boston's international currency business is perfectly legal. The only legal issue was our failure to file the required reports with the Internal Revenue Service. While $1.22 billion over more than four years sounds like a lot of money, and it is, that number is relatively small when compared with our current monthly volume to our domestic corres pondent banks of about $1.4 billion. While Bank of Boston is one of the largest participants in this business, we believe there are U.S. banks whose volume is comparable to or even greater than our own.

Much has also been made of our pleading guilty to "knowingly and willfully" violating Title 31. The U.S. Attorney is reported in the press as suggesting that our guilty plea was an admission that at all points in time we knew we should have filed these reports and that we simply failed to do so. In fact, as soon as we had determined that these reports were required to be filed, we did so for the entire period in question and are continuing to do so. Notwithstanding our action, the fact that one should have known and did not comply with a regulation is tantamount under the law to "knowingly and willfully" being in noncompliance. That is why we pleaded guilty - that we should have known and did not. We did not intentionally avoid complying with Title 31. The plea resulted from extended negotiations with the government to resolve the matter in a fashion that was acceptable both to the government and to the bank.

Finally, a personal note. I have been associated with this institution for 38 years and I have always been proud to say I work for Bank of Boston. I am as proud today as I was the first day I started. Bank of Boston's record of accomplishments, strengths and most of all integrity is a record that thousands of employees around the world have been proud to stand behind for 200 years.

I have asked Gene Tangney, Executive Vice President in charge of bank operations and corporate services, to explain the business side of these currency transactions, and Dick Wiley, Executive Vice President in charge of staff services, to comment on matters relating to the investigation. I will welcome questions at the conclusion of these remarks.

The Business of Currency Shipments
Remarks by Eugene M. Tangney
Executive Vice President
February 11, 1985

Bank of Boston has been engaged in international banking for many years. International banking has always involved the transfer of cash between banks in different countries, and Bank of Boston has historically participated in that business. Part of international banking is the business of providing to foreign correspondent banks United States currency when those banks request such shipments, and the receipt of United States currency from those foreign correspondent banks when they ship it into this country.

Western European banks are our primary customers for this service. These banks in turn maintain their own correspondent banking networks in their local markets and serve as clearing houses for their correspondents in satisfying other banks' requirements for U.S. currency. I will describe the actual steps taken in handling these shipments and receipts as set forth in the exhibits attached. You will note that all shipments were reported on U.S. Export Declaration forms, even though the IRS forms were overlooked.

The transfer of money throughout the world banking system is conducted basically in three ways: 1.) through checks; 2.) through electronic wire transfers; and 3.) through the sale and physical transfer of cash between banks. Currency is by far the smallest medium of the three.

Bank of Boston is one among several, mainly large money center banks, involved in the business of supplying U.S. currency to their correspondents, both international and domestic, and this is a business that we will continue to develop. As New England's largest correspondent bank, we are also the region's largest supplier of coin and currency to regional correspondents in the northeastern United States. Current volumes of currency shipments with our domestic correspondent banks average approximately $1.4 billion monthly. Total transactions for domestic shipments for the same period in question, July 1980 through 1984, were approximately 300,000 shipments for $40 billion, while total international currency shipments for that period were approximately 1200 shipments for $1.2 billion.

DOMESTIC

AVERAGE MONTHLY VOLUME OF MONEY TRANSACTION

Cash $1.2 billion per month - shipments
                                    $ .2 billion per month - receipts

Check Processing $18 billion per month

Checks Paid $26 billion per month

Wire Transfer $157 billion per month - receipt & payment

Total Average Amount Per Month $202.4 billion

OUTGOING

CORRESPONDENT BANK

INTERNATIONAL CASH SHIPMENTS

STEP 1

Foreign bank orders currency (with verification)

STEP 2

BKB orders currency from Federal Reserve Bank

STEP 3

BKB packages currency received from Federal Reserve Bank

STEP 4

BKB prepares U.S. Customs Form describing shipment

STEP 5

BKB deducts amount of shipment from foreign bank's account on BKB's books

STEP 6

Armored car company picks up shipment and delivers to airline, where it is inspected by U.S. Customs Officers

STEP 7

BKB wires foreign bank on details of shipments and arrival time

INCOMING

RECEIPT OF CASH FROM FOREIGN CORRESPONDENT BANK

STEP 1   Receive notice from foreign bank of detail of shipment and arrival time

STEP 2   Armored Car Company picks up shipment through U.S. Customs from airline

STEP 3   Receive cash shipment from Armored Car Company

STEP 4   Count the cash

STEP 5   Credit foreign bank account on our books

<u>Currency Reporting Investigation</u>
Remarks by Richard A. Wiley
Executive Vice President
February 11, 1985

We understand that during the late 1970s and early '80s the Federal government began investigations into compliance by banks with currency reporting requirements. During 1983, the government commenced an inquiry concerning currency transactions at Bank of Boston. However, it was not until the summer of 1984 that it became apparent to the Bank that the inquiry would concern international transactions. At that time, in preparation for an examination of our international area, the Bank began its own review of currency transactions with its foreign correspondent banks. It was discovered that, through error, no one at the Bank had implemented the regulations which had been amended in 1980 to require the reporting of cash transactions with foreign correspondent banks.

In conducting its review of the international reporting issue, the bank retained David McDonald, a Washington attorney, to inquire of the officials of the U.S. Treasury Department responsible for enforcing the law whether such international transactions needed to be reported. He was advised that they did, and as a result the Bank immediately began to file the delinquent reports. No effort was made by Mr. McDonald to terminate the Justice Department's investigation. Mr. Walker, chief enforcement officer at Treasury, is reported in the press as confirming that "neither Mr. McDonald nor Bank of Boston had tried to intercede to get the investigation stopped."

The Bank now has filed reports for all the transactions that went unreported during the period of July 1980 through September 1984 and has instituted administrative policies and procedures to comply with the reporting requirements in the future.

In pleading guilty to one count of non-compliance with the Federal regulation and agreeing to pay the maximum statutory fine of $500,000 for a single count, the Bank negotiated a settlement with the government. The potential penalties could have been far greater if various of the individual violations had been considered as separate counts.

The government has thoroughly investigated the Bank's compliance to date with the Currency and Foreign Transactions Reporting Act. As a result of that investigation, the government has determined not to bring any charges against the Bank other than those relating to the international transactions described in the Information. The plea agreement releases the Bank and its employees from any further liability relating to the reporting by the Bank of currency transactions that were the subject of the investigation. As far as we are concerned, therefore, the case is closed as to the Bank.

The Bank strongly supports the purpose of the government's investigations into illegal activities and at all stages of the investigation has cooperated fully. The government, of course, may at any time investigate transactions of particular customers.

EXHIBIT 3

BANK OF BOSTON

February 11, 1985

Dear Staff Member:

The media coverage following last week's announcement of our failure to report currency transactions with foreign banks has caused all of us embarrassment over the past several days. In view of this, I am holding a press conference today to correct the inaccuracies and misunderstandings contained in this news coverage.

Enclosed is a copy of my remarks before the news media, followed by statements made by Gene Tangney on our currency shipment business and by Dick Wiley on the investigation of our currency reporting failures. I wanted each of you to have all material that I am reporting to the media.

I also am most anxious for you to know that this Bank has in no way intentionally violated the law, nor otherwise in any way acted inconsistently with the high ethical standards which have always governed the affairs of this institution.

Sincerely,

William L. Brown
Chairman

THE FIRST NATIONAL BANK OF BOSTON, Boston, Massachusetts 02106

EXHIBIT 4

Tangney holding bundle of bills: Innocent mistake?

EXHIBIT 5

EXHIBIT 5   **BANK OF BOSTON**

February 12, 1985

Dear Shareholder:

The media coverage following last week's announcement of our failure to report currency transactions with foreign banks has caused us embarrassment over the past several days. In view of this, I held a press conference on Monday of this week to correct the inaccuracies and misunderstandings contained in this news coverage.

Enclosed is a copy of my remarks before the news media, followed by statements made by two of my associates on our currency shipment business and on the investigation of our currency reporting failures. I wanted you to have all material that I reported to the media.

I also am most anxious for you to know that Bank of Boston has in no way intentionally violated the law, nor otherwise in any way acted inconsistently with the high ethical standards which have always governed the affairs of our institution.

Sincerely,

William L. Brown
Chairman and
Chief Executive Officer

The above is a cover letter to a package of information mailed Tuesday by the Bank of Boston to the bank's approximately 16,000 shareholders. The mailing included the statements made at a press conference Monday by bank chairman William L. Brown and two other executives, in which they denied the bank was guilty of any more than a technical violation in not reporting currency transactions with nine foreign banks.

Analysis of the "B" case

One of the best things about Bank of Boston is the strange twist it took while managers are focusing on the fine and cash transfer. William Weld was busy leaking information about connections between the bank and organized crime.

In addition, any further responses will probably involve connections to the Justice Department, which clearly is not playing fair with bank officers.

Ultimately, despite the fact that these were separate incidents, people saw a connection between organized crime and the fine. You can get students to see how foolish it was for Brown et. al. To go forward with their prepared remarks in the face of this new story.

The "B" case speaks for itself and is good for 15 minutes of reading/analysis and 15 minutes of discussion to wrap up.

Chapter 4: Image and Identity

This is a very rich chapter with strong ties to corporate and communication strategy. Students enjoy thinking about image, identity, and reputation so you should have no trouble generating good discussions on the topic.

For the class itself, as I mentioned in the section on image in the last chapter, get a copy of Wally Olins' book, *Corporate Identity* from Harvard Business School Press. In addition, you should gather lots of different examples of logos to use as examples in class. Similarly, Charles Fombrun's *Reputation* (also from Harvard Business School Press) offers a wealth of information for you to use.

The key discussion to have with students is about the notion of image in determining the success or failure of any organization. I give the example of two men, two hotels in my introduction to the chapter, but you can personalize this by talking to students about any two organizations that represent opposite ends of some spectrum. Like Bergdorf Goodman versus Sears for example. Why do we have certain impressions about some organizations and not others? What elements go into creating these impressions?

A good exercise that will take 10 or 15 minutes to emphasize these points is to list three or four companies or products within an industry, like Cadillac, Mercedes Benz, Lexus, Lincoln, Infiniti, and get them to describe differences among companies or products that have similar positionings. In this case, these are all luxury autos, but the Lincoln and Cadillac have a totally different cachet from MB and Lexus. What goes into creating those impressions? This is a fun exercise; personalize it to suit your own local information and what you know best.

Another important point for students to understand is the notion of image versus that of identity. I have defined image as a mirror image of the organization's reality and identity as physical manifestations of that image. This takes a while to understand, but you can bring the point home very easily by using specific company examples. Again, I would urge you to use ones that you know yourself rather than sticking with the ones I talk about.

I have included an article at the end of this chapter that I wrote several years ago with my colleagues to give you more insight into how important names can be. This article points out the connection between name changes and stock price. It is based on very extensive research and can be a nice adjunct to the other information you are covering in this class.

The step-by-step guide to managing identity is another opportunity for an exercise. You can have students work with local companies, or have them conduct such an audit based on public information about a well-known company.

Other Options

Other companies to consider that have made big changes recently are mentioned in the text and should be explored in the context of this case. They include Kmart, which went more upscale; KFC, which tried to become more healthy and perhaps less associated with an old white-haired man than before; and whatever examples are currently available from the time when you are teaching this should also be used.

Another exciting approach is to look at the reputation or image of your college or university and compare it to other institutions. Students will enjoy discussions of the *US News* or *Business Week* rankings. Similarly, the college or university's identity program can be analyzed in the context of the material in this chapter. (See the material at the end of this chapter for more on this.)

If you are really interested in this subject beyond what I have provided in the chapter and in this note, I would strongly urge you to look at some of the books in my bibliography. Lorenz's book, *The Design Dimension*, takes the discussion into the realm of product design as well as what we talk about in this chapter. Forty's book, *Objects of Desire*, focuses on design and society and is a fascinating book to read.

You can also get a local graphic designer to come in and give a presentation when you cover this material. They can talk about the importance of design elements and give specific examples of their work. I do this every year, and find it to be the best way to handle the subject.

GE Identity Program (A) & (B)

Most of the focus for those who do not want to get involved with the above exercises mentioned earlier can be on the GE case. It represents a solid example of one company's attempt to "manage the unmanageable." The "A" case focuses on GE's attempt to reexamine its identity. It raises all of the important questions most of which will be very obvious to your best students.

For example, what is the benefit of a monolithic image for each of the divisions versus a more decentralized approach? Is the current identity so well known that it is impossible to change without creating lots of ill-will for several constituencies? Other pieces of their overall communication strategy will naturally emerge from this discussion.

The questions at the end of the case are comprehensive enough for you to generate lots of discussion about what GE should do.

Get students to think about the value of GE's identity and what the various options presented in the case offer the company. Is the current identity outdated? Will some of the options be too radical?

The "B" case presented following this note explains exactly what happened in the GE case. It is self explanatory. You may want to just teach the material in the "B" case at the end of class rather than have students read and evaluate it. This depends on how much time you can devote to the material.

GE Identity Program (B)

"For the final presentation to the Chairman, we developed three very finished systems: one that was evolutionary and the other two taking steps away from the traditional look to a very radical new approach which had nothing to do with the old identity. People could look at them and begin to get a sense of what each option might be like. In fact, that crystallized opinions very quickly. It was about 80-20; 20% of the management team, about thirty people in all, wanted to move to the radical end. They all tended to be in our high technology businesses. It didn't segment by age, by type of individual; it segmented by the business they were in . . . I was a believer in getting rid of the whole thing, blowing up the trademark. I was radical. I wanted to put a new trademark on the front door. A combination of Landor and the management kept us from doing that, and now, in retrospect, I really think it was the right thing to do."[1]

Richard Costello

"We were pretty excited, to be honest, about some of these breakthrough designs. Ultimately, however, it came back to the fact that the Monogram had such tremendous equity and awareness levels and communications values. It was just impossible to walk away from it.[2]

Patrice Kavanaugh

To give Landor its due, they had done the alternatives in a really high quality fashion. They'd done packaging and signs and cards and letterhead and all that sort of thing. There was a vocal minority that thought we ought to take the more far out modification of the Monogram, to the point that it was unrecognizable. Our concern was that we could lose all identity and that it would be enormously expensive to associate that new identity with all the equity that we'd built up through the Monogram. That was the basis of the decision to make relatively small modifications in the actual appearance of the Monogram. But there was whole-hearted support for the nomenclature and the cleaning up of our appearance and looking as one company."[3]

Paul Van Orden

Ultimately, the decision was made to retain the GE monogram - thus retaining that quality of solidity and reliability - and to communicate the qualities of dynamism and innovation through secondary devices enhancing the Monogram. In other words, to "keep the baby, change the bath water."[4] Landor spent three-quarters of 1987 fleshing out the system to meet their original objectives.

---

[1]Interview with Richard Costello conducted by Peter Lawrence, 18 June 1991.
[2]Interview with Patrice Kavanaugh conducted by Peter Lawrence, 9 May 1991.
[3]Interview with Paul Van Orden, 3 December 1991, conducted by Laurie Poklop.
[4]Interview with Richard Costello by Peter Lawrence, 18 June 1991.

OBJECTIVE: BROADEN AWARENESS OF GE'S DIVERSITY SO THAT PEOPLE HAVE A MORE *ACCURATE PERCEPTION* OF THE COMPANY.

The new identity system gave GE a coherent branding and naming system; it established a logic which had previously been absent and facilitated decision making on branding and naming of components within a brand.

First of all, to address the reality of the corporation's diversity, Landor recommended that in its external and internal communications, the company no longer call itself General Electric, but simply GE. This change was supported by research in which two-thirds of the people who named GE, when asked to name some big companies, called it GE, not General Electric. So the change would not cause confusion.

To make the company appear leaner and simpler, both visually and verbally, a plethora of formal organizational names being used in advertising, brochures, business cards, etc., were shortened to very concise descriptors of competencies. To the degree possible, the rule was to use the highest level of competence that made sense for a particular business, i.e. GE Aerospace, GE Plastics, GE Aircraft Engines, GE Financial Services, etc. While people would not remember that GE was in hundreds of businesses, by using these concise competency terms, it was hoped that they would build awareness of fifteen or so areas of business, thus communicating the company's diversity.

Former Organizational Name
   New Communicative Name

General Electric Aerospace Business Group
   GE Aerospace
General Electric Aircraft Engine Business Group
   GE Aircraft Engines
General Electric Major Appliance Business Group
   GE Appliances
General Electric Financial Services, Inc.
   GE Financial Services
General Electric Lighting Business Group
   GE Lighting
General Electric Medical Systems Business Group
   GE Medical Systems
General Electric Motor Business Group
   GE Motors
General Electric Power Systems Business
   GE Power Systems
General Electric Semiconductor Business
   GE Solid State
General Electric Plastics Business Group
   GE Plastics

A similar logic was used internally to simplify functional titles, which supported the direction of the company to become less bureaucratic. For example, the person in charge of the major appliance business had been called Vice President and General Manager of Major Appliance Business Division. Under the new system, that person's title is Vice President, Major Appliances.

> We were striving internally to become less bureaucratic, to have fewer layers of management structure, increasing the span of control of the manager, so that instead of having seven people reporting to a manager, we have fifteen or sixteen. We were cleaning up the processes so that there were fewer approvals. Cleaning up the way we identified ourselves internally went with the grain of that thought. This was another step in being less of a bureaucratic, cumbersome company. We're cleaner, we're one, we're going to have more simple identification of our business.[5]
>
> Paul Van Orden

Next came the issue of how the company would deal with acquired brands. Patrice Kavanaugh gives the following description of how corporations deal with branding issues:

> There are basically two extremes, if you think in terms of a spectrum. On one extreme, you have a company like IBM, where the brand that's used at the corporate level is also the brand that's used at all their product levels. The opposite extreme is represented by Bristol Meyers or Proctor and Gamble, where the corporate brand is completely invisible to the public and, all of their visibility is exclusively through their brands. It allows them to create two brands in the same category, like Bufferin and Excedrin, which compete against each other and thereby increase the company's overall market share.
>
> Then you have companies that do a mixture of the two. Disney, for example, has some of its products and brands share the corporate brand while others don't. For example, Touchstone, the more mature theme film brand, has no

---
[5]Interview with Paul Van Orden, former GE Vice President, on 6 December 1991.

relationship back to Disney, because they're trying to create some separation.

It can be very difficult to support the Bristol Meyers strategy, because you have to have lots of promotional dollars to support all those brands. And an IBM-type strategy can be just as difficult unless you're in one business that allows you to expand as much as you want to remain viable. So, most companies end up somewhere in between.[6]

GE historically had been where IBM was, but it was moving. The question was, how far would it move and how? Landor developed five levels of identification which GE could use to identify conceivably every business it would ever enter or acquire: (Examples shown are for purposes of illustration only.)

1. GE linked to a competence term. Encompassed 80% of GE's businesses.

2. The Monogram + Proper Name. Used when it is beneficial to retain the affiliate's existing name and a lesser degree of association with GE is desirable.

3. GE Monogram Endorsement. Used if the company acquired a business with powerful brand which would still benefit from being linked to GE.

4. GE Verbal Endorsement. Used if an acquired company had strong equity in both its visual and its verbal expression, or if for other reasons the company didn't want GE so closely tied to it.

5. GE Invisible. Used in cases where there is no benefit in linking GE with an affiliate. NBC is an example of this. Concerned that GE would be seen as controlling the news if it linked itself too closely to NBC, it was decided to retain NBC as a separate entity.

To help the company determine which level is appropriate for a business, Landor developed an elaborate decision tree addressing business, industry, image, and identity issues. In terms of business issues, questions are asked such as, do you have control over this organization, and are you committed to this business? If GE doesn't control an acquired company, it is recommended that they not link themselves too closely to it, because they risk losing control of their image. In terms of commitment, GE had historically gotten in and out of several businesses. This system allowed GE not to link itself too closely to a business it was not committed to for the long term.

Through its extensive research, Landor rated the image value of particular industries. For example, aerospace, communications, and medical systems industries were rated with a high image value for the targeted qualities of dynamism and innovation, while appliances, construction equipment, and financial services provide a lower image value for these traits. Because the company is trying to communicate that it is dynamic and innovative, if they were acquiring a company in an industry that is not particularly dynamic, a lower level of association with GE would be appropriate. Similarly, through research Landor developed ratings of performance expectations of GE in a range of industries. Whether or not GE is likely to be thought of as doing well in a particular industry would lead to higher or lower level of association.

Finally, in terms of identity issues, questions are asked such as: Is the equity of the affiliate's existing identity strong or weak? Is awareness of the name and logo high? Is the name associated with a leadership position in terms of product and service quality? What would be the impact on the company if GE were prominently associated with the affiliate? A negative association always leads to a higher level (#4).

OBJECTIVE: MAINTAIN GE'S IMAGE OF RELIABILITY AND IMPROVE PERCEPTIONS OF ITS INNOVATION AND DYNAMISM.

The GE Identity Program Manual succinctly describes how the new GE signature communicates the qualities of reliability, innovation, and dynamism:

Reliability if conveyed by:
- continuing use of the Monogram, a 100-year-old symbol that is familiar and
- trusted.
- standardizing the color of the Monogram to Platinum Grey, creating a classic and distinguished presentation, and
- using a serif typeface, ITC New Baskerville, suggesting traditional qualities.

---
[6]Interview with Patrice Kavanaugh conducted by Peter Lawrence, 9 May, 1991.

Dynamism and innovation are conveyed by:
- Using a signature that provides a contemporary environment for the Monogram. The Graphic Signature features:
  —*the Laser Line*, suggesting high technology,
  —*the italic typeface Univers*, suggesting forward movement, and
  —*an asymmetrical layout*, conveying movement with its visual tension.
- Selectively using a portion of the Monogram on a large scale - the Dynamic Monogram - suggesting the Company is "too dynamic to be contained."[7]

OBJECTIVE: UNIFY THE COMPANY'S VISUAL AND VERBAL EXPRESSIONS THROUGH A CONSISTENT AND HIGH QUALITY APPLICATION OF THE CONTEMPORARY PROGRAM STANDARDS.

The Landor design team worked out applications for every conceivable visual and nomenclature situation - print advertising, brochures, stationery, checks and business forms, trucks, packaging, signs, and exhibits. At this point, the Advisory Council broke up into small groups to help define the breadth of each media category and the practical limitations and requirements imposed by each kind of application.[8]

The most tangible deliverable Landor presented to GE was a two-volume manual documenting all the standards. The first volume, distributed by late autumn of 1987, was devoted to general standards and trademark applications. The second was devoted completely to applications and followed a few months after the first. Because GE had so many businesses spread throughout the world working with so many consultants, they felt it was important to show as many examples as possible, leaving as little as possible to people's imaginations. The manual was designed as a out-sized loose-leaf notebook. The large format allowed space for the necessary displays and specifications and indicated the importance of the program. In addition, the loose-leaf format permitted economical printing of any adjustments and additions that might be made to the standards.

By early 1988 each business began implementing the standards of the new corporate identity system, supported by a communications manager who had participated first hand in the development of the program through the Advisory Council. Each business was responsible for developing its own roll-out schedule. Schedules were influenced by such factors as current budgets, new product launches, a new advertising campaign, etc.

Media that are the most easily and economically implemented—such as stationery, print advertising, new brochures, etc.—were the first converted to the new identity system. Other media that are more expensive to implement—such as signs and vehicles—were converted once funds could be allocated or according to pre-existing maintenance schedules. For example, if a vehicle fleet was due to be repainted in twelve months, then it would be converted to the new look at that time. In this way, GE instituted a "rolling change" for the new identity system. That is, its various media were implemented over a period of time, rather than all at once; thus, the implementation was carried out in as cost efficient a manner as possible.

GE's businesses were introduced to the program standards via on-site Identity Introduction presentations. For each major business, in the United States and at several international locations, GE corporate identity management and Landor presented an overview of the program standards to selected marketing and communications managers and their staffs, as well as key outside vendors. A subsequent question and answer session addressed the program standards.

Shortly after these presentations, the manuals were distributed throughout the company to the appropriate individuals and implementation began according to each business' roll-out schedule. In addition to the manuals, posters were distributed summarizing the program for display in office/studios. A videotape was produced, detailing highlights of the development process and strategy; this was distributed widely inside the Company.

One of the largest businesses, GE Appliances, established its own internal corporate identity council. Vic Alcott, Manager of Advertising and Design for GE Appliances, had been a member of the Advisory Council, and implementation of major areas of the identity program came under his responsibility. To accomplish this, be brought together a team of about a dozen people representing design, purchasing, sales, promotion, consumer service, and patent council. The group stayed in place for approximately two years and worked to execute the program, keep a lid on costs, and develop a sense of ownership of the plan among people with various departmental responsibilities.

---

[7] GE Identity Program, Volume 1: Basic Standards, p.ii.
[8] Bartels, Donald H., "The GE Identity Program: A Historical Review," p.50.

One of the biggest challenges from the beginning was what I call the cost equation. You can't tell management you need X million dollars to implement some corporate identity program. You still have to meet bottom line goals. So how do you phase it in and begin to execute it as quickly as possible and make it very visible, but not generate a lot of incremental cost? I saw that as our #1 challenge.[9]

Vic Alcott

Some changes were easier to implement fairly quickly, like adapting the type style and signature guidelines in advertising. Other changes took place according to regular schedules. For example, in exhibit design, new shows are continuously designed throughout the year, and elements such as dynamic monogram were integrated fairly quickly. Other changes, such as those effecting product or vehicle design, were more long-term. The program effected product design in terms of graphics and terminology which appeared on appliances. Similar to the principles of the simplified nomenclature system, the basic criteria governing words and graphics on products are that they will create an overall statement of quality and innovation and will communicate to the user how to use the product. They will have functional copy, not promotional copy. Particular graphic elements are evaluated as to their effectiveness on individual products. For example, a thin, laser red line on a microwave oven helps to create a streamlined appearance.

Once the team had communicated the guidelines internally, it took on the challenge of implementing the program with external suppliers. To do this, they distilled the two-volume identity manual into approximately fifty pages, covering the highlights of each of the basic media. Then they held a seminar with forty to fifty of their major suppliers and got them to begin working with the system—"put it into real day execution."

Getting it under control; simplifying it; making whatever modifications had to be made along the way; making sure that it doesn't get out of line from a financial perspective; and getting people to feel comfortable with it and therefore take ownership: these are the key ingredients of making a corporate identity program work well in the real marketplace quickly.[10]

Landor continued to work with GE on "identity system maintenance"—monitoring the implementation of the identity system through on-site workshops conducted at each of the fourteen major businesses approximately every eighteen months. Over a period of several months prior to the workshops, Landor evaluated visual materials produced by each business, then reported back the results to each group. Through a slide presentation, Landor presented, first, how the identity system was being implemented company-wide and, second, how the particular business was performing in terms of following the identity guidelines. Workshop participants were also encouraged to bring materials to the workshops for on-the-spot consultation. In the first such Identity Review, which took place in 1989, a few businesses showed excellent results, while as a whole the company's implementation was judged to be very good, particularly considering its decentralized organization structure.[11]

According to Patrice Kavanaugh:

The workshops are really effective in motivating people to continue following these guidelines. They are a reflection of the corporation's ongoing commitment to the identity program, and help keep the program on track. Identity is like any other corporate asset. You have to give it attention and maintain it over time. These workshops seem to be an effective way to do that.[12]

Has the GE Identity Program been a success? The following comments represent a variety of perspectives on the value of corporate identity:

Paul Van Orden, Executive Vice President, GE:

The GE identity, as former chairman Owen D. Young once said, 'may be our least tangible yet most valuable asset.' To sustain the #1 or #2 position of all our businesses in today's tough business environment, we must leverage every asset and competitive advantage we own. We

---

[9] Interview with Vic Alcott, Manager of Advertising and Design, GE Appliances, 2 December 1991.

[10] Ibid.
[11] Ibid., p. 52.
[12] Interview with Patrice Kavanaugh conducted by Peter Lawrence, 9 May 1991.

can't afford to be misunderstood; we can't afford our leadership position to be overlooked.[13]

Richard Costello, Manager of corporate Marketing Communications, GE:

I could argue quite vigorously that there has been significant day to day cost savings by implementing a clean, clear, orderly, narrowly defined program. We have had millions of dollars being spent on people reinventing the light bulb, or more specifically, reinventing how you do a sign outside. By limiting choices, we've improved not only the quality of the output, but we've improved productivity as well. When we audited business cards and stationery, even in corporate headquarters, there were ten different designs. So even at that very pragmatic level of standardizing stationery, there is a cost savings.

At a strategic level, I would argue that the company had done a superb job over a century of creating whatever it was that people perceived and valued about GE. That was the reason that we decided to keep the monogram—because there's 100 years of investment behind that. However, over that time there had been some practices or just simply sufficient changes that it was not as appropriately positioned for today's world and today's company as it might have been. So I would argue that we then invested for a couple of years a significant sum of money, that in the scheme of a $50 billion corporation is peanuts, to position ourselves for the next 20 years.[14]

Vic Alcott, Manager of Advertising and Design, GE Appliances:

As we began to expand it internationally, through working with customers or acquiring new companies on a global basis, one of the first things they say is, isn't it remarkable, all you people at GE have the same business card. It's such a simple thing, but what it says to people on the international scene is that here's a company that is concerned about its identity; no matter how big or small, it is communicated. Be it a business card or an expensive product display or a television commercial there is a clear, single idea that you get about this company from all those media. It pays off as it begins to get bigger and broader.

If your objective is to establish an image for a brand as being a leader in a given industry, and as one that provides genuine relevant innovation in its product to that industry and maintains a very high quality standard of execution that has a rub off in sales and margins, profitability over time. It's hard to single out that that was the result of a given signature or graphic system, but the fact remains that that forces the consistence which results in an executional quality and a perception of a customer when they look at all those products and they see that design consistency. It pays off, it builds, it has added value.

Roger Morey, Vice President, GE Motor Sales:

Ten years from now, we'll look back and realize the identity program is one of the best things the company ever did.[15]

Patrice Kavanaugh, Account Executive, Landor Associates:

The hardest job I think we have to do in 'selling' companies on the value of design is proving its value to the bottom line. If you've got dozens of consulting firms, design firms, and in-house designers constantly creating new looks and coming up with new themes, all of that time and effort and energy costs the company money. If you come up with a set of guidelines that establish consistency, while still allowing sufficient flexibility, you're giving people a template. Our argument is that, giving them that template, one, you're insuring that the company is communicating what the corporate message is, but two, they're further up on the design line than they would be if they were always starting from ground zero.[16]

---

[13] Bartels, p. 46.
[14] Interview with Richard Costello conducted by Peter Lawrence, 18 June 1991.
[15] Bartels, p 52.
[16] Interview with Patrice Kavanaugh conducted by Peter Lawrence, 9 May 1991.

Reprint

Anspach
Grossman
Portugal
Inc

Identity
Consultants

711 Third Avenue
New York, NY 10017
212 692 9000

77 Maiden Lane
San Francisco, CA 94108
415 781 7337

TUCK TODAY

The Name Game:
How Corporate Name Changes Affect Stock Price

By Professors Paul Argenti, Robert Hansen, and Scott Neslin

Much has appeared in the media about name changes in the past year because companies — indeed, some very large, well-known companies — are changing their names more than ever. Yet, despite all the attention focused on this trendy subject, little has been done (particularly in the academic community) to study the effects of this expensive and time-consuming process. The few academic studies that have been done suggest that name changes are associated with small positive effects on the company's stock price around the time of the name change announcement. These studies suffer, however, from small data bases and a lack of control for events concurrent with the name change that can confound measurement of the name change's effect.

We undertook a study of the effect corporate name changes have on stock prices for Anspach Grossman Portugal Inc. (AGP), a corporate identity firm located in New York. Because of the large data set provided by AGP — a complete listing of all corporations that had changed names since 1960 — we felt that we could provide results supplementing those of earlier studies. This article explains in detail the conceptual framework we used to conduct the study, our methodology, and the results of our analysis.

IH → NAVISTAR

Libbey Owens Ford → TRINOVA

Continental Telecom Inc. → CONTEL

UNITED STATES GYPSUM → USG

CONSOLIDATED FOODS CORPORATION → SARA LEE CORPORATION

First National City Bank New York → CITIBANK

I. Conceptual Framework

We identified two mechanisms by which a name change could affect the price of common stock. One of these acts directly through the investment community; the other works through the company's business customers:

**A firm changes its name
(or proposes such a change)**

Mechanism 1

The investment community hears about the change

The investment community judges the implications of name change

Mechanism 2

Customers hear about the change

Through their actions, customers can affect earnings per share

Stock price is either affected positively, negatively, or not at all

---

Although the second mechanism clearly is important, we realized that it would be virtually impossible to analyze except on a case-by-case basis, because the mechanism would operate over an extended period of time. Its effect would be diffuse and, therefore, difficult to measure.

The first mechanism, however, would be expected to operate around the actual time of the name change. In our analysis, the "investment community" includes stock specialists, other insiders, and the general investing public. Our sense was that the specialists and insiders could affect the stock price before an announcement and the general public would exert its influence afterwards. In fact, investors will anticipate how customer reactions will affect earnings and stock price in the future and, therefore, they will impound those expectations into present stock prices. Our reliance on this weak form of market efficiency underlies our considering only Mechanism 1.

In devising a conceptual framework for the study, we also needed to make decisions about whether to analyze only those companies that had "pure" name changes (i.e., no other events, like dividend announcements, happening at the same time), or to look at those with concurrent events.

We encountered difficulties in both cases. Those companies with pure name changes would be very limited in number and thus might not produce statistically significant results. On the other hand, companies that changed their names and had concurrent events would tend to confound things and dilute the effects of name changes alone. In addition, the number of concurrent events would likely be large and, therefore, difficult to classify. Yet, companies with concurrent events would provide a much larger sample and, thus, more significant results. More importantly, these companies would be representative of the typical name change scenario. Thus, we decided to look at both sets of companies and to explore methods for minimizing the problems associated with each case.

Finally, in terms of the conceptual framework, we needed to make decisions about what characteristics or kinds of name changes would be important. For this information, we relied heavily on AGP's guidance provided through a detailed report and follow-up discussions. Specifically, we used AGP's classification of corporate name changes to examine whether different types of name changes had different effects.

II. Methodology

Event studies

Event studies are *the* major way in which financial economists examine the effect on security prices of firm-specific events and test the informational efficiency of securities markets. This methodology arose right after the initial development of the theoretical models for determining asset prices (e.g., the capital asset pricing model [CAPM], which is a framework for analyzing the relationship between risk and rates of return).

A list of the published papers using event-study methodology would be extremely long. It has certainly passed the test of general academic acceptance. Furthermore, there is a well-developed theoretical justification for event-study methodology.

The basic idea underlying the methodology is that in the absence of any unanticipated firm-specific information, a firm's stock will yield a return just high enough to compensate investors for holding that stock. This "normal" or "expected" return is predicted by the CAPM and reflects what the market as a whole earns with an adjustment for the firm's risk. A stock will yield a return different from the expected return only to the extent that unanticipated firm-specific information has appeared during the period.

Announcements or releases of such information are referred to as "events." Events involving bad information will cause a stock's actual return to be less than expected, and the reverse is true for events of good information.

If we then define the "excess" or "abnormal" return to be the actual return less the expected return, we can classify events as containing good or bad information according to whether we observe positive or negative excess returns, respectively.

The last step is to calculate excess returns. A simple and reliable technique is to subtract the market's return (overall average for all stocks listed on the NYSE) from a stock's actual return. Intuitively, we are "adjusting for the effect of the market as a whole" and are left with only firm-specific excess returns, all of which must be due to unanticipated informational events.

Table 1. Type and Number of Name Changes

In order of frequency, here are the fifteen types of name changes we studied in 355 companies. The numbers in parentheses indicate the number of companies studied for each name change type.

	Before	**After**
1. Removal of a limiting descriptor (95 companies)	Hershey Chocolate Corporation Sun Oil Company St. Regis Paper Company	Hershey Foods Corporation Sun Company, Inc. St. Regis Corporation
2. Newly created or selected name (71 companies)	Swift & Co. First National City Corp. American Metal Climax Inc.	Esmark, Inc. Citicorp Amax Inc.
3. Adoption of initials (41 companies)	Union Twist Drill Company Radio Corporation of America Shoe Corporation of America	UTD Corporation RCA Corporation SCOA Industries, Inc.
4. Simple truncation (eliminating the non-essential) (31 companies)	Ashland Oil & Refining Co. Harris-Intertype Corporation Foremost-McKesson, Inc.	Ashland Oil, Inc. Harris Corporation McKesson Corporation
5. Addition of merger partner, acquirer, or acquisition's name (22 companies)	Phibro Corporation Knight Newspapers Inc. Amerace Corporation	Phibro-Salomon Inc. Knight-Ridder Newspapers Inc. Amerace Esna Corporation
6. Adoption of an acronym (of the previous name) (14 companies)	National Biscuit Company Continental Oil Company Pepsi-Cola Company	Nabisco, Inc. Conoco, Inc. PepsiCo, Inc.
7. "Verbal escalation" (use of presumably more impressive words) (12 companies)	Genstar Limited Dun & Bradstreet	Genstar Corporation Dun & Bradstreet Companies Inc.
8. Change to a descriptive name, or addition to an existing description (12 companies)	SuCrest Corporation Purolator, Inc. National Aviation Corporation	Ingredient Technology Corp. Purolator Courier Corp. National Aviation & Technology Corp.
9. Adoption of a brand name as the corporate name (12 companies)	Consolidated Foods Corporation Charter New York Corporation California Packing Corp.	Sara Lee Corporation Irving Bank Corporation Del Monte Corporation
10. Adoption of a personal name (11 companies)	A-T-O Inc. Associated Spring Corp. Saturn Industries, Inc.	Figgie International Inc. Barnes Group Inc. Tyler Corporation
11. Change of description (10 companies)	Interlake Iron Corporation Mission Equities Corporation Wallace Business Forms, Inc.	Interlake Steel Corporation Mission Insurance Group, Inc. Wallace Computer Services, Inc.
12. Replacement of initials (8 companies)	VWR United Corporation SOS Consolidated Inc. ELT, Inc.	Univar Corporation Core Industries Inc. Dutch Boy, Inc.
13. Adoption of an acquirer's or an acquisition's name (7 companies)	Lum's Inc. Leasco Corporation Gulf Oil Corporation	Caesars World, Inc. Reliance Group, Inc. Chevron U.S.A., Inc.
14. Legal status change or similar technicality (5 companies)	M.D.C. Corporation LITCO Corporation Bates Manufacturing Co.	M.D.C. Holdings Inc. LITCO Bancorporation BAV Liquidating Corp.
15. Reversal of an earlier name change (4 companies)	U.S. Plywood-Champion Papers Inc. Acme Markets, Inc. Amerace Esna Corporation	Champion International Corp. American Stores Company Amerace Corporation

Thus, in the case of our study, we would look for abnormal returns associated with the event, name change. The difficulty with this study in relation to other event studies is twofold. First, event studies usually do not take into account concurrent events because they deal with "cleaner," more discrete information, such as dividend announcements, which have an obvious economic impact. Second, most event studies also deal with events for which information cannot leak out (such as earnings information), and which occur on a specific day. Despite these problems, this study fit very obviously into the realm of other event studies.

Selection of day zero
As mentioned earlier, one of the biggest problems we had with this study was determining what day would serve as "day zero," or the day on which information about the name change became public. AGP provided us with an initial listing by effective dates. So many other legal and communication-oriented events have occurred by this time that we decided not to use effective dates. (For example, Consolidated Foods Corporation's change to Sara Lee Corporation became effective on the New York Stock Exchange on April 2, 1985, yet *The Wall Street Journal* had already announced news of the change on February 1, 1985.) Furthermore, investors' reactions to the name change are what cause stock prices to change, and investors will react as soon as information on the name change comes out. By the time the change becomes effective, all reactions may have ended.

We also thought about using surveys to find out when mailings went out to shareholders for approval or to solicit dates of press releases. Given the large sample (714 companies initially), however, and time constraints, we determined that this was infeasible.

Therefore, we chose *The Wall Street Journal (WSJ)* announcement dates as those easiest for us to find and closest to the actual event. We also decided to look at sixty days on either side of this day zero as a way to capture and isolate the actual day on which information became public.

Our conclusion is that information about name change does not become public on one particular day (as wih dividend announcements), but over a period of time. Conversations with market specialists backed up this assertion. Thus, at the very least, stockholders and insiders (like specialists) might find out about a name change at different times from the general investing public.

Coding of concurrent events
Through the *WSJ* Index, we were able to find not only information about initial public announcements, but references to other events that occurred on the same day (concurrent events). Thus, for each company, we looked first in the Index, then followed up by looking for the specific articles mentioned to find concurrent events. Using some judgment, we grouped all concurrent events into classes so that we could statistically control for the effect of the concurrent events.

Final selection of sample
Although we began with 714 companies, only 448 had an announcement in the *WSJ* Index, which narrowed our focus substantially. In addition, we had to cut out companies for which we could not find out information both sixty days before and after day zero. We were limited in this regard by what was available on our data base — the 1985 CRSP (Center for Research on Security Prices, a research group based in Chicago that provides daily returns and volume for NYSE stocks) tape. This data base began in 1962, which eliminated more companies, and ended in 1985, which further cut the sample.

We also cut several companies that merged into, or were acquired by, other companies and dramatically altered the nature of the original company. Thus, our final sample included 355 companies, 60 of which had no concurrent events besides name change.

Statistical analysis
The statistical analysis for this study was designed to achieve two objectives: first, to estimate the potentially different effects of the various types of name changes, and second, to control for the effects of events occurring the same day as the name change announcement. A regression model was formulated and estimated to achieve these goals.

The model was made feasible by the character of the data available. Most name changes occurred simultaneously with at least one concurrent event, although there were some "clean" name changes. Among the name changes occurring jointly with other events, the particular events or combination of events varied for a given type of name change. For example, acronym name changes did not always take place concurrently with earnings reports. Sometimes there were concurrent earnings reports, but other times there were investment announcements, financing news, etc.

This lack of perfect correlation between particular name changes and particular events allowed us to disentangle the effects of the name changes from the effects of concurrent events. If the data had been such that, say, acronym name changes had always been implemented simultaneously with an earnings report, we never would have been able to disentangle the name change for the earnings effect.

III. Results

The most important finding in our study is that we are now convinced that name change *does* have an effect on stock price. We also believe, however, that the *type* of name change is important, rather than just name change in general. (See Tables 1 and 2.)

For the entire sample of 355 companies, we found significant positive effects beginning three days before the *WSJ* announcements (day zero). The effect is about 1%, which is significant at the 5% level. The effect continues to accumulate, reading 2.3%, 33 days before the *WSJ* announcement. There was some indication of a positive effect occurring after the *WSJ* announcement, but the result was not significant at the 10% level.

The above result is very important. It says that, across all 355 companies, after controlling as best we could for concurrent events, a corporate name change has a positive association with stock price. (Incidentally, this is the same finding being reported by other researchers.) We also found, however, that the type of name change is more important than name change in general. To summarize what we found about different types of name change:

1. We discovered effects both before and after *WSJ* announcements.

2. Effects tend to show up within two weeks of the announcements.

3. *Positive effects* are much more likely for the following types of name change:
   - Adoption of acronym
   - Adoption of initials
   - Adoption of personal name
   - Adding name of merger partner/acquisition
   - Removal of a limiting descriptor
   - Replacement of initials
   - Simple truncation
   - Verbal escalation

4. Negative effects are rare but were found for:
   - Adoption of a brand name
   - Adoption of acquirer's/acquistion's name
   - Change to description

5. We found no effect for:
   - Change of description
   - Legal status change
   - Newly devised name
   - Rollback of earlier name change

Table 2. Highlights of the Study

The most important finding of this study is that the researchers are convinced that name change has an effect on stock price, and that positive effects are more common than negative effects. The following graphs illustrate those effects for the periods before and after initial *Wall Street Journal* announcements:

Statistically Significant Positive Effects
(Period Before WSJ Announcements)

All firms (3 days before*)	+ .9%
Acronyms (6 days before)	+3.0%
Add name of merger partner (1 day before)	+3.0%
Initials (8 days before)	+2.5%
Remove limiting descriptor (8 days before)	+1.9%
Simple truncation (1 day before)	+1.8%

Significant Positive Effects
(Period After WSJ Announcement)

Personal (9 days after)	+4.2%
Verbal Escalation (3 days after)	+2.8%
Initials (7 days after)	+2.6%

*Denotes day relative to *WSJ* announcement that the effect first becomes statistically significant. For example, the average firm's stock price increased .9% cumulatively between the date of the *WSJ* announcement and 3 days prior. For firms using acronyms, the average cumulative effect is 3.0% at 6 days prior to the announcement.

IV. Conclusion

The most important conclusion of our study is that corporate name changes appear to affect the price of a corporation's stock. The effect generally appears within two weeks of the name change, so the evidence is that the market judges the information represented by the name change without waiting for a shift in actual earnings.

Three important cautions, however, preclude companies from rampantly changing their names. First, our statistical analysis detected an association between name change and stock prices, but association does not guarantee causality. There is always the possibility that, despite our attempts to control for concurrent events, some third event, correlated with the name change, actually caused the price to change. Second, our regression results represent *average* effects. For example, not every single acronym name change resulted in a stock price increase: only the average stock change was positive. Third, we can't project the results of this study beyond the time frame 1962-85. What generally occurred during this period may not hold up in the late 1980s.

Despite these caveats, our conclusion is that, after a careful and thorough analysis of 355 name changes, it appears that such name changes affect stock prices. The "name game" is therefore more than a fact: it is associated with the actual financial worth of the corporation.

Business Schools Enhance Identity with Logos

Although one could hardly expect Tuck's stock price to rise in response to a new logo, the search for a School "graphic identifier" that could unify a decades-old proliferation of Tuck symbols was approached with the same studied caution that attends the renaming of a billion-dollar corporation. "We wanted to present a single targeted and coherent picture to the world," says Dean Colin Blaydon.

The wider context of the decision was the increasing awareness of graphic image on the part of top-ranking schools, more and more of which (most recently Wharton and Carnegie-Mellon) have been following in business' footsteps with the adoption of new logos.

The logical place to start was at the top—with the communications and design consultants Anspach Grossman Portugal, who had been responsible for International Harvester's recent rebirth as Navistar, Libby-Owens-Ford's transformation into Trinova, and Consolidated Foods' adoption of the name of one of its tastier products—Sara Lee. Principal Joel Portugal is also a 1958 Dartmouth graduate, and thus familiar with the setting and the tradition.

Under the direction of Blaydon and Tuck Director of Communications Paul Argenti, the company carefully outlined a proposal that would define the kind of identifier to be sought: one that would be a shorthand means of communicating Tuck's image; that would use the name as a core ingredient; that would adapt itself to uses relating it to Dartmouth College; and that would convey a "strong sense of tradition"—specifically by a seal, if possible.

An extensive review of existing current and historical media, both at Tuck and other competing business schools, interviews with the School decision makers, and a careful analysis of the possible usages followed. "We wanted to create something that was compatible with Tuck's tradition, history, and closeness to Dartmouth," relates Blaydon, "but would also capture the modern corporate spirit."

The result combines elements of Tuck's main building facade (resonant with the Georgian and Greek Revival architectural images that abound on campus), its proximity to the Connecticut River (borrowed from the Dartmouth seal), its venerability (the 1900 founding year), and the traditional shield shape. Still, it projects a contemporary feel due to the strength of the lines and the succinctness of its wording: TUCK At Dartmouth. Agrees the Dean, "We're extremely pleased with what they came up with."

113

PRODUCTION

Managing CORPORATE IDENTITY

THIS ESSAY OFFERS readers an understanding of what the terms "image" and "identity" mean and describes a process for managing a corporate identity program that moves from performing and audit through implementation. Argenti also notes several identity mistakes and suggests how to avoid them.

By Paul Argenti

We all choose certain kinds of clothing, drive particular cars, and wear that special watch to express our individuality. The towns we live in, the music we prefer, the restaurants we frequent all add up to an impression – or identity – that others easily distinguish.

Compare these two examples. The grey-haired gentleman in the Jaguar is dressed in a blue Brooks Brothers suit and sports a Rolex President. The middle-aged man in the Toyota has on a pair of blue jeans and black turtleneck and tells the time with a Seiko digital. Even for people who have only lived in the U.S. for a few years, these quick glimpses allow them to come to some instant conclusions about what these two characters are like. And more information about where they live, their religion, and their occupations would help form a much clearer identity.

The same is true for corporations. Walk into a firm's office and it takes just a few moments to capture those all-important first impressions and learn a good deal about the company. It is no wonder, then, that designing and managing this "identity" is a crucial business concern. In addition, if the effort is a challenge at

PROFESSOR PAUL A. ARGENTI HAS BEEN ON THE FACULTY OF THE TUCK SCHOOL AT DARTMOUTH COLLEGE, WHERE HE TEACHES BOTH MANAGEMENT AND CORPORATE COMMUNICATION, FOR THE PAST NINE YEARS. HE IS ALSO A VISITING PROFESSOR AT THE INTERNATIONAL UNIVERSITY OF JAPAN AND THE HELSINKI SCHOOL OF ECONOMICS.

the personal level, it is easy to imagine that it is significantly more difficult within organizations.

One reason for this complexity is that there are, as personal experience confirms, many potential identity options. Last year while teaching in Asia, my wife and I treated ourselves to one of life's great pleasures – a weekend in a suite at the Oriental Hotel in Bangkok. There, newspapers (the *Asian Wall Street Journal* and the *Herald Tribune*) were ironed to eliminate creases; hotel staff were omnipresent to the point of running down the hallway to open the door lest patrons should actually have to use their keys; laundry arrived beautifully gift-wrapped with an orchard accent; each night our pillows were adorned with an English poem on the theme of sleep; and, outside the lobby, Mercedes limos were lined up ready to take us anywhere at any time of the day or night.

A few weeks later I returned to the U.S. and was giving a lecture to a group of executives at a resort in the Midwest. A newspaper (*USA Today*, of course) appeared on the outside doorknob squeezed into a plastic bag; the staff was invisible and unavailable to bring room service in under 45 minutes; my pillow was adorned with a room-service menu for the following morning and a piece of hard candy; the vehicle waiting to whisk guests to various destinations was a Dodge van; and for flowers, the resort provided plastic varietals in a glass-enclosed case that played "Feelings" when the top was lifted.

Both hotels have strong identities; both appeal to particular constituencies; and both provide roughly the same level of service using distinctive approaches. These kinds of choices are the heart of the matter, contributing to and shaping the "personalities" of these hotels and, more generally, conveying the profile and content of any institution.

Just what goes into creating such impressions? Is this a recent trend? How do organizations distinguish themselves in the minds of customers, shareholders, employees, and other relevant constituencies? And, above all, how does an organization manage something so seemingly ephemeral as an identity?

Corporate Identity: A Recent Trend?

Corporate identity may appear to be a recent trend – emerging from the need for definition in a complicated world – but, in fact, identity programs have been around for a very long time. In ancient Egypt, the Pharaohs used their signatures as a symbol of their administration. Anyone who has been to Luxor can attest to the fascination Ramses IV had with his "logo." It appears virtually everywhere and is especially noticeable because his cartouche is primitive and bold, dominating earlier symbols on columns and buildings.

More contemporary historical examples of corporate identity are evident in the eighteenth-century U.S. and French revolutions. As a facet of those battles, both countries changed their identities with the development of new flags, national anthems, uniforms and, in the case of France, with a new execution device – the guillotine. During the the middle decades of the twentieth century, Nazi Germany terrified the world with its identity program. What is valuable to remember is that, although today we regard the swastika as something abhorrent, the same symbol obviously had strong positive connotations to earlier generations of German nationalists.

In terms of individual behavior, the cross and Jewish star are critical symbols in Western civilization. Throughout the world, they are instantly recognized and elicit a spectrum of emotional responses. A case in point is Martin Scorcese's disturbing film, *Goodfellas*, where the protagonist has to hide his gold cross when he first meets his Jewish in-laws. After his marriage, he is draped with both the cross and the star, and the people in the audience, most of whom are familiar with the Judeo-Christian tradition, realize the transformation that has occurred within the character.

Such symbols, however – be they a Pharoah's cartouche, a nation's flag or a sign of a person's religious commitment – are just one dimension of the identity picture. They receive a lot of attention because of our increasingly visual focus and exposure to this type of shorthand in television, magazines, annual reports, and the endless barrage of brochures we see at work and at home. And as a parallel, corporations, from start-ups to industry giants, as well as not-for-profits and universities, give at least some thought to these issues. Yet despite this awareness, it is a much smaller group of executives and managers that understands a broader definition of identity and how to exploit those perceptions as an essential organizational asset.

What is Corporate Identity?

Most of those who have written on this subject come from the graphic design discipline and spend an inordinate amount of time describing why identity is much more than the design itself. They are right but tend to overcompensate, translating identity into an all-encompassing concept that touches everything the organization does. The approach is sometimes hard to grasp and often impossible to put into a strategic framework.

> **The primary basis** *for corporate identity is the reality of the organization itself.*

Identity, whether corporate or personal, is defined as individuality. For some that means trying to be different; for others, conformity. Whatever the reality is gets communicated – consciously or not – to various constituencies who subsequently form perceptions about their experiences. The process has many components.

REALITY

The primary basis for corporate identity is the reality of the organization itself. This is frequently hard for anyone but the CEO or president to grasp. What is the reality of an organization as large as Exxon, as diversified as Mitsubishi, or as monolithic as General Electric? Certainly the products and the services, the people, the buildings, the symbols, and other objects contribute to this reality. While there are inevitably differences in how the elements are perceived (as we will see in a moment), it is this cluster of "facts," this collection of tangible things, that provides the organization with a starting point for creating an identity.

COMMUNICATION STRATEGY

A communication strategy is the process by which

the corporate reality/identity is conveyed. If that strategy is coherent, the organization is understood by various constituencies in the best possible light. In this effort, design, public relations, and both formal and informal messages such as the way a store is decorated and the attitudes towards customers, all reinforce the same image. But achieving this unity is far from easy and studying each component of an effective program – organizational objectives, constituency analysis, and message strategy – gives some indication of the nuances involved in the undertaking.

ORGANIZATIONAL OBJECTIVES – Usually, if a person searches for corporate reality in a mission statement, the conclusions are so bland as to be indistinguishable from one another. Top management, on the other hand, is traditionally compelled to be explicit about a company's goals and directions, and this language can serve as the stepping stone to define, enhance or alter a firm's identity. Those responsible for the communications strategy should talk to the CEO, find out what the corporation is trying to do, and then use that information to establish key identity objectives. For instance, the mission statement of one company I worked with said that its goal was "to present a mosaic of the organization in our communications." When I asked a vice-president what he meant, I discovered that the underlying intent was to increase sales.

CONSTITUENCY ANALYSIS – Determining which constituencies are relevant and finding ways to explain a corporation's identity to each, without sounding like people who talk out of both sides of their mouths, can be an imposing task. Often, a message that sounds good to one constituency may not appeal to another. Communicators, then, need to be careful about the messages they select and how they frame those ideas to address different constituencies. As an example, when K mart changed its retail identifier in September 1990, it had to raise expectations about what the change meant to certain groups while explaining to others that the logo on an individual store might not change until five years down the line. Careful analysis, including a clear definition of who the constituencies are, what they know about the organization, how they feel about it, permits a corporation to develop approaches tailored to specific audiences. Traditionalists might believe beneficial change is unnecessary window dressing. Alternatively, progressive constituents might see the same move as too limited.

MESSAGE STRATEGY – Most corporate identity programs include design changes. This may include new logos, symbols and color changes that appear on buildings, uniforms, and hundreds of other media. Organizations try very hard to make these formal identity manifestations unique in order to distinguish themselves from competitors. Nonetheless, on many occasions – oil and gas companies come to mind – the differences are overwhelmingly symbolic. Are there any real distinctions between Mobil and Texaco gasolines? There may actually be slight discrepancies in formula, yet when I think about these companies, the major variations seem limited to the logos and Mobil's focus on corporate advocacy versus Texaco's support of opera.

In a similar vein, it is interesting to investigate the mission statements of three or four companies in an industry where the product is virtually interchangeable. More than likely, the contrast will be minuscule. But if the corporations do, indeed, have separate identities, the best places to find these profiles are in the brochures, policy statements and other physical expressions of their respective corporate realities. In addition, other informal messages abound in the myths, atmosphere, decor and even security procedures of the particular firms. To illustrate, the team that developed the Apple Macintosh removed themselves physically from the rest of the company, changed their work habits, and developed an entirely different *esprit de corps*. Or, in advertising agencies, creative departments generally have a different feel than the more businesslike atmosphere of account executives.

PERCEPTIONS

Perception is the third vital aspect of identity, and constituents form perceptions based on the messages companies send out. If these notions accurately reflect an organization's reality, the identity program is a success. If the perceptions differ dramatically from reality (and this often happens when companies do not take the time to analyze whether or not a match actually exists), then either the strategy is ineffective or the corporation's self-understanding needs modification.

Through research, the corporation can determine how different constituents perceive the current identity and any changes the organization is contemplating. These investigations, however, must be more than anecdotal information picked up in a few focus groups. A concerted effort takes time, money, and patience. Instead of relying simply on qualitative investigations (such as focus groups), companies need to conduct quantitative studies as well. It is not unusual for a firm to rely on the observations of a few people asked at random about their feelings, but a more appropriate undertaking might be an extensive and scientific survey, sending questionnaires to customers and carefully interpreting the findings.

Considering the resources involved in implementing an identity program, this could easily be considered an investment.

Throughout the process, corporations must shun cosmetic changes. Identity is not simply public relations; most analysts are pretty good at looking behind an image that does not seem to ring true. In UAL's case, executives invested great sums of money to create a new firm named Allegis, but the company remained what it was initially – an airline – rather than a broader travel organization with hotels and other accoutrements. In another example, USX is still a steel company despite its attempt to hide that fact behind the Big Board call letters. And Sears continues to conjure up the idea of a department store long after attempts to diversify beyond its core business.

This does not mean that change is impossible. Transformations do occur. We have only to study the AT&T logos from Angus S. Hibbard's 1889 design through 1984 when the company was split up to see the metamorphosis. But these generations of visual material are only the symptom, a sign of new realities rather than the new realities themselves. They represent a dynamic process, a growth, a shifting in priorities that is often difficult to define and perhaps more difficult to manage. Articulating and communicating this vision is the identity challenge.

Managing the Unmanageable

The dual nature of identity – embodied in things yet inextricably tied to perceptions – creates a special dilemma for decision-makers. In a world where attention is generally focused on quantifiable results, the emphasis here is on qualitative issues. And devising a program that addresses these elusive but very significant concerns requires an approach that balances thoughtful analysis with action. The path outlined below suggests a method used successfully by many.

STEP 1. CONDUCT AN IDENTITY AUDIT. To begin, an organization needs to assess the current picture. How does the general public view the organization? What do its various symbols represent? Does its identity accurately reflect what is happening, or is it simply a leftover from days gone by?

To avoid superficial input and objectively respond to these questions, consultants must conduct in-depth interviews with top managers and those working in areas most affected by change. They review company literature, advertising, stationery, products and facilities. They research perceptions among the important constituencies, including employees, analysts and customers. The idea is to be thorough, to uncover relationships and inconsistencies and then to use the audit as a basis for potential identity changes. In this process, executives should look for red flags. Typical problems include symbols that conjure up images of days gone by and just generally incorrect impressions. And once decision-makers have the facts, they can move to create a new identity or institute a communication program to share the correct and most up-to-date profile.

The recent experience at K mart is illustrative. This company's stores are part of the American landscape, so much so that it is one of the most recognized corporations in the country. Johnny Carson has talked about "blue-light specials" on his late-night show, and the Oscar-winning movie, *Rain Man*, had several less flattering references to the firm. With over 2,000 stores throughout the United States (80% of the population in the U.S. lives within five miles of a K mart), visits from 180 million shoppers a year, and over $30 billion in sales, the K mart of 1990 had very few problems with recognition.

What it did have, however, was a symbol that reflected the K mart of the 1960s. Like a worn, gray-flannel suit, the logo seemed comfortable, but after 28 years, changes in the stores and throughout the organization motivated designers, vendors, customers and reporters to plead with CEO and Chairman Joseph Antonini to update the corporation's symbolic image.

In this case, Ken Love of Anspach Grossman Portugal conducted the identity audit. After talking to customers, vendors, suppliers, and analysts and examining the way in which the old identity was used, he concluded that the retail identifier needed to be changed. K mart is different from the company represented in the original mark. In addition, attitudes about design have shifted. The result is a modified logo that will be implemented in every store, on all signs, and in advertising over the next five years. But that is not all. As a precedent to putting up the new sign, the company is also spending several billion dollars to refurbish stores so that, as a single message, the change in symbol will be complemented by significant interior enhancements.

STEP 2. SET IDENTITY OBJECTIVES. Having clear goals is essential to the identity process. These should be set by senior management and explain how each constituency is supposed to react to specific identity proposals. For instance: "As a result of this name change, analysts will recognize our organization as more than just a one-product company;" or, "By putting a new logo on the outside of our store, customers will be more aware of dramatic transformations inside." What is important is that emphasis be placed on constituency response rather than company action.

In another example, the oldest graduate school of business in the world found itself with an identi-

Evolution of a Symbol

1903
1907
1909
1915
1936
1963
1982

SOURCE: ANSPACH GROSSMAN PORTUGAL

ty that had little to do with the reality of the institution in the late 1980s. Administrators and faculty were using five different logos, including a pine tree, a literal rendition of the school's main building, and several variations of the Dartmouth logo. In addition, the official name of the school, The Amos Tuck School of Business Administration at Dartmouth College, was too long and confusing. This led to humorous renditions of the name, such as the infamous "Truck School."

As suspected, the audit indicated that Tuck's overall awareness and name recognition were suffering. To improve the situation, two objectives were outlined: first, to come up with a more manageable name that all constituencies would use and second, to design a logo that would differentiate the graduate school from the college. The School is now "Tuck at Dartmouth," which eliminates the confusion about how a graduate school could be a part of a college. And the new logo, developed by Gene Grossman, incorporates the founding date of the graduate school (rather than the college) and a contemporary symbol within a traditional shield framework.

STEP 3. DEVELOP DESIGNS AND NAMES. Once the audit is complete and objectives established, the next phase is design. If a name change is needed, consultants start to come up with alternatives. Sometimes options can number in the hundreds, although inevitably certain ones stand out as more appropriate. The criteria for selection depend on several variables. For example, if the company is undergoing a global expansion, the addition of the word "international" might be the answer. If, however, a firm has a lot of equity built into one product, changing the name of the corporation to that of the product might be the answer, as happened when Consolidated Foods became Sara Lee.

A degree of autonomy is also valuable during this part of the process. On one program I was involved with, the CEO kept offering suggestions, making it awkward, if not impossible, for designers to be serious about exploring other possibilities. In the end, the CEO's design won out and we wondered why he had bothered to hire professionals in the first place.

At the same time, there must be a balance. Beyond the outsider's conception of what an organization is all about, a manager's own instincts should be a part of the final decision. In some cases, designers and identity consultants are perfectionists or idealistic, presenting ideas that are unrealistic or too avant-garde.

To typify the focus of this design dialogue, I show a series of Texaco logos. While this is a bit different from the exploration just described, it does show the variety that can emerge in what otherwise might be considered straightforward circumstances. Making sure this kind of diversity is a facet of the identity discussion is a key to success at this stage of the process.

STEP 4. DEVELOP PROTOTYPES. Once the final design is selected, consultants develop models using the new symbols or names. For products, they prepare prototype packages and show how the brand image is used in advertising. If it is a retail operation, they often build a model to show what the store will look like. In other situations, the identity is applied to everything, including ties and T-shirts.

During this phase, it is not uncommon for managers to get cold feet. As the reality of change sinks in, criticism mounts, from some quarters because they have not been involved in the process and from others because they do not have a good sense of the evolution and meaning of the design. At times, negative reactions on the part of constituents can be so strong that proposals have to be abandoned.

To overcome this failure, it is important to have a diversity of people and viewpoints involved in the identity process. The one *caveat* is to avoid accommodating different ideas by diluting concepts. A company should not accept an identity that is simply the lowest common denominator. Two ways to deal with the task are to either let a strong leader champion the new design, or set up a committee (sometimes the board) to work on the program. In either approach, keep people informed and invested in the project from the beginning. I once worked with an organization that assigned the identity effort to a single board member. When that person proudly came back with the design, it was unanimously rejected. Not willing to give up, a committee was formed that solicited assistance from the entire board. Not surprisingly, when this second design was up for a vote, it was unanimously approved.

STEP 5. LAUNCH AND COMMUNICATE. Given the time and the breadth of the group required to develop an identity, news about future changes can easily be leaked. In the K mart process, hundreds knew about the effort, and managers worried that the new logo would appear in *Advertising Age* weeks ahead of the launch. Fortunately, the story stayed under wraps until the day of the announcement, and was only exposed when a savvy photographer spotted hundreds of carts with the new logo sitting in a parking lot. Of course, he took pictures and promptly sold them to *USA Today*. Sometimes such publicity is a positive event, as it can create excitement and a sense of anticipation.

Still, the chance occurrences are no substitute for a formal introduction. To build drama into the announcement, public relations staff should be creative in inviting reporters without giving away the purpose – one company I know sent six-foot pencils and a huge calendar with the date of the press conference marked off. And once at the meeting, the design should be clearly displayed in a variety of contexts, and senior executives should carefully explain the strategy behind the program. As additional communication tools, corporations might want to avail themselves of video news releases and satellite links. Whatever the choice, it must be remembered that effectively presenting an identity is a complex problem. It is much too easy to interpret the change as cosmetic. To avoid this, most companies seek professionals to help orchestrate this showcasing process.

STEP 6. IMPLEMENT THE PROGRAM. The final stage is implementation. This can take years in large companies and a minimum of several months for small firms. Resistance is inevitable, but what is frequently shocking is the extent of ownership constituents have in the old identity. Think about how long it took to get lights in Wrigley Field. I have also encountered similar reluctance from secretaries who do not want to use a new block format and from older Dartmouth alumni who could not understand how the traditional Indian symbol could possibly have been offensive. A standards manual is useful in showing staff and managers how to use the new identity consistently and correctly. Beyond this, someone in the organization needs to monitor the program and make judgements about when flexibility is allowed and when it is not. Over time, changes will need to be made in some standards, for instance, when a modern typeface chosen by a designer is not available in certain countries.

As a few final words, I note that most managers who have not been involved in developing an identity program tend to underestimate its value. I have found that those in the financial side of the operation, in particular, often think that corporate identity is rather silly and trivial. Some of this hesitation emerges from a lack of understanding about what corporate identity is and what it does for an organization. In response, I can only say that I am certain that an inappropriate or outdated identity can be as damaging to a firm as a weak financial performance. People seek consistency, and if perceptions about a corporation fail to mesh with reality, constituents take their business elsewhere.

Executives, then, need to be fully aware of the tremendous impact of corporate identity, and they must learn how to manage this critical design resource. Success in this area is a catalyst for and a symbol of change, the dynamic process that keeps companies thriving. Success also matures into pride and commitment – among employees, among consumers and among the general public – irreplaceable assets in our intensely competitive business environment. ◆

Reprint 9121ARG52

Suggested Readings

T. F. Garbett, *How To Build a Corporation's Identity and Project Its Image*, Lexington: Lexington Books, 1988.

A. Forty, *Objects of Desire*, New York: Pantheon Books, 1986.

C. Lorenz, *The Design Dimension: The New Competitive Weapon for Business*, Oxford: Basil Blackwell Ltd., 1986.

Chapter 5: The Corporation is the Message

Teaching corporate advertising is easy to do because such rich examples are available for you to use. For more general information, I would rely on Garbett's book, *Corporate Advertising*, which I mentioned in the book. It will tell you everything that you could ever possibly want to know about the subject.

Prior to teaching this class, I start about a month before collecting lots of good examples to use in class. Business magazines are a good source for corporate ads as are liberal-oriented magazines like *New Republic*, *New Yorker*, *Atlantic Monthly*, etc. Try to find ads that fall into the different categories that I list in the chapter. For instance, I would look for some that are aimed at the financial community, some aimed at clarifying or expanding on image, some advocacy ads, etc.

Most copy shops can now produce color transparencies, which makes the reproduction of these ads easier than ever before. For those who would rather use slides, however, they are still the best way to display ads in class (you should check to see if you need permissions, however, before reproducing ads).

You can find the best television ads on Sunday morning television, on *Meet the Press* for example, as well as on the nightly network news broadcasts. One recent Sunday on *Meet the Press* gave me all I needed to use for the class and included a great example from GE. In addition, virtually any company or ad agency would be delighted to have you show ads for them. Apple's current ad campaign was a typical example of what's available.

Show lots of the examples, and simply let students talk about them. Try to see if the company's strategy is clear (it usually isn't), if it can be easily categorized (usually not so easy), and whether the design and copy work together to form an effective ad.

Another way to deal with the problem of finding ads is to assign the chapter and let students find examples for a homework assignment. Tell them each to bring in four or five ads and you will be well on your way toward building a collection that you can use the following year when you come to this lecture. Be sure to make arrangements for making them into slides or using them on overhead transparencies before class.

You can also use the examples that I have provided in the book if you would rather not take the time to hunt down other advertisements. They represent a few different kinds of ads and are very good examples for you to use. A look at each will be useful for us to consider how they fit into my categories and for you to get the idea about how these ads work.

Corporate Advertising Exercise

Have students study the ads at the end of the chapter and answer all six of the questions in the exercise.

RCN ad: "No Empire Lasts Forever"

This is an image campaign by an upstart telecommunications company competing directly with monopolists in the telephone and cable industry. Using a noose around Lenin's neck to draw an analogy between the fall of communism and the changes in the telecommunications industry, Angotti, Thomas, Hedge has created an image campaign that also sells RCN's superior service. Also notice RCN's starman logo and tagline, "The Live Wire in Communications."

Mobil

This is Mobil's more contemporary corporate advocacy campaign. Have students compare it to the ad on p. 103, which has more copy and shows Mobil's more traditional approach to advocacy. Is the ad with less copy more or less effective? Does anyone really read or believe these ads?

Absolut Kitty Hawk

Absolut was a relatively obscure and unpopular Swedish vodka prior to Chiat Day's incredibly successful image campaign. Children collect the ads and hang them in their bedrooms, books have been published filled with Absolut ads, and people compete for ideas in the campaign. Collect other ads currently running and compare with this one. My current favorite is Absolut Psycho with a torn shower curtain in the shape of an Absolut bottle. Discuss the importance of creativity as you analyze this campaign.

Benetton

Next we see the relatively controversial Benetton ad that ran in 1993 in which the chairman appeared naked to make a point about how you can donate clothes to the needy. Only an Italian with the amount of money and caché of Benetton can get away with stuff like this. How about the chairman of Exxon trying this one? Think about how ingenious this philanthropic ad was. As people turned in their old Benetton's they would have to buy new clothes!

Milk ad

The campaign for milk, which focuses on celebrities with milk mustaches, is a hybrid product and image ad. I like to include an industry rather than company specific ad to get students thinking about now marketing communications is connected to corporate communications.

Get students into a discussion about all of these ads and don't forget that they have a few study questions that they were supposed to answer anyway. As I mentioned earlier, between the ads you collect, what you get them to collect, and the ones I show in the book, you should have no problem getting this class to succeed.

For Further Information ...

For those of you who do not come to this area with business background, I would strongly recommend that you look at a chapter on advertising in a more general sense in a marketing textbook like Kotler's *Marketing Management*, which I noted in the bibliography to this chapter. You will probably have to answer some questions about the differences between product and corporate advertising and this is the best way to get yourself to feel comfortable with the whole thing.

Chapter 6: Managing Media Relations

The point of this chapter is to show how the new corporate communication function deals with media versus the old way of dealing with the media. The original title for the chapter in the first edition, "No More Press Releases," said it all. Media relations professionals today need to get away from a focus on press releases toward a more strategic, targeted effort.

To understand this chapter, you need to know a bit about what it was like in the old days. I have given a brief account of what I see as the major changes, but you might want to pick up a public relations book from the library if you are unfamiliar with old style flakkery (see *Effective Public Communications*, Cutlip and Center, Prentice-Hall). For a more contemporary and effective history read *PR! A Social History of Spin*, by Stuart Ewen (Basic Books, 1990).

I think the best way to make this material come alive is to get a real media person in to your class. No matter what school you teach at and no matter where you are located, you should be able to convince a local journalist to come in and talk about what they do to write stories. Getting it straight from the horse's mouth is the best way to hear about how the media works. The better the journalist, the better the class will go.

If you feel uncomfortable turning your class over to a journalist, however, you can certainly deal with the material in other ways. For example, do some of the research on a reporter yourself and talk about how you would approach the reporter if you were trying to pitch a story. Or get students to do it. Have them follow a reporter for a few months to see what style the reporter uses and how you would advise someone to approach the reporter.

The rest of the material in the chapter is rather obvious, so let's focus on the case instead.

The Adolph Coors Company

This case gives students a birds eye view of what it is like to be under fire by *60 Minutes*. I think that of all the cases in the book it is by far the most foolproof if you follow my advice about how to teach this material.

I have sometimes heard complaints about using older cases, but this one is really a classic. Students universally love this case whether you are teaching upper-level undergrads, MBAs, or executives. Overall, that the product is well known, but the *60 Minutes* incident forgotten makes it particularly delightful to teach this case.

First, get students to identify the problems. Some are very obvious, like "*60 Minutes* is coming to do an interview and we have to decide how to respond," but others are more difficult. Here is what your students are likely to come up with:

1. Coors seems to discriminate against women, gays, and minorities. This comes through in this case as a result of several things, but one of the main influences is that the Coors brothers are so conservative.

2. Joe Coors is a Reaganite/John Bircher. So what? Get into a discussion about how conservative most business people are, but we don't see them being boycotted or persecuted. This makes for a fascinating discussion about company personalities versus the companies themselves. Should the company try to distance itself from these conservative views? Isn't it the right of all Americans to hold whatever beliefs they want?

3. The industry is maturing and Coors now faces stiff competition from Anheuser-Busch. Everyone in the U.S. knows enough about beer (especially students!) to get into a discussion about the beer industry. Try to show that the strategy for communication also depends on what's going on in the world around the company.

4. The company has no experience with advertising or public relations. Coors was essentially still a private firm at the time of the case and has little of the experience its counterparts would have had.

5. The people in charge of communications are not experienced enough to deal with this kind of problem. Richards was basically an accountant and her boss was a fund-raiser for a university. It is a good example of how not to staff a corporate communication department.

6. The AFL-CIO is a formidable opponent and in some ways a bigger organization than the company itself. Although Coors may have the upper hand at the local level, the larger union organization is making this the focus of its attention to take a stand after Ronald Reagan busted the air traffic controllers.

7. The Coors company has used unfair hiring practices and seems to treat its workers like they are children. Allegations of unfair practices are likely to come up. For example, the company used lie detector tests and asked weird questions. It had search and seizure policies that seem to come out of the dark ages.

8. The company has a history of busting unions. This doesn't help its image with workers, but how will the general public feel about its anti-union stance?

9. The company only became public within the last seven or eight years and lost 50% of its value within three years. This is the kind of information that will make any CEO's hair curl. The last thing they need is *60 Minutes* when they are fighting to keep their stock price up.

10. Going public makes them a more public institution and they haven't really figured that out at the time of the case.

11. The boycott is a real bummer. How would you like to have a tough organization like the AFL-CIO on your case telling consumers not to buy your products?

12. *60 Minutes* was the most popular show on TV at the time of the case (it still is) and it has over 24 million influential viewers. In addition, Mike Wallace is the toughest in the business. It's like the cannibals coming to the feast.

13. The producer has already told Richards that he wants to tear the company to shreds. How can you possibly get a fair shake from this guy?

Communication Strategy

Use the corporate communication strategy model (from Chapter 2) to analyze the case. What should Coors' objective be? Who are the most important constituencies? What are the best channels to use for each? A strategic approach works very well in analyzing this case.

You might want to focus, in particular, on credibility. Coors had a "mystique" for credibility, but little focus on communication as a private company. Now that it's public, what has changed?

Go back to this model after using the "B" case. The list on p. 2 shows what the company's objectives were. Ask students to decide which were met (all but the union objective).

Solutions

So, what to do in the face of such a nasty situation? Your job is to get students to choose sides in a debate that should focus on whether Coors should follow an open-door or closed-door policy. Let's take a look at each option.

   Closed-door. This is what you would have said if you were in Richards' shoes at the time of the case. Coors doesn't seem to have a prayer given all of the problems that we outlined above. When students take this position, get them to tell you what they would do instead of going on *60 Minutes*.

Usually, they will say stuff like, "We will try to get another journalist to tell the real story at Coors!" Right. Encourage them, but then point out that it's unlikely that you would get any fairer deal with anyone else. And, who is bigger than this?

They might also say that they will go on, but only if they can do a live interview or if they have control over the editing. Again, they are living in a dream world if they think this way today. CBS is much better off if you don't show up at all rather than having you come in and take away their prerogative to edit the program any way they want.

Any of the arguments that they come up with on this side of the fence are likely to be pretty weak, but you need to get them to think about what they would do instead of going on. Don't let them simply weasel out of *60 Minutes* and leave it at that.

   <u>Open-door.</u> Despite the focus in the case on keeping things quiet, most students who have really read the case and chapter 6 are more likely to suggest that Coors open up the doors and face the music. Get them to explain how they can use the ideas from chapter 6 to make this a successful venture.

1. Research the producer. The producer is king at *60 Minutes*, what has he done before?

2. What do we want to get across to 24 million viewers?

3. The Coors brothers are going to need some serious training lest their conservative views start spilling over on national TV, thereby weakening the whole case.

4. What is Sickler and Co. likely to do? Get them to think about where we are really vulnerable and how you would really deal with a situation like this. What can you say about the allegations?

5. How do we follow up after the show?

Following all of the above, which should take about an hour to develop, you need to show the program to let them know what really happened. It is still available from Coors public relations department in Golden, Colorado (contact Anita Russell, VP-Corporate Communications, phone 303-277-3615). The program is a complete surprise in that it ends up praising the Coors company. How did this happen?

The "B" case

The whole thing is laid out so beautifully by Richard that you really don't need to do anything more than let them read the "B" case to find out what she did. It takes 10 or 15 minutes to read and then I have them discuss it a bit more making sure to let them see how powerful a good media relations program and some strategy can be in a situation like this.

As I said earlier, it works like a charm if you know the material well and follow my advice.

Source Perrier

I have also included this three-part role play I wrote because it gives you a chance to teach another class on media and to get students doing something experiential.

On the day you intend to use this, give one-third of the class the executive's role, one-third the *FNN* reporter's role, and one-third the *Hard Copy* reporter's role. Don't let them share information between groups. You, however, know that the reporter from *FNN* is positively disposed to business in general and isn't going to roast the people from Perrier, while the other reporter is more like a *60 Minutes* type.

Also the reporter from *Hard Copy* has some information that even the executive doesn't have which can really be hurtful. Get the executives to prepare by reading Mary Munter's, "How to Conduct a Successful Media Interview" from *California Management Review*, April 1983.

Give them 45 minutes in class to prepare. Break them into groups of five within each subgroup. Videotape interviews with one executive and a reporter from *FNN* and *Hard Copy*. Then you can show and analyze the tape immediately with the entire class using Munter's article to give feedback on delivery and the material in chapter 6 to give feedback on strategy.

Adolph Coors Company (B)

THE AMOS TUCK SCHOOL | DARTMOUTH COLLEGE

Adolph Coors Company (B)*

The following is the complete transcript of a speech given by Shirley Richard, director of corporate communications, at the International Association of Business Communicators annual conference on May 12, 1983.

INTRODUCTION

The winds of change are blowing, and as we progress into the information age, investigative journalism is something which will affect all of us--either as consumers, members of special interest groups, business persons, or members of the general public. Organizations -- and especially businesses -- will be forced in the years ahead to deal with investigative reporters in an open and forthright manner.

Adolph Coors Company, the nation's sixth largest brewer, has changed its news media policy from being a "no comment" company to a company with an open door policy. The purpose of this address is to discuss a case history involving Coors and "60 Minutes."

There are certain ways you know when it's a bad day....One of these is when "60 Minutes" calls.

IDENTIFICATION OF THE PROBLEM/OPPORTUNITY

1. Since 1977 Coors had been the victim of a vicious labor-related boycott designed by AFL-CIO officials to put Coors out of business.

2. Mike Wallace has gained a reputation as television's major exponent of adversary journalism and had been accused on occasion of not reporting all the facts (particularly with regard to business). There was concern about the news angle "60 Minutes" could take because Coors had a reputation for being a conservative company that took controversial political stances. In addition, Joe Coors for many years had been a supporter of Ronald Reagan and was a member of Reagan's "kitchen cabinet." Because of the unemployment situation in America, Reagan's policies were being seriously questioned. Joe Coors was also reported to have been responsible for the appointments of controversial James Watt (former Secretary of the Interior) and Anne Gorsuch (former EPA administrator). Furthermore, Coors required a preemployment polygraph of all employees, which was an emotional issue with many segments of the general public.

---

* This case was prepared by Paul A. Argenti, The Amos Tuck School, Dartmouth College. All rights reserved. Do not reproduce without written permission.

3. Awareness levels about boycott issues were low in states where Coors was not sold (thirty states). Since Coors was considering a major expansion into the Southeast, there was a risk of raising awareness about negative corporate issues.

4. The AFL-CIO boycott against Coors appeared to be working. Awareness levels of boycott-related issues throughout the marketing area were high. Formal research performed in 1981 showed that Coors's corporate image had slipped badly. A comprehensive public relations program was in effect to combat the problem, but progress being made to change attitudes was slow.

5. The facts were on Coors's side. The labor-related boycott was based largely on falsehoods. An open-door policy with "60 Minutes" could result in helping set the record straight.

6. Morale among distributors and employees was eroding because they believed Coors's management was not doing enough to combat the boycott.

7. If "60 Minutes" decided to do a feature about Coors, it could be disastrous for Coors not to participate.

After considering the facts, Joe and Bill Coors made a decision to open Coors's doors to "60 Minutes" and conduct an interview with Mike Wallace.

PLANNING FOR THE INTERVIEW

Target Audience:

Primary   Beer consumers, potential beer consumers, and opinion leaders with neutral or slightly negative attitudes toward Coors who would comprise a portion of the "60 Minutes" audience of twenty-plus million households.

Secondary   Employees and independent Coors distributors.

Objectives:

Turn a potentially negative report into a positive one by providing an open and candid forum for the "60 Minutes" investigative reporting team. Unlike other organizations' responses to "60 Minutes," Coors didn't want to merely "survive" the investigation, but instead set out to take advantage of this opportunity to set the record straight.

We established some message objectives which were based upon overall corporate objectives and identification of image problems in the market. These are extremely important in any interview situation. These are key points we would make if we had free air time. This is the heart of dealing successfully with investigative reporters. The message objectives we established were:

1. Coors has fair hiring practices and is a good place to work.

2. The boycott is unfair and is carried on by a few rejected union officials.

3. Coors cares about its employees, its products, its community, and its country.

4. Coors is not anti-union.

5. Coors makes a unique quality beer.

Plan Elements:

1. Make sure certain officers were adequately prepared prior to the Wallace interview.

2. Maintain an open door policy with "60 Minutes" throughout the investigation.

3. Perform informal and formal research to measure results of the broadcast.

4. Share "60 Minutes" with employees and distributors after the show's airing.

Budget:

We established a budget which was spent primarily for professional telecommunications training. Establishing a budget is essential for all PR programs.

Execution (by the Corporate Communications Department):

1. Preparation

   a. Requested a letter from Mike Wallace stating the subject matter of his investigation.

   b. To properly prepare for any investigative reporter, you should know as much about the program and its host as possible. To prepare for Mike Wallace's visit to Coors, we learned as much about "60 Minutes" as we could. The success of "60 Minutes" is attributed to its investigative portions and especially the hard-hitting, inquisitorial approach of Mike Wallace, who has been with the show since its debut on the CBS network in the fall of 1968. The show reaches approximately forty million Americans each week.

   Allan Maraynes was the producer for the Coors investigation. According to Palmer Williams who recently retired after thirty-one years with CBS -- the last fourteen as deputy to Don Hewitt -- the founding father and executive producer of "60 Minutes":

   > "Producers are the be-all and end-all of everything that happens on this show. They are the twenty-three skilled entrepreneurs who do a great deal of research and collar people for interviews and arrange schedules and beat their correspondents over the head all year long. Good camera crews and good editors improve pieces, but it is the producer who does the donkey work at every level, and it's his neck that's out. If his case--and that includes his big-name correspondent--doesn't perform up to expectations, it's a blot on the producer."

   After we learned this information, we traveled to New York to visit the producer, Allan Maraynes, to learn more about him and how "60 Minutes" worked. We obtained tapes of Mr. Maraynes' recent productions, and we contacted other corporations that had been the subject of an investigation by Allan Maraynes. In all cases, we learned that Allan Maraynes was a professional who researched the facts thoroughly and produced a fair story.

   c. Obtained tapes of recent speeches and information about David Sickler, the AFL-CIO official who headed the Coors boycott.

   d. Researched and gathered all facts surrounding every issue which could be brought up by Mike Wallace.

e. Obtained permission from Mike Wallace for the Coors Television Department to film all aspects of the "60 Minutes" visit to Coors. It's good to have a record of questions asked and responses.

f. Prepared Bill and Joe Coors for the Mike Wallace interview with professional spokesmanship training using actual reporters. These techniques would apply to any interview situation for any company.

1. Reviewed message objectives and explained technique of bridging from Mike Wallace's questions to positive points about the company. (Emphasize that audience will not see actual bridging of message objectives during the "60 Minutes" film they will see because of editing. Explain that the message objectives were communicated through-out the entire "60 Minutes" investi-gation, including when we transmitted all informa-tion to producer in response to his requests.) Example of bridging: Mike: "Joe Coors, you give to right wing groups, including Anita Bryant, to help stamp out gays. You are the acknowledged leader of the Colorado Crazies, including James Watt. You sneak into the back door of the White House when Ronnie's secret kitchen cabinet meets. Wouldn't it be better to get out of politics and just make beer?" Answer: "I don't agree with your statements, Mike. The reason I'm involved in politics is that I care about America--people may not agree with me philosophically, but they can't argue with the fact that I care. But more importantly, the com-pany I represent cares about its employees and cares about providing a good place to work.

2. Reviewed interview strategy:

   - During an inter-view, you have rights...Advised Joe and Bill of their rights with Mike Wallace, i.e., the right to set their own pace, the right to be comfortable, the right to have Mr. Wallace repeat a question if they are uncomfortable with it, the right to ask Mr. Wallace for more information or why he may be asking a certain question. We reminded them that this interview would be a two-way conversation between them and Mike Wallace.

   - Reminded Joe and Bill to remember the "real audience" would not be Mike Wallace but the millions of viewers who would be watching the broadcast. We urged them to use language the person at home could understand.

   - Cautioned them to listen carefully to the entire question.

   - Advised them to smile and not be afraid to show a sense of humor.

   - Some don'ts that were reviewed:

     - Don't fall for Mike Wallace's technique, the "pregnant" pause. You feel compelled to fill the space--lots of errors occur here.

     - Don't become hostile, no matter how hostile Mike Wallace might become. We emphasized that more points could be made with the real audience by keeping cool.

     - Don't say "no comment." We advised them that if they couldn't answer a question, to say so but tell the audience why.

- Don't belabor a point. We told them they probably would not get Mike Wallace to agree with them anyway on most points.

- Don't be patronizing. We encouraged them to avoid comments like, "That's a good question," or "I'm glad you asked that." We also advised them not to ask, "Does that answer your question?" It would be an open invitation for Mike Wallace to say no.

3. Reviewed interview techniques:

- Some types of questions, fav-orites of investi-gative reporters (particularly the broadcast media), should not be answered in the form they were asked. We told them to answer the question their way, then bridge to a positive objective.

Examples:

- A or B Questions--The answer doesn't have to be yes or no, either/or, black or white. It may well be C--or D, E, or F. Example: "Your sales are down. Is this because? a. Of your Johnny-come-lately marketing campaign? or b. Lack of commitment on the part of your inde-pendent distributors? Answer: Our sales are off due to tough competitive pressures in the market-place. But the reason we'll be successful in the long run is because we make a unique quality beer.

- Absent Third Party--We told them they didn't have to attack, defend, or explain someone who was not present. Example: "August Busch of Anheuser-Busch has made a statement to the effect that your company lacks breadth and depth at the top man-agement levels. Could you comment on that?" Answer: I don't have knowledge of August Busch's statement, but I can tell you that at the top man-agement levels we're committed to providing a good place to work.

- Irrelevant--We told them they did not have to answer any irrelevant questions. Example: "Mrs. Coors is a born-again Christian--how do you reconcile that with the fact that you support causes that are costing Americans their jobs?" Answer: We're not here to talk about Mrs. Coors, but we are here to talk about the unfair boycott carried on by a few rejected union officials.

- Loaded Preface--We advised them to watch out for long questions that contained outrageous statements from which they may want to disassociate themselves. Example: "We all know that Coors is anti-union, anti-gay, anti-minority, and anti-people. It is also generally agreed that your marketing campaign has been ineffective against your major competitors. Even some of your distributors have questioned your leadership--calling Coors a rudderless ship at sea. Yet, you've often said that survival is the name of the game--how can you expect to survive?" Answer: I don't agree with your statements. There are a lot of misunderstandings about Coors, and that's why we're here. We will survive for a number of reasons, but primarily because: a. We make a unique product, and b. We care about our employees and provide them a good place to work.

4. Actual interviews were conducted with Joe and Bill by professional reporters before television cameras and lights in the setting where the interview with Mike Wallace would take place. We reviewed and critiqued the videotapes and each officer. We prepared a follow-up memorandum summarizing the key points. It's interesting to note that Mike Wallace agrees with this approach to preparing for an interview using outside reporters. He once said, "It makes perfect sense to me because people should have every opportunity to make the best case they can for themselves."

5. Other--Recognizing that audiences respond emo-tionally rather than intellectually, it's impor-tant to make a good impression with appear-ance and mannerisms. Some things were considered:

- Joe Coors's glasses

- Whether to wear coats and ties

- Whether to use make-up

- What type of chairs to sit in; where chairs should be placed

- The importance of smiling, no matter how hostile Mike Wallace might become

g. Engaged Harbicht Research Inc., of Arcadia, California, to perform formal research with beer consumers to measure the impact of the show in Los Angeles and Denver:

Wave I - Immediately prior to broadcast (9/21-26)

Wave II - One week after broadcast (10/1-4)

Wave III - Four weeks after broadcast (10/28-31)--Wave III was intended as a measure of long-term impact of the program.

h. Engaged Manning, Selvage & Lee to perform a media audit in Los Angeles.

2. Open Door Policy

a. Invited Allan Maraynes, producer, to visit the brewery and ask questions of any employee he wanted about the working conditions at Coors.

b. Prepared extensive chronology of Coors's labor relations history.

c. Responded immediately to all requests for information. (Note: the actual interview with Bill and Joe Coors was held in May; the show was not aired until September 26. There were continuing follow-up requests for information throughout the summer.)

d. Conducted an employee "brown bag" luncheon with Mike Wallace where employees at random told Mike Wallace their opinions about Coors.

What followed was a series of questions and answers between Mike Wallace and over a dozen Coors employees. These were all filmed by "60 Minutes" and comments from three employees eventually appeared in the segment aired in September.

The "60 Minutes" broadcast "Trouble Brewing" was aired on September 26, 1982. We didn't know until we saw the show what was in the program.

EVALUATION

Mike Wallace and his producer were professionals in every sense of the word. They explained what type of story they wanted to do, and then they set about doing it. They were never hostile or antagonistic, although Mike Wallace was tough in his questioning. According to Neilsen, 20.8 million households saw the program; it was the number two show of the week.

We met our objective to turn a potentially negative story into a positive one as evidenced by the following:

- Coors received more than eight hundred letters expressing viewers' thoughts about the program--only six were negative. We also received hundreds of phone calls supporting Coors. In addition, according to CBS the thousands of letters it received about the broadcast were overwhelmingly in favor of Coors.

- A review of the script showed that all message objectives were communicated at least once.

- According to the formal research, one out of five beer drinkers saw the show. The change in attitudes among the minority who saw it was large enough to cause a notable shift in the total sample.

- The media audit revealed that 90 percent of the media saw the show. All believed the story was positive for Coors. Importantly, the people with some of the strongest anti-Coors feelings six months earlier showed the largest change in attitude.

- Many organizations lifted their boycotts as a result of the broadcast. These groups included Hispanic groups, colleges, and gay editors in San Francisco. Also, pro-Coors editorials appeared in several newspapers.

FOLLOW UP

- Negotiated with "60 Minutes" to purchase rights to reproduce and distribute tapes for employees, distributors, and opinion leaders. The transmittal to distributors suggested ways to use the tape in their markets to capitalize on the positive impact.

- Made available to employees the tape of the employee brown bag luncheon with Mike Wallace.

- Held an open house with management and employees to share the "60 Minutes" broadcast. Shared "60 Minutes" updates with employees and distributors through employee and distributor publications.

- Sent copies to distributors of the support letters we had received from consumers in their markets and asked them to follow up. We also answered each letter personally.

- Placed ads in several local papers reproducing the editorial which had been run by that paper with a note of thanks for supporting Coors.

CONCLUSION

Adolph Coors Company faced its biggest communication challenge ever in 1982 when Coors was the subject of a "60 Minutes" investigation by Mike Wallace. Our objective was to turn a potentially negative report into a positive one by providing an open and candid forum for the "60 Minutes" team. We successfully accomplished our objective.

TRENDS

There are a number of emerging issues in which business plays a part and that have substantial impact on the public. A quick reading of major periodicals provides some indication of what these issues are: America's shift from an industrial society to an information society; multinationalism with both domestic and international ramifications; corporate governance at all levels; increasing reliance on public referenda and consumer protection. There is also a rapid development of new power centers throughout our society. Special interest groups have come to occupy a position of significant political and social importance. Employees, too, are flexing their muscles.

Forming a backdrop to this is the pervasiveness and the influence of the news media, which have become a center of power in America. Although investigative reporting is not new, the journalists of today come prepared with better understanding of the workings of business and they also have the resources of large media organizations. The outcome of all these changes--the new issues, the rise of new power centers, and the enlarged influence and reach of the media--has been to bring previously private organizational problems into the public domain. Unlike the earlier muckraking, investigative reporting of the '80s will attempt to interpret more thoroughly and accurately all of these massive changes in a targeted manner. It is an opportunity for an organization to communicate positive messages about itself.

It is also an opportunity for organizational communicators to expand their roles by keeping abreast of all changes and expectations related to the public interest. Communicators can interpret these changes to management and then become involved in the decision-making process to help ensure that the company's policies are perceived to be in the public's best interest. The organization then will be better prepared to respond to its stakeholders and survive in this changing, information-oriented society.

Source Perrier S.A.
Media Role Play Exercise

Source Perrier S. A. Media Role Play Exercise*

Executive Role

On February 9, 1990, Ronald V. Davis, president of Perrier Group of America Inc. in Greenwich, Conn., removed Perrier's sparkling spring water from distribution in North America. A lab in North Carolina had picked up traces of benzene, a carcinogen, in several samples a few days earlier. The following day at a news conference, Mr. Davis announced that Perrier would be off the market for two to three months.

Perrier and the brands it acquired from Beatrice in 1987 commanded about 24% of the $2.2 billion U.S. market for bottled water at the end of 1989. But Perrier had been losing share at the end of the 80s to such European rivals as Evian, which analysts predicted would profit heavily from the benzene scare. A Sunday *New York Times* article on February 11th quoted customers and restaurant owners who were switching brands before the benzene scare. The manager of a fashionable New York restaurant said: "I think Perrier is finished. We can write it off."

Rumors started circulating in the press in the following week about the source of the problem. Several articles claimed that sabotage was responsible for the presence of benzene, and others claimed that a Source Perrier official said that the company believed the contamination occurred because an employee mistakenly used cleaning fluid containing benzene to clean machinery used on the bottling line that filled bottles for North America.

On February 14th at a news conference in Paris, company officials announced the expansion of its recall to the rest of the world and acknowledged all production lines for its trademark sparkling water had been contaminated in recent months by tiny amounts of benzene. Officials also said for the first time that benzene occurred naturally in Perrier water and that the chemical made its way into the bottle because workers had failed to replace filters designed to remove it.

Health officials in the U.S. and France said the benzene levels found in Perrier did not pose a significant health risk. Even so, some marketing experts said the discovery could have seriously damaged Perrier, which had gone to great lengths to position its water as naturally pure.

Throughout the crisis, Perrier executives were characterized as nonchalant. Frederick Zimmer, Perrier parent company president, even contended that "all this publicity helps build the brand's renown."

You are a group of advisors to Mr. Davis. Your job is to advise and train him for television appearances in the United States. One member of the group will be selected to play the role of Mr. Davis.

---

* This case was written by Professor Paul A. Argenti, The Amos Tuck School of Business Administration, Dartmouth College © 1992.

THE AMOS TUCK SCHOOL — DARTMOUTH COLLEGE

Source Perrier S. A.
Media Role Play Exercise*

Reporter, Financial News Network

On February 9, 1990, Ronald V. Davis, president of Perrier Group of America Inc. in Greenwich, Conn., removed Perrier's sparkling spring water from distribution in North America. A lab in North Carolina had picked up traces of benzene, a carcinogen, in several samples a few days earlier. The following day at a news conference, Mr. Davis announced that Perrier would be off the market for two to three months.

Perrier and the brands it acquired from Beatrice in 1987 commanded about 24% of the $2.2 billion U.S. market for bottled water at the end of 1989. But Perrier had been losing share at the end of the 80s to such European rivals as Evian, which analysts predicted would profit heavily from the benzene scare. A Sunday *New York Times* article on February 11th quoted customers and restaurant owners who were switching brands before the benzene scare. The manager of a fashionable New York restaurant said: "I think Perrier is finished. We can write it off."

Rumors started circulating in the press in the following week about the source of the problem. Several articles claimed that sabotage was responsible for the presence of benzene, and others claimed that a Source Perrier official said that the company believed the contamination occurred because an employee mistakenly used cleaning fluid containing benzene to clean machinery used on the bottling line that filled bottles for North America.

On February 14th at a news conference in Paris, company officials announced the expansion of its recall to the rest of the world and acknowledged all production lines for its trademark sparkling water had been contaminated in recent months by tiny amounts of benzene. Officials also said for the first time that benzene occurred naturally in Perrier water and that the chemical made its way into bottles because workers had failed to replace filters designed to remove it.

Health officials in the U.S. and France said the benzene levels found in Perrier did not pose a significant health risk. Even so, some marketing experts said the discovery could have seriously damaged Perrier, which had gone to great lengths to position its water as naturally pure.

Throughout the crisis, Perrier executives were characterized as nonchalant. Frederick Zimmer, Perrier parent company president, even contended that "all this publicity helps build the brand's renown."

You are a group of reporters for the *Financial News Network*, which is regarded as having a pro-business slant. You all have MBA degrees from prestigious schools and studied CorpComm as part of your b-school curriculum. Prepare for a two-minute interview in a talk-show format. One member of the group will be selected to play the role of a television reporter who will interview Mr. Davis.

---

* This case was written by Professor Paul A. Argenti, The Amos Tuck School of Business Administration, Dartmouth College © 1992.

THE AMOS TUCK SCHOOL   DARTMOUTH COLLEGE

Source Perrier S. A.
Media Role Play Exercise*

Reporter, "Hard Copy"

On February 9, 1990, Ronald V. Davis, president of Perrier Group of America Inc. in Greenwich, Conn., removed Perrier's sparkling spring water from distribution in North America. A lab in North Carolina had picked up traces of benzene (a poisonous liquid shown to cause cancer in laboratory animals) in several samples a few days earlier. The following day at a news conference, Mr. Davis announced that Perrier would be off the market for two to three months.

The situation at Perrier had all the elements of an extraordinarily difficult crisis-management challenge. Unlike Tylenol's recall in 1982, Perrier's difficulties came from an internal mistake. Thus, critics questioned how forgiving consumers would be. In addition, Perrier's unusually long absence from the market would severely test the loyalty of many Perrier customers who were accustomed to drinking the brand daily.

Perrier and the brands it acquired from Beatrice in 1987 commanded about 24% of the $2.2 billion U.S. market for bottled water at the end of 1989. But Perrier had been losing share at the end of the 80s to such European rivals as Evian and San Pelligrino, which analysts predicted would profit heavily from the benzene scare. A Sunday *New York Times* article on February 11th quoted customers and restaurant owners who were switching brands before the benzene scare. The manager of a fashionable New York restaurant said: "I think Perrier is finished. We can write it off."

Perrier decided against mounting a public relations campaign to inform the public of exactly what went wrong. Thus, rumors started circulating in the press in the following week about the source of the problem. Several articles claimed that sabotage was responsible for the presence of benzene, and others claimed that a Source Perrier official said that the company believed the contamination occurred because an employee mistakenly used cleaning fluid containing benzene to clean machinery used on the bottling line that filled bottles for North America.

On February 14th at a raucous news conference in Paris, company officials announced the expansion of its recall to the rest of the world and acknowledged all production lines for its trademark sparkling water had been contaminated in recent months by tiny amounts of benzene.

---

* This case was written by Professor Paul A. Argenti, The Amos Tuck School of Business Administration, Dartmouth College © 1992.

Officials also said for the first time that benzene occurred naturally in Perrier water and that the chemical made its way into bottles because workers had failed to replace filters designed to remove it.

Perrier insisted its famous spring in Vergeze, France, was unpolluted, but the company's explanations seemed to raise more questions than they answered. Immediately after the recall, Perrier executives had made several contradictory statements about the problem and appeared to make light of it. Asked why Perrier expanded the recall, Chairman Gustave Leven responded at the news conference with a joking reference to Perrier's ad slogan in France: "Perrier is crazy!"

Throughout the crisis, other Perrier executives were also characterized as nonchalant. Frederick Zimmer, Perrier parent company president, even contended that "all this publicity helps build the brand's renown."

At the first U.S. news conference on February 10, Mr. Davis had said the contamination was limited to production lines making water for export to the U.S. "The problem is only in the U.S.," said Mr. Davis. But on February 14th, Mr. Leven said Perrier had known as early as February 9th that all its production lines had been contaminated by benzene at one time or another over the last few months. Mr. Zimmer, the parent company's president, insisted Perrier had never said anything different.

In a related development, Mr. Leven scoffed at suggestions he or his company might be concerned by an insider-trading investigation launched February 14th into Perrier option trading. French securities industry regulators said they were looking into trading that occurred just before Perrier announced the benzene contamination on February 9th.

Trading in options to sell Perrier shares at 1800 or 1900 French francs ($315.80 or $333.30) was abnormally heavy just before the negative announcement. The trading was similar to short-selling. Perrier shares tumbled to just 1413 French francs by the February 14th close, sharply boosting the value of options to sell at the higher price. Traders said that those who acquired the options stood to make profits equal to $1 million.

You are a group of television reporters for the *Hard Copy* television show, which is regarded as having an anti-business slant. The network is known for its hard-hitting investigative reporting. Prepare for a two-minute *Sixty Minutes*-style interview with Mr. Davis. One member of the group will be selected to play the role of a television reporter.

Chapter 7: A Random Walk Down Wall Street

Investor relations, or IR as it is commonly called, is such a specialized field that you must read another text to understand what is really going on. I would recommend two different ones for this purpose. First, Mahoney's *The Professional's Guide to Financial Marketing and Communications* and then Little and Rhodes's *Understanding Wall Street*. These include much more detail about the different aspects of IR.

As I mentioned in the blurb on this material in chapter 3, you should also try to get someone into your class who is an expert in this area. Most large public companies have someone working on this area exclusively that you can invite in to talk to your class about what the typical day is like. Even if they cannot come, try to get someone who does this for a living to talk with you briefly over the phone. For me, actually talking with people who do this was worth much more than all I have read.

Another way to get information is call the National Investor Relations Institute (NIRI) (Phone: 1-703-506-3570). They will give you lots of different stuff to focus on. The SEC (Phone: 202-942-8088) also has a booklet that talks about the documents I discuss at the beginning of the chapter.

You could also attempt to build alliances with the finance faculty in your school or university. They know about the importance of this area and might be able to help in the same way that an IR professional could. And, finally, I would try to get hold of one of the many consultants who work in this area on things like annual report writing, developing contacts with analysts, and other related matters.

Once you have done these things, well in advance of the class, you should also attempt to collect as many annual reports as possible. Try to get a range of them from a variety of industries displaying many different styles. You can get any company's annual report you want in the United States for free. Sometimes the *Wall Street Journal* will have a little tear sheet that allows you to write away for many annual reports from a variety of companies both domestic and international.

Put some thought into what you want to focus on. For example, if you are in Texas, you might want to focus on oil companies, or if you are in New York, you could be more interested in banking. You can cover virtually any industry you desire. But you must plan for this in advance.

Once you have the annual reports, you then need to look at them in two different ways. First, look at the overall design. Which ones stand out?

Why? The Marvel comic report is an obvious one because it is written like a comic book, but what makes other reports stand out in terms of design? Is it color? Is it use of design elements? Pictures?

Then look to see what the company has to say in the non-financial section of the report. Analyze the comments based on the company's financial performance (for those without financial backgrounds, you might want to consult with your accounting faculty for help). Does what they say up front jive with the numbers in the back? Are they trying to hide something? Bring examples into the classroom to make this session come alive.

Finally, you can give the students an assignment that will allow them to focus on the last part of the chapter. Have them develop an IR program for a company that they can find something about either through information in the library or by interviewing people in the company itself.

Topic Outline

Given that this is the most difficult topc in the book from the perspective of most communication's professors, I am including the following outline, which I have used to teach the session in my elective.

I. **Investor Relations Overview**

   A. **Types of Investors**

   - individual (shareholders of record/street-name or beneficial holders)
     - $2 trillion of capital, 20% in equities
     - hold approximately 55% of equities
     - *Advantage*: diversified shareholder base → less volatility (stability → investor appeal)

   - institutional (pension funds, mutual funds, insurance co's, banks)
     - $5 trillion under management, 50% in equities
     - hold approximately 45% of equities
     - larger holdings
     - trade more actively
     - can have greater impact on stock price volatility
     - *Advantage*: easier to target/communicate with

   - insider

   B. **The Angle of Presentation**

   - growth stock—anticipated steady growth in earnings
   - income stock—steady stream of dividend income
   - industry play—assessing attractive dynamics
   - value stock—currently undervalued by market

   C. **Valuation Methods**

   - value—the "right" stock price, assuming most productive use of Company's assets
   - multiples (EPS, CF, REV, BV)
   - discounted cash flow (free cash flow = NI + DEP - CAPEX)
   - break-up

   D. **The IR Team**

   - typical components (CEO, CFO, Director of IR, staff)
   - access to senior management (IR Director and financial community)
   - access to operating management (IR Director and financial community)

II. Stock Marketing in General

A. Basic Qualities of a Stock Marketing/IR Program

- providing information that analysts need to recommend stock and investors need to buy it
- information-based
- avoid typically slick marketing/promotional methods
- proactive
- focused
- targeted

B. Disclosure Issues

- *Disclosure* - the handling of *material information*
  - *SEC definition*: any information that might influence an investor to make a buy, sell or hold decision
  - *Courts' definition*: information is material if there is "substantial likelihood" that a "reasonable investor" would consider it important in the "total mix" of information

- *Proper disclosure* - reaching sufficient media sources to ensure adequate coverage to reach attention of investor body (often via newswires, ie., Dow Jones, Reuters, Associated Press, UPI, etc.)

- *Structured disclosure* (mandated by 1934 Securities Act) - 10K, 10Q, 8K, prospectus, proxy, registration statements, audited financials, MD&A

- *Unstructured disclosure* (addressed in 1933 Securities Act - implicit obligations under anti-fraud provisions) - annual and quarterlies, letters to sh's, press releases, speeches, investor meetings, phone conversations

- Rules of thumb:
  - If it's material and finalized, you're obligated to disclose
    - Board vote
    - letter of intent
  - If it's not finalized, you may choose to disclose, but are then obligated to continue commenting as situation develops
  - No obligation to comment on market rumors <u>not attributable to the company</u>; however, the exchanges encourage companies to dispel unfounded rumors leading to unusual market activity
  - *Avoid selective disclosure of material information at all costs*

- Segment disclosure requirements (10% of assets or revenues)

C. **Credibility Issues**

- The IR professional's biggest asset
- Know your company
- Know your industry

III. **Providing the Information: Financial Community Relations**

A. **Contacts/Targets**

- The Buy-side
  - institutional analysts
  - fund/portfolio managers
  - individuals
- The Sell-side
  - research analysts
  - institutional brokers
  - individual brokers (registered representatives)

B. **Methods/Tools**

- Ways to reach institutions

  - day-to-day phone contact; one-on-ones with buy-side and sell-side
    - the estimate game
    - research reports
    - timing of comments vis-á-vis reporting periods
  - formal meeting formats
    - addressing analyst/broker societies
    - addressing brokerage-sponsored industry conferences
    - hosting tours/presentations/one-on-ones at company offices, mfring sites
    - hosting company meeting in NYC, Boston, etc.
  - an aside on speeches—writing and giving
    - determining the speaker
    - direct, brief
    - "plain speaking"
    - speaker preferences
    - a/v aids
      - appropriate to corporate image/financial topics
      - timing rule of thumb: 6 slides/minute
      - avoid filler slides

- Ways to reach individuals

  - direct mail to affinity groups (current shareholders, employees, customers, suppliers)
  - brokerage community (direct mail, corporate profiles)
  - general visibility through media relations
  - National Association of Investors Corporation (NAIC)
    - 163,000 members
    - average portfolio of approximately $110,000
  - American Association of Individual Investors (AAII)
    - 140,000 members
    - average portfolio of approximately $110,000

- Ways to reach both institutions and individuals

  - financial reporting (ongoing)
    - annual report/10K
      - principal shareholder communication document
      - not technically required under SEC disclosure rules (10K is)
      - typically contains:
        - strategic information in letter to shareholders
        - operational information in review of operations
        - financial information in financial review, MD&A, statement
      - risk of over-designing
    - quarterly report/10Q
      - quarterly financial report providing continuing view of financial position during year
      - timeliness
      - relevance
    - proxy
      - official notification to shareholders of matters to be voted on at annual meeting
      - can return vote by proxy
      - recent SEC policy revisions
        - executive compensation disclosure
        - total return to shareholders comparison
    - earnings/news releases
  - annual meetings
    - review of fiscal year
    - forum for Q&A

United Technologies (B)

INVESTOR RELATIONS AT UNITED TECHNOLOGIES (B)

United Technologies' Investor Relations strategy focused on three major initiatives: launching a concerted effort to reposition UTC in the minds of investors and analysts as a commercial, consumer-driven company rather than as an engineer-driven aerospace company; projecting the image of a business culture that delivered on its promises; and sending out line managers and executives from the company's businesses to meet analysts face-to-face.

Repositioning the Company

In a real sense, these initiatives were an attempt to redefine the image of the company as a whole. The objective was to sell the future in the global post-cold war business environment of the 1990s. As Steve Page, executive vice-president and CFO of United Technologies, put it:

> A year ago, we had an aerospace side that was coming down, and commercial businesses that were growing. And when we went out to talk about the company, we would say, "We lost a billion dollars of revenue at Pratt & Whitney."
>
> Why were we telling *that* story? We *made* $2 billion in revenue in the commercial businesses and we *lost* $2 billion of revenue in aerospace. We were telling a story of decline instead of growth. So we turned it around and started talking about growth. But it wasn't easy to get George to do that; it's more fun to talk about a 777 engine—that's hot technology. A Sikorsky helicopter that can fly backwards at 86 miles an hour—that's technology. Now we talk with the same enthusiasm about a scroll compressor or an elevator as a jet engine.

Top management decided that for too long UTC had been associated primarily with its troubled aerospace businesses in the minds of its key constituencies, and that the company was followed by too narrow a range of aerospace analysts. As a result, UTC began to aggressively

---

This case was written by James Rubin, Instructor in Business Administration and Theodore M. Forbes, Instructor in Business Administration. Copyright © 1997 by the University of Virginia Darden School Foundation, Charlottesville, VA. All rights reserved.

promote its Otis and Carrier businesses. Both were generating healthy profits, both were in growth industries, and both were well positioned in the burgeoning markets of Asia and Eastern Europe. This emphasis on the positive side of the UTC story would begin to reposition the company, not only in the analyst community, but also among institutional and individual investors.

Although UTC had historically been regarded primarily as a defense/aerospace play, this identity was, in the minds of UTC's IR professionals, dragging down the growing franchises. The new story was of a restructured, lean global player, quickly expanding into new markets and building on a history of technical excellence. Steve Page described what UTC was trying to accomplish:

> Aerospace companies historically have P/E ratios of 10 to 12. The commercial companies, like Carrier and Otis, are at 16 to 18, if they were pure stand-alones. So some of what we've done is subtle: if you go back and look at the 1992 and 1993 annual reports, we lead with the aerospace companies; but in 1994, we lead off with Otis and Carrier, more commercial companies. Does that make a difference? I'm not sure, but I want people to know we're Otis and Carrier as much as Pratt. Now we go to electrical product conferences as well as aerospace conferences. Angelo is trying to get electrical products analysts to follow us, not just aerospace/defense analysts. I'm focusing on the commercial side, which accounts for 58 percent of our business.

The effect of such a repositioning could be swift and dramatic, and the potential power of changing the analysts' minds about the company was vast. Page zeroed in on the core strategy:

> We want to have another multiple point or two on our P/E ratio. If we can get one more multiple point by having people think differently about us, all the shareholders win. How do you achieve that? By shifting the focus away from the aerospace sector, and by getting non-aerospace/defense analysts to follow us. We want to change the mix. We'd rather have multi-industry analysts following us, conglomerate or commercial, electrical equipment analysts. Some of these things you can *manage*; they don't just happen.

Delivering on Promises

The management team readily acknowledged that the company's credibility was less than perfect. After several years of not meeting its earnings estimates and experiencing management problems, the investment community had grown suspicious. Refocusing attention on the company's successful businesses was a start, but UTC also had to prove wrong the notion that the company couldn't deliver on its promises. Steve Page recalled a meeting with George David in which they discussed this:

I said, "George, there are some things we just have to do better, and they're real simple. We have to tell them what's going on." In the past when we had a problem, we thought if we didn't talk about it, maybe something good would happen. We don't do that any more. If we're having a problem, we talk about it early on so there are no surprises. "Here's the problem. Here's how we're going to fix it." We did this with Hamilton Standard last year; we had a leadership crisis, and we went out and said, "Here's the problem. Here's what we're going to do." George replaced the president, and then went in and replaced the CFO. A crisis in leadership is unacceptable. We expect performance if you say you're going to do something.

With this new strategy in place, the investment community began to change its mind about UTC. As Page tells it:

George and I both said, "In 1993 we have to make it. And *really* make it. Every single quarter, right through to 1994. And we don't have any reason not to do it." So we came out and said to the Street, "We're going to do $3.30 a share in 1993"; and we started to make every quarter of $3.30. As a result, during 1993 the stock, on flat earnings, went from $40-something to $60-something, because we made every single quarter. People said, "Wait a minute; you mean they said they were going to do it, and they're doing it? That's a change."

As UTC met its targets quarter after quarter, Wall Street began to think differently about the company. Messina described the change in mood:

You make your first quarter, second quarter, third quarter of 1993, and all of a sudden a pattern starts to develop. As you make the numbers each time, you begin to lay out the longer-term objectives. You show you're continuing to make progress, and you get more and more believers in the company. They start to say, "This is no longer just a restructuring story, where the company restructured and had some benefits. Now it's a company that really is managing its businesses better, and it has good businesses; it's got strategy and global growth."

Involving Line Management

One of the key planks in UTC's strategy was putting the heads of the various business units out in front of the analysts who helped shape Wall Street's impressions of the company. This accomplished two key objectives. As Messina put it:

Our goal was twofold: one was to let the investors see the people who were running our operations and develop more confidence in them, and the other was for our managers to get a taste of Wall Street and what investors expected. It is one thing to present a business plan internally in the company, and another to get out in front of the investment community and tell them what your company or operating division is going to do for the year.

The impetus for this move came directly from the top of the company. David's shareholder agenda quickly became a key element in United Technologies' culture. David made sure that all the top executives shared his commitment to the shareholders and to the company's investors. The managers, in turn, found meetings with analysts a useful way to get a fresh perspective on the company. Messina recalled:

> One of the things that changed was UTC's management. We didn't just go out and tell our story; we also asked questions. What are the shareholders' concerns? What would investors like to see? So we got a lot of feedback that we never asked for before. In the past we built walls around the company—we were going to do what we wanted and we didn't seek external input. Today, we go and seek out that external input. When Steve and George meet with institutional investors, they ask, what are your concerns? What would you like to see happen with the company?

Results

One by one, "hold" positions moved to "buy" and "strong buy," and a wider variety of firms began tracking the stock. Out of thirteen top brokerage houses in May 1995, nine had moved to a buy and only four remained on hold positions. Perhaps the most pointed tribute the analysts could pay UTC's IR initiative and core performance came in the words of once-skeptical Prudential. As Gary Reich wrote in April 1995, when UTC's 52-week high had hit 72:

> "It is easy to fall into the trap of trying to value UTC in line with similar companies. However, we can argue at this point that no company can be valued similarly to United Technologies. The company has come through a long hard restructuring. This includes most of their management.... With earnings on the rebound and about to expand substantially, we will use the assumption that, in the future, the shares of United Technologies can and will sell at a market multiple. Under that assumption we can arrive at a price 12 months from now of $84, which would represent a multiple of 13.3 times our earnings model."

Dean Witter's analysis confirmed that management's message was, by 1995, getting across:

> "In our opinion, management is doing an excellent job of transitioning United Technologies to a predominantly commercial company, with 58 percent of sales international, 58 percent commercial, and only 18 percent to the U.S. government. We believe that this year's prospects for Otis, Carrier, and UT Automotive are excellent as Europe recovers, high growth is maintained in Asia, and profitability in North America improves."

With UTC at around 130 in November 1996, this sounded like a pretty good recommendation (see Exhibits 1 and 2).

But the IR team at UTC did not rest on its laurels during a rise that outstripped enthusiastic analysts' projections, for a key to future long-term strategy would be addressing the question of just who owned the company, and whether or not the shareowners were well aligned with strategic objectives.

Exhibit 1

INVESTOR RELATIONS AT UNITED TECHNOLOGIES (B)

UTX Stock Prices

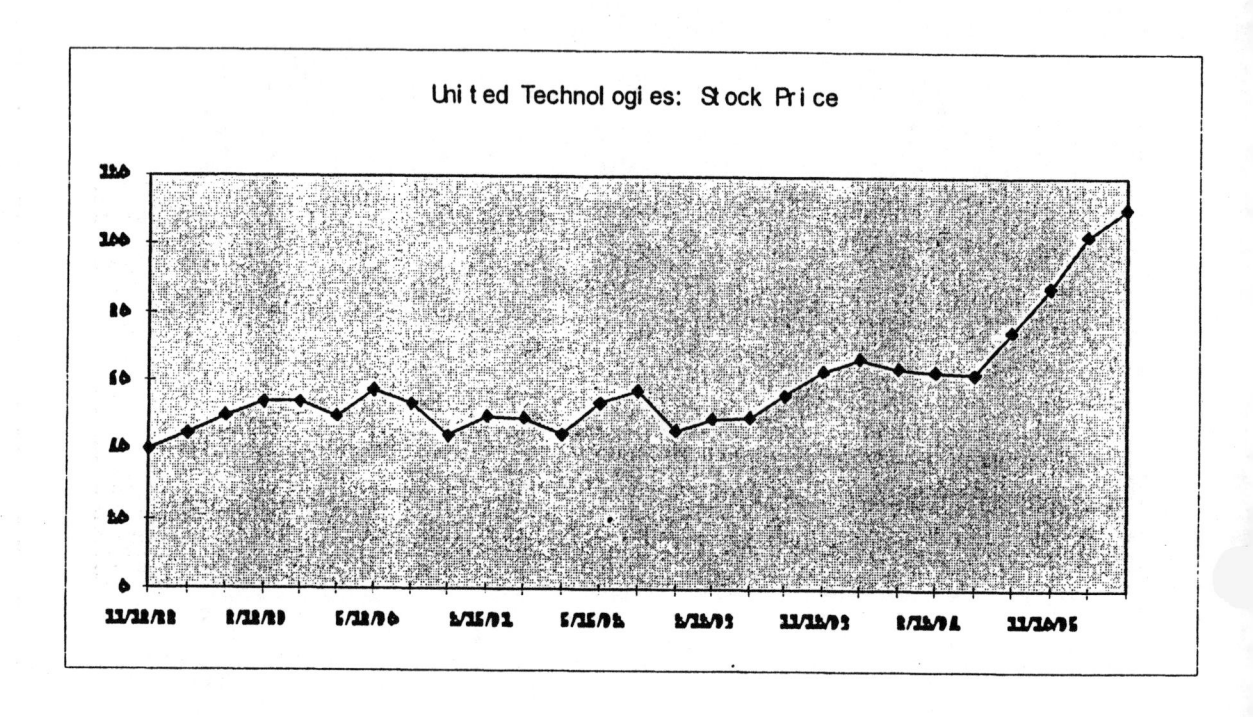

-7-   UVA-BC-0121

Exhibit 2

INVESTOR RELATIONS AT UNITED TECHNOLOGIES (B)

UTX P/E Ratios

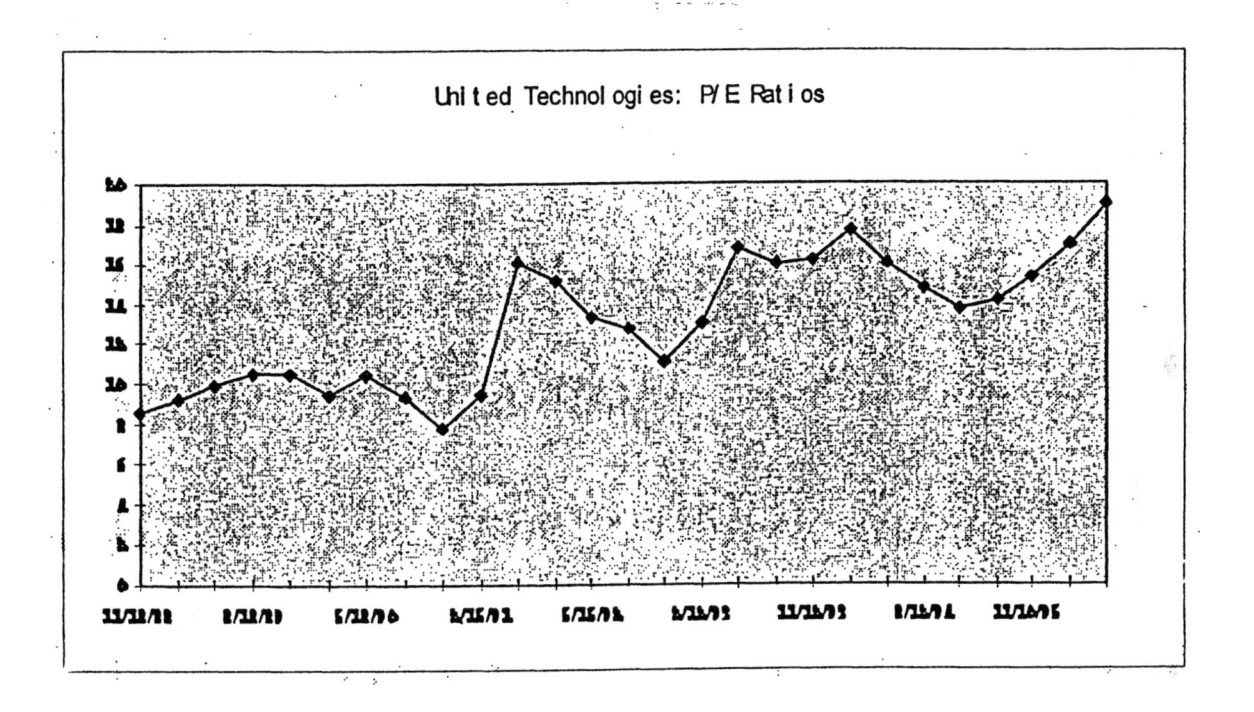

United Technologies Teaching Note

INVESTOR RELATIONS AT UNITED TECHNOLOGIES (A and B)

Teaching Note

Abstract

In late 1992 and early 1993, the managers in charge of investor relations at United Technologies were faced with a financial community skeptical about the future performance of the company's stock. While the stock market had doubled between 1986 and 1992, UTX on the New York Stock Exchange stagnated in the mid-40s. Mainly tracked by aerospace analysts, the once core holding in many portfolios had "lost the affection" of Wall Street through past management's several restructurings and forecasting of earnings that did not meet expectations set by the company. The new management team has the advantage of a strongly articulated mission from CEO George David who has substantially turned around the company. The problem for the investor relations team, CFO Steve Page, and IR director, Angelo Messina, lies in the challenge of restoring the capital market's belief in the company's future. They must effectively communicate how the company has repositioned itself from an aerospace conglomerate to a commercial customer-driven, global corporation. The A case takes students into the highest levels of investor relations management; the B case sets out the specific strategy used to attain remarkable results.

Description and Background

This case is meant to be cross-functional, showing the relationship between the finance and corporate-communication functions of a major corporation in the Dow Jones Industrials. The primary lesson students are meant to take away is that in today's world of ever-increasing complexity in moving information, corporations with a strong sense of mission and identity take a proactive stance in financial reporting through investor relations, one of the subfunctions of corporate communication. While it does not attempt to be a rigorous finance case as such, it does hope to show the way that effective management of the IR function can affect a company's relationship with analysts on the buy and sell side, and the way that Wall Street perceives and values a company.

The case proceeds mostly through the words of the key managers in IR, CFO Steve Page and IR Director Angelo Messina, who with the leadership of CEO George David, rebuilt UTC's

---

This teaching note was prepared by James Rubin, Instructor in Business Administration. Copyright © 1997 by the University of Virginia Darden School Foundation, Charlottesville, VA. All rights reserved.

credibility in the capital markets. They not only turned the company around, but moved the analyst community from a "wait-and-see" situation, to a "strong buy." Excerpts from analyst reports act to give students a sense of audience as well as a second point of view in the case. After a series of restructuring and failures to make good on predictions of earnings, in 1994 the company began to move with general market trends on a 1 percent increase in profits, and at the time of this writing, hit the 130s, split, and is moving up through the 60s.

On the macro level, the message the IR team has to send is closely aligned with George David's central mission, which is not only keeping the company's shareholders firmly in mind (the company at present is one of the first to include its stock price under the name of the company on its web site), but repositioning the corporation from a vulnerable aerospace defense conglomerate to a consumer-driven, innovative commercial corporation. David had been president of Otis Elevator, and was inspired by Japanese *kaizen* (lean manufacturing) at a time when UTC was still perceived as a engineer-driven aerospace company whose R&D budget was not necessarily tied to the current markets. In the recession, in one way or another, all of their business's growth had been called into question—Pratt & Whitney, Sikorsky, and Hamilton Standard through the end of the cold war and endless talk of downsizing national defense, as well as trouble in the airline industry following deregulation; Otis and Carrier in the recession of the 1980s, through the decline in domestic building.

As president of Otis, then COO and CEO, David pursued an aggressive globalization strategy with entry into emerging markets in virtually every country in the world. What Page and Messina knew was that while analysts still held the door open in aerospace for a long-awaited upgrading of the commercial airline fleet and solid positioning in the spare parts and maintenance business, the commercial businesses were an increasingly important part of the company. With such changes in image and identity as, for example, placing Otis and Carrier before Pratt &Whitney and Sikorsky in the 1994 *Annual Report*, Page and Messina aimed to expand the kind of analysts that tracked the company in order to broaden awareness of its new direction. They had to get out the "new story" of UTC's future to find a more appropriate value when the stock of other similar conglomerates was rising. Their success was striking as more analysts began to track the company, and analysts's reports moved from skepticism to enthusiasm that UTC, once a core holding in Dow Jones Industrial portfolios, had really turned itself around this time. Students should be brought up-to-date not only through the B case which describes in detail the IR strategy, but also through the company's superb web site and its provocative "Be There First" ad campaign which redefines and, in a sense, unifies the company's old and new strengths—technological innovation and globalization.

Case Discussion

Study questions for Investor Relations at UTC might include:

1. How do analysts arrive at a value for UTC's stock?

2. What are the obstacles facing the IR managers?

3. What strategy should the managers pursue to have the company appropriately valued?

4. Who are the audiences for their communications?

Opening (20 minutes)

First, the students should lay out case facts and eventually reach the point that the market had shifted and UTC had not kept pace with the trend toward overall growth. By examining excerpts from recent UTC annual reports that break out the earnings of the various divisions, and through the words of the managers, they should discuss how UTC is perceived in 1992 and how the perception of investors has not caught up with the fact that 58 percent of the business is now commercial. At some point early on, students could be asked how the stock's value is arrived at—i.e., EPS × Multiple—but how is the multiple determined and by whom?

The second stage of the opening case discussion should turn on two key concepts: the importance of credibility in communicating with the financial community and the necessity of proactively communicating a company's mission at a time of redefinition. This latter point could branch out into a discussion of other large companies such as GE, Xerox, Kodak, Ford, IBM, and so on, who have all struggled with redefining their image.

Credibility (20 minutes)

The next stage of discussion might begin with the question, How does UTC reestablish credibility? While it is a subtle subject to discuss, Steve Page stresses the importance of credibility on Wall Street. Brought in from Black & Decker by David, Page had an impeccable reputation with the financial community, and this is surely one of the "intangibles" in discussing the value of a conglomerate with first-year students first learning technical tools of valuation.

Still, Page and Messina's accomplishment lies in their recognition that UTC had made too many promises it hadn't kept and implemented a restructuring that was supposed to be the last, only to see something go wrong—as one wag put it, "UTC always had one engine moving in the wrong direction." They correctly perceived their task as restoring confidence and credibility in UTC's relationships with the capital markets, either by making the earnings they projected or quickly communicating an instance when they fell short. Beyond this, both by listening carefully to the buy and sell sides and by strategic presentations at analyst meetings, they were able to convince investors that the company was back on the right track, and that David's final restructuring had brought discipline to the conglomerate.

Hand out the B Case (20 minutes)

Ask students what specific steps IR took to address their problems. How it was a careful and strategic communication aligned with overall mission? The B case tells in the managers' own words how they repositioned UTC from a vulnerable defense conglomerate to a cutting-edge consumer-driven global company; the change in tone in analyst reports tells the story of their accomplishment. Their more subtle achievement was to communicate the ways in which UTC had no pure play, and in the words of the Prudential analyst, needed to be considered in its own right. Herein lies another fine point: the way a changing company's valuation may be reconsidered in light of the different EPS multiples that different kinds of companies trade at. Top management at UTC felt the company was undervalued in 1992, and subsequent events have proven them prescient. Again, students can be brought up to date through press releases from IR, the company's web site, and annual reports.

A visit to UTC's web site (http://www.utc.com), which includes recent press releases and sophisticated investor relations information, is well worth the closing 15 or 20 minutes of class time to show the increasingly open climate of the flow of financial information to internal and external constituencies, and to suggest what the company has to do to maintain its high perfromance.

Take-aways

Many will admit that the stock market is moved by "intangibles" but that these intangibles can also be tracked accurately by technical analysts. The final "take-away" of this case for students should be an appreciation of the complexity of the growing and increasingly open IR function, the difference between press release and proactive engagement in the perception (and ownership) of a company. A company has to perform, but without proactive communication this performance may be overlooked. The case also demonstrates how, in an age of ever-increasing speed and exactitude of measurements, the human factor of visionary leaders who are also effective communicators like George David and Steve Page, and effective managers like Angelo Messina, can still make all the difference in managing the shift from the old story of public relations to the new story of corporate communication.

Chapter 8: Communicating Internally

Everyone says that employee communications is the most important part of any corporate communication program today. I have recently worked with a few companies on this exciting area and can tell you that even the ones that are committed to changing the way they communicate with employees have a lot to learn.

This chapter gives you a fairly straightforward account of the best thinking out there on employee communications, but you can do lots of fun exercises to help students sort through how to become more two-way in their communications.

<u>One-Way/Two-Way Exercise</u>

Start with the One-Way/Two-Way exercise that I have included at the end of the chapter. Make transparencies of each and then do the following. Pick a fairly outgoing student to run the exercise and allot about 15 minutes at the beginning of the class.

Put the following on the overhead projector (see OHTs, chapter 8) or write it on the blackboard:

<u>Figure 1</u>

Elapsed
Time
Accuracy

Perceived Accuracy		Actual	
5 correct	#	5	#
4 correct		4	
3 correct		3	
2 correct		2	
1 correct		1	

<u>Figure 2</u>

Elapsed
Time
Accuracy

Perceived Accuracy		Actual	
5 correct	#	5	#
4 correct		4	
3 correct		3	
2 correct		2	
1 correct		1	

Then let the student describe Figure 1 from the back of the room making no eye contact and only communicating one way. Then have the students vote on whether they think they got 1-5 right. List the responses as indicated above, measure time, then show them the right answer on the transparency and get accurate account of what they really got.

Have the same student come to the front and describe Figure 2 (make sure to tell them Figure 2 is different), but this time have the students answer any questions they have. Measure time and as above the elements before and after.

Here is what you should find. Two-way communication takes more time, but people feel more confident and are more accurate as a result of two-way communication as compared to one-way communication.

This gets the discussion focused on being two-way right from the start. You can also, however, get them focused on other material in this chapter. For example, how have workers changed over the last twenty, thirty, forty, fifty years? If they have read an early work of fiction in the beginning of the semester, you can focus again on that here. Upton Sinclair's *The Jungle* is excellent for this purpose because it shows how awful the work environment was in the early part of this century.

Get them to talk about their own values, too. Are they going to commit their lives to some corporation? What would motivate them to feel comfortable working in one environment versus another? You can also talk with someone in the human resources area of a local company on these matters.

Another thing to get from the outside is some samples of company newsletters. Usually these are so bad that you may not have anything good to say, but every once in a while, you will find an innovative company that has put some time into developing a strong company newsletter. Use the various ones you collect to make some point about newsletters similar to what I cover in the chapter.

Norwich Software

Again, as with many of the subspecialties in this book, you can always get an employee communications specialist in to discuss this subject with the group if you know someone who seems to be doing a good job for a fairly large company.

Norwich Software is based on a real case, believe it or not, and it points out exactly how not to deal with laying off a good workforce in a company that has lots of *esprit de corps*.

Bernstein is shirking her own responsibilities here. Get the students to come up with solutions to John's problems that will help them use the material in the case while at the same time dealing with some of the political and other problems introduced.

Although it is a short, hypothetical case, it hits all the right buttons. I have had lots of interesting discussions about this little case based on the material in the chapter. Get them to focus on the problems, as always, first. Here is what the best of them are going to come up with.

1. The boss is shifting down responsibility for her problems.

2. The company doesn't have a strong corpcomm person and is about to give the bad one they have the axe. What should you do about this given what you now know about corpcomm?

3. How will the unaffected respond? What can you do about this?

A good strategy for Norwich Software should include:

1. A way to stratify employees into constituencies.

2. A way to deal with the loss of the corpcomm vice president.

3. A way to deal with the reputation of Bernstein after it hits the fan.

4. A way to save your own job.

Brown & Sharpe

I have included the Brown & Sharpe case here, which appeared in the first edition. It is still a classic and makes a great alternative to Norwich for a more sophisticated audience or a great second-day discussion on employee communication. Here is the case, the "B" case, and teaching notes.

One-Way/Two-Way Exercise

FIGURE 1
(for one-way communication)

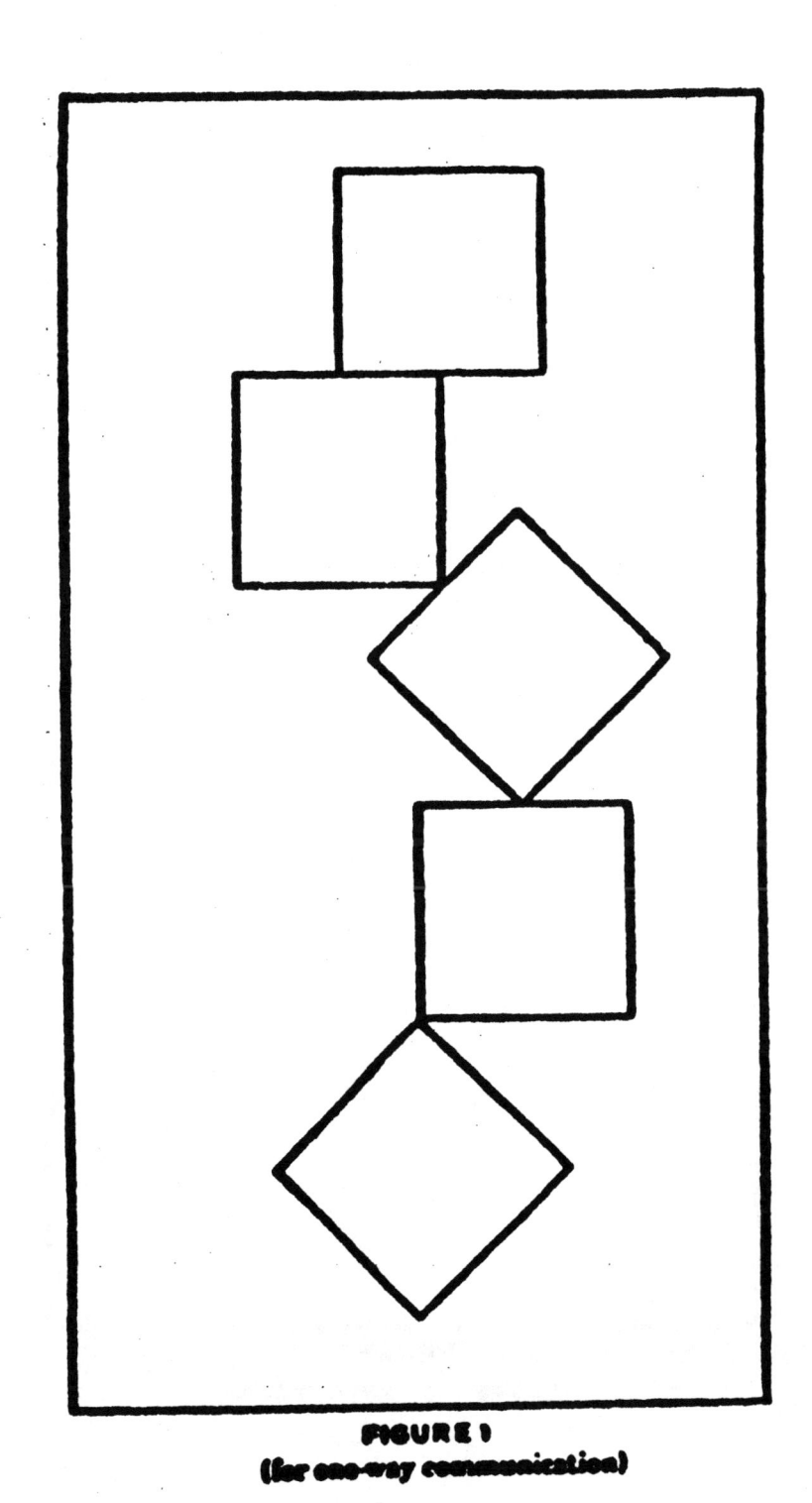

FIGURE 2
(for two-way communication)

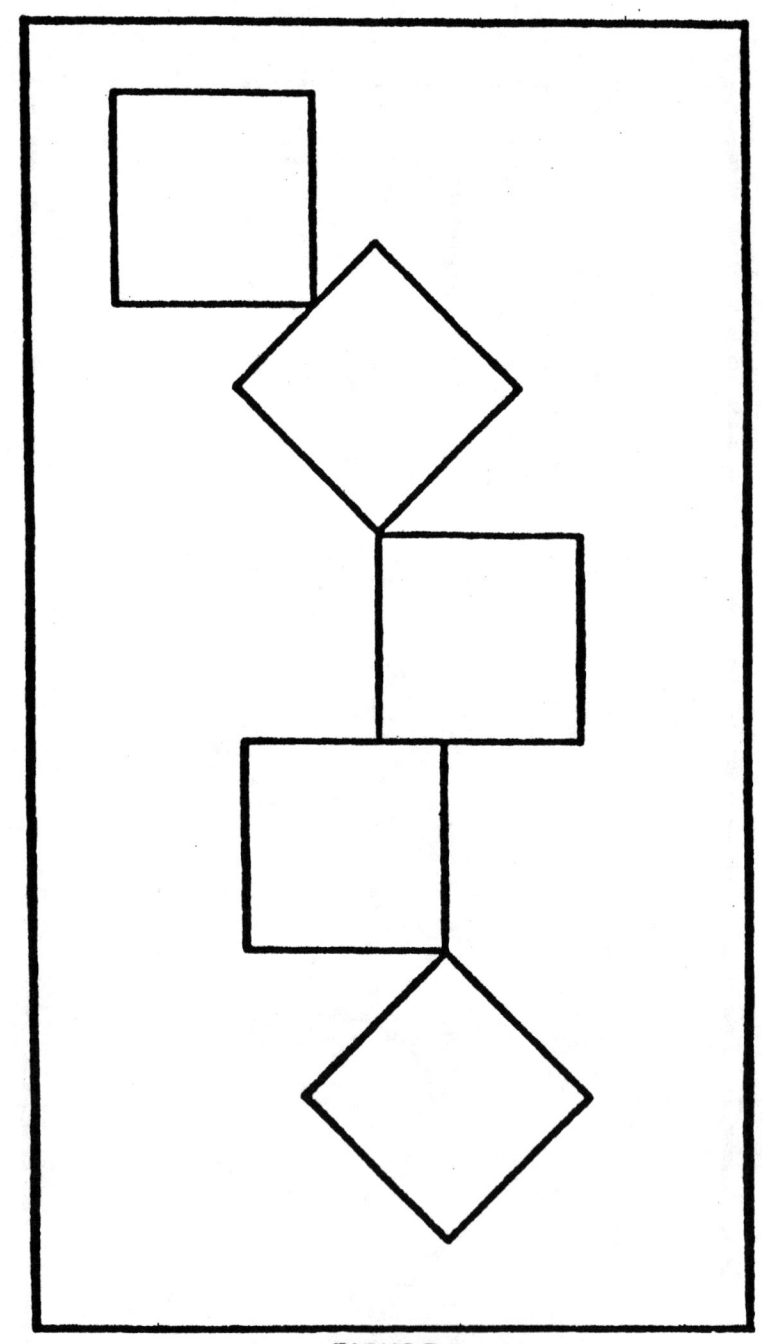

FIGURE 2
(for two-way communication)

Brown & Sharpe

Brown & Sharpe*

John Gordon, Director of Industrial Relations for Brown & Sharpe Manufacturing Company, drove up to the barbed-wire fence of his company's Precision Park facility one morning in early June 1982. The entrance surrounding the Rhode Island manufacturing concern's major plant looked more like a prison than a machine tool operation. A strike by the International Association of Machinists (IAM) was then in its seventh month. A particularly violent winter and spring had passed as a result of the company's decision to hire "replacements" in February 1982, four months after the strike began (see Exhibit 1).

As Gordon drove by the vast array of state, local, and company-hired security guards, he thought back to a phone call he had received the night before from Dick Jocelyn, Brown & Sharpe's Manager of Labor Relations. Apparently, the IAM had just hired a sophisticated labor organizer from New York named Ray Rogers. Rogers was head of a consulting firm called Corporate Campaign, Inc.

Jocelyn was concerned because Rogers' Corporate Campaign tactics had been instrumental in forcing the J.P. Stevens & Co. management to recognize the textile workers union after a 17-year struggle. These tactics included the rallying of community, religious, and political support. In addition, Rogers' Campaigns were covered extensively by local and national media. For example, the J.P. Stevens organizing fight appeared in the pages of local papers in South Carolina and in the national business press—the Wall Street Journal and Business Week. In Jocelyn's view, the man was dangerous.

When John Gordon and Dick Jocelyn met for their daily session that morning, they resolved to work out a strategy that would minimize the effect of Rogers' unorthodox tactics. Among their many concerns was how to respond to the inevitable media coverage that was about to descend on the company.

---

* This case was prepared by Paul A. Argenti, Amos Tuck School of Business Administration, Dartmouth College. The case is intended for class discussion rather than to reflect either effective or ineffective handling of a management situation.

BROWN & SHARPE HISTORY

The multinational machine tool company began as a watch and clock-making venture. In 1833, father David and son Joseph R. Brown opened their business in Providence, R.I. Apprentice

Lucian Sharpe joined the firm in 1848 and formed a partnership with the younger Brown in 1851.

The B&S partnership became a renowned technological pacesetter. The partners produced the first Vernier caliper, sewing machines and needle bars, the first universal milling machine, the universal grinding machine, the formed tooth gear cutter, and other products including horse hair clippers. Brown, a brilliant inventor, developed many products that remained virtually unchanged over the next century, while Sharpe ran the business operations.

B&S incorporated in 1868 and soon shifted its priorities to meeting demand. For the next 50 years, plants were expanded or built, and employment swelled. By 1920, over 7,500 Rhode Islanders worked for the company. The business, however, was cyclical and followed national economic trends (see Exhibit 2). The all-time employment peak of 11,119 occurred during WWII; the all-time trough of 1,295 occurred during the Great Depression.

Current Chairman Henry D. Sharpe, Jr. (Lucian's grandson) first became corporate president in the 1950s.. When he took control he was 26 years old and a budding journalist. By the 1960s, the company moved corporate headquarters from Providence to Precision Park in North Kingstown, joined the New York Stock Exchange, and acquired a foreign subsidiary.

Both Chairman Sharpe and President and CEO Donald Roach were active leaders in the Rhode Island community. Sharpe served as a Brown University trustee and as a Providence Journal-Bulletin director. Roach, a Harvard Business School graduate, served as director of the second largest state bank -- Rhode Island Hospital Trust National Bank.

During the 1970s, Roach introduced computer technology into B&S products. In 1978, the B&S DigitCal replaced the 19th century caliper as a precise measuring device. The DigitCal was the first such microchip tool placed on the market anywhere.

By the 1980s, lines of business included pumps, machine tools, and measuring devices. Manufacturing operations were located stateside in Rhode Island, Michigan, and North Carolina, and abroad in Switzerland, the United Kingdom, and West Germany.

President Roach attempted to reduce general business cycle effects on the company. As early as 1972, he advocated bridge-building, which minimized work force reductions and built inventories during economic downturns. Over 500 employees' jobs were saved within the next two years. Roach's interest in employee effectiveness led to a company study in 1979-80. The industrial relations staff studied B&S's Rhode Island operations and found that employee motivation and productivity could be improved.

HUMAN RESOURCE DEVELOPMENT AT B&S

Industrial Relations Director John Gordon viewed employee effectiveness as a management problem. Gordon, a Columbia MBA and former Ciba-Geigy Pharmaceutical human resources manager, defined motivation as "the desire by an employee to want to do what you want him to do." He divided motivation into a commodity element and a discretionary element. The employees' commodity element was their ability to "perform to the minimum acceptable standard to avoid being discharged." The employees' discretionary element, however, was their willing cooperation to "do things beyond minimum expectations." Gordon sought to capture the discretionary element (see Exhibit 3).

After completing the management study, B&S started to implement its human resource plan. The company founded a newspaper to communicate corporate concerns. The newspaper included messages from President Roach and divisional managers; employee recognition for cost-saving suggestions, good work, and athletic league participation; and articles about the effects of local, national and international events on the company. In the newspaper, Roach expressed his concern with Rhode Island's extraordinarily high workers' and unemployment compensation costs, as well as increasing energy costs. The B&S President also emphasized the company's need to compete with the Japanese machine tool industry that was rapidly gaining its share of the American market. To respond to these problems, the President sought improved employee motivation and productivity. He declared:

> "First, we intend to keep everyone much better informed about the business....This newspaper is an important first step in that direction. We have also started a newsletter for supervisors....

"Second, we will also try to do a much better job of listening. The Vice Presidents and I will start holding small group meetings....

"Third, all managers will be invited to attend a series of sessions....[about] working together more effectively."

According to Gordon, employees recognized these managerial efforts. He said that they sensed management was trying to change.

Union leaders said they saw the program as representing another managerial effort -- to destroy the union. They viewed the company's new emphasis on individuals as an anti-union ploy. In particular, they claimed Roach complicated employee grievance procedures -- leading to increasing arbitrations, and a deteriorating labor-management relationship.

According to Bob Thayer, business representative for the local district of the International Association of Machinists and a former B&S employee, "Something started to change in 1975. The latitude of industrial relations to adjust difficulties was getting condensed. The grievance procedure was being bastardized and the case load to personnel was on the increase." In short, the labor leader saw a deterioration in the previously cordial relations with management.

Thayer pointed to public evidence of management's changing sentiments. In the August 1981 company newspaper, management described two companies and asked, "Which is the better company?" (See Exhibit 4). Labor interpreted Company A as a non-union prototype and Company B as the existing union shop. The comparison inflamed labor leaders. Representative Thayer sent a letter to Gordon in response, but never received a reply (see Exhibit 5). Thayer claimed the "Ivory Tower" management had revealed its anti-union attitude.

LABOR RELATIONS AT BROWN & SHARPE

Prior to the 1970s, labor relations at B&S were notably absent of the strife that was to make the 1981 strike the largest and longest running strike in the United States. Labor characterized relations with management prior to 1975 as firm, but fair. Aside from some minor skirmishes during WWI and again during Henry Sharpe, Jr.'s first year as President (in 1951), the company had never faced a prolonged strike.

Contracts were renewed every two years until the 1970s. In 1975, the company endured an eight-week strike. Since the company settled with the union just before unemployment benefits were to be distributed, labor felt that management wanted the 1975 strike. Labor leaders felt that a strike was B&S's easy and cheap way to deal with a downswing in the industry at that time.

Although the 1977 negotiations were settled without a strike, the 1979 negotiations led to a three-day walkout. With the national economy in an upswing, management felt that the union was able to win a generous settlement. Labor felt that the 1979 strike would never have happened if "Those charged with responsibility in 1979 had full latitude to negotiate a contract," said Thayer, who was then president of the B&S local. "The direction was coming from top management, not labor and industrial relations directors."

NEGOTIATIONS: 1981

As management approached negotiations in 1981, they felt confident about conducting successful collective bargaining sessions with labor. According to President Roach, everything was done correctly. First, B&S offered a generous wage package, with 11, 10, and nine percent raises in three successive years. This offer far surpassed industry and general business standards. Second, the company emphasized its commitment to Rhode Island. Management claimed that workers were scared about B&S's possible departure, especially with the unhealthy business environment in the state. Yet B&S wanted a Rhode Island workforce that would be flexible and responsive to increasing foreign competition.

During the negotiations, management and labor were not concerned with the wage package; they primarily focused on two new "flexibility" articles. Article 15.2 declared company supervisors' rights to assign employees to specific tasks, as long as the work fell in the same labor grades, occupational codes, shifts, and seniority groups. Management designed the article to stop what they viewed as inefficient job preference or machine seniority practices, where workers could decide what specific parts of their jobs to perform. Article 9.4(i) allowed for mandatory employee transfers. If no employees responded to B&S's request for temporary job volunteers, then the company would assign these jobs. The assignments would be limited to 30 days (maximum), and workers' seniority, based on their permanent jobs, would remain unchanged. Workers' pay also would remain unchanged, unless they filled jobs normally held by higher labor grade workers. In the latter cases, replacements' pay would increase during the assignments.

Labor did not understand why these flexibility articles were needed, how the revised articles would increase worker flexibility, or how they would help B&S respond to foreign competition. In fact, labor interpreted these articles as union-busting measures. Consequently, they saw a rapidly approaching dead-end with management. They had cooperated, conditionally approving 85 percent of the company's demands. The union would not, however, approve the remaining measures, which they called a "death blow."

Management also perceived a dead-end attitude embodied in union Business Representative Thayer. Industrial Relations Director Gordon commented that although Thayer had worked at B&S previously, Thayer was unaware of recent changes and a refocusing of the workforce toward flexibility. Dick Jocelyn, a University of Rhode Island graduate who served as negotiator and labor relations manager, said he failed to receive any response on these flexibility articles from Thayer. As the contract expiration date approached, Jocelyn expressed shock at Thayer's refusal to extend negotiations.

Thayer saw management as arrogant and inflexible. Thayer stated that Jocelyn talked of "absolutes" and that he would not listen to negotiating strategies or compromises proposed by the union. Although Jocelyn did offer a one week extension, Thayer felt that management's position on the issues as "absolutes" made an extension a futile effort. In addition, Jocelyn's last-ditch ploy -- to send management's final offer directly to workers the day before contract expiration -- signaled an unwillingness to modify agreements.

Union leaders also felt that Gordon, who sat in on negotiations, had a distaste for the union. "He showed his contempt and frustration for us through his body language," said Thayer. From labor's perspective, Roach, Gordon and the 1970s generation of management at B&S were out to get the union from the very beginning of negotiations in 1981.

THE 1981 STRIKE

The International Association of Machinists' District 64 voted overwhelmingly to strike, effective October 18, 1981. The machinists began their daily picket outside B&S's Precision Park, and five were arrested within the first four hours. Local police stationed themselves nearby as did a private security force hired by the company. As the fall turned into a frigid winter an increasing amount of violence occurred. Strikers were frustrated by the length of the walkout and by B&S's hiring of strike replacement workers. Nearly every day nails were thrown on the pavement in an attempt to stop management employees' cars. Everyone was fair game. Even the car driven by Gordon's secretary was attacked while she sat helplessly inside; strikers lifted and shook the car from side to side. According to newspaper reports, stones were often thrown at windows and names were called, particularly at those workers whom strikers recognized.

Union leaders claim, however, that very little of the violence was caused by striking workers. They saw the company's inability to get an injunction, which would have placed the blame on strikers, as an indication that their ranks might have been infiltrated. One labor leader said, "I wouldn't put it past Gordon to hire someone to throw rocks at the appropriate time."

Strikers also suffered amidst the violence. Newspapers reported that a 62-year-old female striker died from a stroke after overexposure to the cold air. In February and March violent activity peaked, directly triggered by the arrival of replacement workers. When picketers continued to block the main entrance to workers on March 22, local police sprayed pepper gas at them. This event reminded local journalists of Rhode Island's labor struggles in the 1930s.

THE B&S ENVIRONMENT: 1982

"When there's a strike, there's a level of group cohesion....that gives you a starting point," observed Gordon. Supervisors, non-striking workers, and newly hired replacements all worked together to run operations as smoothly as possible and to protect the plant against the strikers.

Inside Precision Park, the focus was on business as usual. Supervisors concentrated on important contracts and also delegated more responsibilities. The supervisors came to understand their operations better than before the strike and discovered many possibilities for savings. Since everyone was needed to operate the equipment, management employees and strikebreakers assumed many responsibilities. In addition, Gordon explained that the replacements, hired through management referrals, rapidly developed company loyalty.

From the beginning of the strike, management employees also provided many strike-related services. They maintained daily surveillance of the property and photographed strikers' activities. Managers personally drove replacement workers through the picket line, according to Roach, because these workers bore the brunt of strikers' resentful attacks. Through good formal and informal communication, Gordon proclaimed, "Morale was never higher."

In his B&S newspaper column, President Roach stated that the B&S workforce could change its direction. He had living proof of employee flexibility, pointing in his column to those who readily changed their jobs according to production needs. Management, running the facility as part of strike contingency plans, had helped to create the business efficiencies Roach had sought.

CORPORATE CAMPAIGN, INC.

In June 1982, B&S managers learned that the IAM had hired labor organizer Ray Rogers to help the strikers. The managers were troubled by the potential power of Rogers' Corporate Campaign, Inc.

Rogers founded the Corporate Campaign in the late 1970s as an outgrowth of a concept that ultimately led the J.P. Stevens Company to accept unions at 10 of its southern plants in 1980. Working for the Amalgamated Clothing and Textile Workers Union (ACTWU) at the time, Rogers masterminded a successful strategy to disrupt J.P. Stevens' relationship with the corporate and financial community. Rogers' strategy was to apply pressure to financial concerns that did business with Stevens or that had Stevens' directors on their own boards. This pressure remained until those companies worked toward change in Stevens' labor policies.

Labeled as unorthodox by both advocates and critics alike, most of Rogers' tactics in part stemmed from methods developed and proclaimed by the late Saul Alinsky, a popular organizer in the 1930s and author of Rules for Radicals.

Speaking at a major eastern business school in 1983, Rogers told a group of first-year MBA students: "The overriding issue that should be raised to the highest levels of public and political debate -- but never is -- is who controls the flow of the huge concentrations of money and to what ends. The response determines whether we improve the quality of life for all living things, or whether we face social, economic, and quite possibly nuclear, holocaust."

In an article Rogers wrote during the summer of 1981 for Business and Society Review[1], he stated:

> There are means other than long, costly strikes and boycotts to challenge powerful institutions that are irresponsible in their social and economic policies. I am referring to a "corporate campaign," an approach that should become as important a confrontation strategy in the future as strikes, boycotts, and other forms of protest have been in the past.

A total corporate campaign considers all avenues of pressure and would include the possibility of a strike, a boycott, and other traditional tactics. However, these would be timed and coordinated as part of an overall conceptualized strategy to maximize their effectiveness. A corporate campaign attacks a corporate adversary from every conceivable angle. It takes on the power behind a company. It shows clearly how to cut off the lifeblood of an institution. Its proponents recognize that powerful institutions are both economic and political animals and must be challenged in both the economic and political spheres. It moves workers' and poor people's struggles away from their own doorsteps to the doorsteps of the corporate power brokers.

The original corporate campaign aimed at helping workers represented by the Amalgamated Clothing and Textile Workers Union (ACTWU) gain union contracts at J.P. Stevens & Co. This campaign focused on the company's corporate headquarters and on those institutions heavily tied into Stevens interests through interlocking directorates, large stock holdings, and multimillion-dollar loans.

In the Stevens campaign we wanted to cause those institutions heavily tied in with Stevens interests to exert their considerable influence on the company to recognize the rights and dignity of the workers and to sit down and bargain in good faith. We realized, however, that the "targeted" institutions and individuals would exert their influence only when they realized it was in their own primary self-interest to do so. To make it in their

---

[1] Reprinted by permission from the Business and Society Review, Summer 1981, Number 38, Copyright © 1981, Warren, Gorham and Lamont Inc., 210 South Street, Boston, Mass. All Rights Reserved.

primary self-interest we had to draw these institutions into the Stevens controversy -- so that their own image, reputation, and credibility were seriously jeopardized with large segments of the population important to their overall growth and prosperity. The ultimate goal of the corporate campaign was, if necessary, to polarize the entire corporate and Wall Street community away from J.P. Stevens, thereby pulling that company's most crucial underpinnings out from underneath it.

A company like J.P. Stevens cannot survive in a vacuum; it must be able to continue to spread its influence within the corporate and financial community if it is to maintain a stable level of business, much less grow and prosper. Once corporate and financial America turns off against a company like J.P. Stevens, unless that company is bent upon its own self-destruction, there is no place for it to go but the bargaining table. None of the big institutions that fight organized labor wants to face extinction. They only have to be convinced that unless they recognize the legitimate concerns of the labor movement, they will lose a great deal more than they have to gain.

We must recognize that banks and insurance companies have great influence over other corporations. First of all, banks and insurance companies control enormous amounts of stock in other corporations. They have voting power over this stock and can vote against management if they do not like the direction a corporation is taking. They can initiate stronger action by dumping large amounts of a corporation's stock on the market. When major financial institutions hurriedly sell a company's stock, it signals to the rest of the financial community that there is something wrong with the policies and direction of the company. The stock will probably decline in value, and no one else will be in a hurry to buy it. Banks and insurance companies also have a critical influence over other corporations when they decide to extend credit, or tighten credit terms, or deny credit entirely. Finally, big banks and insurance companies influence corporate America as well as each other by having their directors sit on the boards of other corporations. In this fashion they can have direct say over the policies and actions of these companies, or they can threaten to leave the board.

On the other hand, officials of a company serving on the board of a bank or insurance company can have tremendous pressure exerted on them to change their policies or face being pushed off a board.

Corporate Campaign tactics were used against other companies as diverse as Farah Manufacturing Company and the Yale University Bookstore during the late 1970s and early 1980s. By May of 1982, the IAM felt that it was time for Rogers to try his hand at Brown & Sharpe. The regional offices put Rogers in touch with the local IAM strikers; Rogers arrived in Rhode Island with his associates the first week of June.

JUNE 8, 1982

After several days of deliberation, management at Brown & Sharpe knew that they needed a detailed strategy to counteract Rogers' Corporate Campaign. Rogers had already spoken the previous weekend to 1100 of the 1600 striking workers at a mass meeting.

One of the concerns John Gordon and Dick Jocelyn considered at any early morning meeting was how to respond to the local and national media. Don Roach and Henry Sharpe, Jr. had already spoken with a New York public relations firm; both were undecided about whether to go on the offensive (as advised) or remain silent.

Gordon's secretary interrupted the meeting to tell him that Peter Gosselin, a staff writer for the <u>Providence Journal-Bulletin</u>, was on the phone asking for a statement about Rogers' arrival. John Gordon took a deep breath.

QUESTIONS

1. Identify problems in the Brown and Sharpe case.

2. How would you characterize employee relations and communications at Brown and Sharpe?

3. Should John Gordon adopt an open or closed door strategy with the media?

EXHIBIT 1

The Evening Bulletin — City

Partly cloudy tonight and tomorrow
Low tonight high 20s, high tomorrow 40s.
Details on Page A-3.

119th year, No. 57, 32 Pages

Providence, Rhode Island, Monday, March 22, 1982

© 1982 Providence Journal Co. · 30¢, $1.40 per week by carrier

Violence at Brown & Sharpe

BATTLE ZONE: Using a "pepper fogger," police spray tear gas over strikers blocking the main entrance to the Brown & Sharpe plant in North Kingstown this morning.

—Journal-Bulletin Photo by JIM DANIELS

EXHIBIT 2

Cyclical Trends as Reflected in Recent Financial Data

<u>Five Year Financial Data</u> (Historical, in thousands except share & employee data

	1982	1981	1980	1979	1978
Net Sales	$149,827	$205,356	$227,472	$193,250	$148,540
Net Income	(13,547)	6,040	13,649	10,494	5,271
Share Price (yr. end)	10.630	18.000	28.000	27.125	13.640
Cash dividends declared per share	.6800	1.3200	1.200	.9000	.5833
Number of employees (yr. end)	3,032	4,089	4,172	4,147	3,532

<u>Five Year Financial Data</u> (Historical, reclassified to reflect the effects of discontinued operations)

	1982	1981	1980	1979	1978
Net Sales	$143,770	$195,018	$216,312	$182,420	$139,271
Net Income	(12,039)	5,909	13,025	10,133	5,165

<u>Five Year Financial Data</u> (Average 1982 dollars, current costs, reclassified to reflect the effects of discontinued operations and to conform to SFAS70: (Financial Reporting and Changing Prices: Foreign Currency Translation")

	1982	1981	1980	1979	1978
Net Sales	$143,770	$206,972	$253,386	$242,582	$206,056
Net Income	(15,184)	347	7,870	6,081	NA
Share Price (yr. end)	10.63	18.49	31.33	34.11	19.43
Cash dividends declared per share	.68	1.40	1.41	1.20	.86

(from B&S annual reports)

EXHIBIT 3

Is it reasonable for the company to expect...

1. That every employee comes to work every day on time?

2. That every employee gives a fair day's work?

3. That every employee produces the quantity and quality of work that is expected?

4. That every employee performs his or her job in a safe manner?

5. That every employee abide by the Company rules?

(from B&S news, 9/80)

EXHIBIT 3 continued

Would Brown & Sharpe be a better place to work...

1. If all employees knew exactly what's expected of them?

2. If every employee who failed to meet the performance standards was helped to meet them?

3. If every employee did not have value judgments made about him or her as a person, however poor the performance might be?

4. If every employee was given the fairest possible break and was given the benefit of the doubt when a doubt exists?

5. If every employee "belonged" as a member of a section and a department, knew what the goals were, and knew how each was doing?

6. If every employee was treated as an individual and approached in terms of his or her individual needs?

7. If every employee knew where he or she fits in the organization?

8. If every employee was told how he or she was doing?

9. If the Company listened to what employees say without recrimination, even when what employees say is negative?

10. If every employee was recognized for his or her contribution?

11. If every employee was asked and given the reason why, rather than being told?

12. If every employee was developed until he or she was making the optimum use of his or her capabilities?

Which is the better company?

As a customer:
Which company would you buy from?
As an investor:
Which company would you invest in?
As an employee:
In which company would your future be more secure?

	COMPANY A	COMPANY B
MANAGEMENT SYSTEMS:	Efficient systems provide concise, accurate and timely information which supports sound decision making.	Outdated systems produce untimely and frequently inaccurate information that cannot be consistently relied upon in the decision-making process.
MANAGEMENT STYLE:	High standards of performance expected, but style is supportive.	Standards of performance variable. Style is punitive.
CAPITAL INVESTMENT:	Long-term commitment to continued reinvestment in the most productive equipment.	Very little investment in new equipment. Result: low productivity and poor quality.
RESEARCH AND DEVELOPMENT:	Continued investment in improved and new products to maintain and enhance competitive position.	Limited investment in new products resulting in reduced sales because of outdated product lines.
COMMUNICATIONS:	All employees know what the goals are and how they're doing. Management listens to employee concerns.	Management doesn't communicate anything and never listens to employee concerns.
EMPLOYMENT STABILITY:	Employment is kept as stable as possible to the extent that the company can afford it. Reductions in the workforce, when necessary, are by performance.	Workforce expands and contracts based on business cycles. Extensive and frequent layoffs take place by seniority. Result: Many of the best performers are not retained.
PROMOTIONS:	Earned on the basis of performance.	By seniority.
WAGE INCREASES:	Earned on basis of performance and contribution.	Not related to performance.
FLEXIBILITY:	Employees extremely responsive in work assignments, transfers, and scheduling to meet both immediate and longer term business requirements.	Rigid work practices restrict the company's ability to respond quickly to changed conditions, raising costs and allowing competitors to capitalize on opportunities.
LABOR DISRUPTIONS:	Work stoppages virtually non-existent, allowing company to plan effectively and customers to rely on the company as a continuing source of supply.	Frequent work stoppages erode customer confidence in the company's ability to deliver on schedule, polarize the workforce, lower efficiency, and limit the company's ability to plan.
QUALITY:	Increased sales result from company's high quality reputation. Strong understanding in all functions that quality of work is a key to success in the marketplace.	Prevalent "what-you-can-get-away-with" attitude results in customer skepticism about the company's concern for quality, reflected in a loss of repeat business and higher warranty cost.
PRODUCTIVITY:	Continuing improvements in productivity have controlled product cost, allowing the company to price products competitively.	Limited improvements in productivity make the company a high-cost manufacturer, resulting in non-competitive prices for their products.

EXHIBIT 5

International Association of Machinists and Aerospace Workers
AFL-CIO
DISTRICT LODGE NO. SIXTY-FOUR

78 KENWOOD STREET, CRANSTON, RHODE ISLAND 02907

Tel. No. (401) 944-4580 — 4581

August 31, 1981

Mr. John Gordon, Director Industrial Relations
Brown & Sharpe Mfg. Co.
Precision Park
North Kingstown, R. I. 02852

Dear Mr. Gordon:

    On behalf of all IAM&AW members employed at Brown & Sharpe Mfg. Co., I feel compelled to respond to the Article – "WHICH IS A BETTER COMPANY?" – published in the B & S News of August, 1981.

    It becomes obvious after reading the Article that the connotations and perceptions drawn are a direct attack on the collective bargaining system, recognized not only in this country, but universally, as a system that given its due, works in the best interest of all parties concerned.

    Reference between Company "A" and Company "B" is a typical example of a Company without a collective bargaining agreement and one with an agreement.

    The twelve items addressed in the article, even if they were given a positive view, certainly does not represent what collective bargaining has meant to Brown & Sharpe Mfg. Co. and its unionized employees.

    The history of collective bargaining between the Company and the Machinists Union, given a careful review, reflect a posture between the parties best portrayed as when various challenges affecting the parties need addressing. Sound labor relations have been implemented, and examples of this are evident when one considers the move from the Providence location to the new plant in North Kingstown. Also the adoption of the New Form Standards which were negotiated and adopted in 1953. More recently, a serious problem arose when McDonnell-Douglas removed Brown & Sharpe Mfg. Co. from its list of bidding manufacturers. As you know, when we mutually addressed these problems, both productive and worthwhile resolves benefiting all were attained.

    For one to question a seniority system which is no more than a recognition of an employees service to the Company, is to suggest a system which does not recognize or value long service.

EXHIBIT 5 continued

To question wage increases by contract vs performances is totally an 18TH century viewpoint. Unions' became a reality because those who determined earnings based on performance felt few, if any, were worthy of a wage increase.

I could continue on in rebuttal of this unjust article but I will choose what I think is a more productive approach. I would request that Brown & Sharpe Mfg. Co. review our total record of labor relations and hopefully, they will recognize a work force that has always been responsive to placing Brown & Sharpe Mfg. Co. in a viable position in the market place.

In closing I would like to quote statements by former President's of the United States - Abraham Lincoln and Dwight D. Eisenhower ----

Abraham Lincoln: "All that serves labor serves the nation. All that harms is treason...If a man tells you he loves America, yet hates labor, he is a liar...There is no America without labor, and to fleece one is to rob the other."

Dwight D. Eisenhower: "Only a fool would try to deprive working men and women of their right to join the union of their choice."

Very truly yours,

Robert V. Thayer
Business Representative
District #64, IAMAW, AFL-CIO

RVT/v

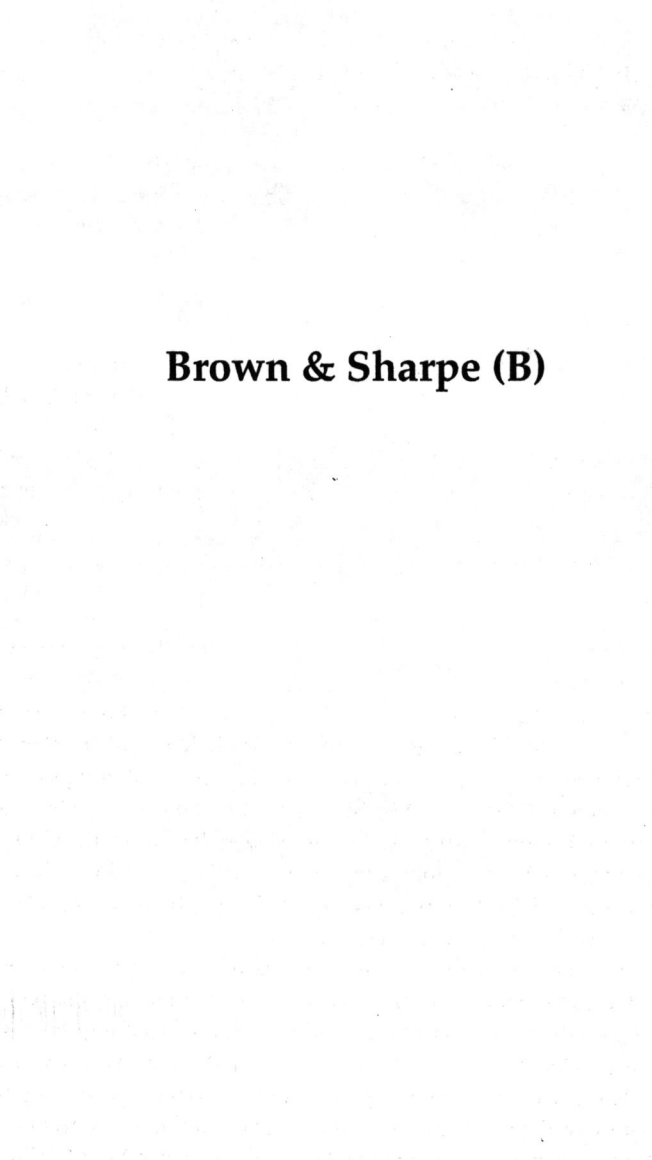

Brown & Sharpe (B)

Brown & Sharpe (B)*

"It is an interesting development," responded John Gordon, director of industrial relations for Brown & Sharpe Manufacturing Company, to a *Providence* (R.I.) *Journal-Bulletin* reporter who asked about labor organizer Ray Rogers's recent arrival. In June 1982, the International Association of Machinists (IAM) hired Rogers to help the local District 64 settle its seven-month strike against B&S. Gordon, by remaining silent, set the tone of company communications during that summer.

ROGERS'S CAMPAIGN STRATEGY

Ray Rogers began the corporate campaign for the machinists' union by organizing a June 10 rally. About 1100 (of 1600) strikers attended and heard Rogers explain campaign strategy. First, the union would pressure Rhode Island Hospital Trust National Bank to remove B&S President Donald A. Roach from its board of directors. This strategy would continue until Roach either helped settle the strike or actually was dumped from the board. The strikers planned to picket the bank, threaten the bank with account withdrawals, and solicit other social groups to pressure the bank. Rogers used the same strategy in his 1978 J.P. Stevens & Co. campaign. The protesters successfully pressured Manufacturers Hanover Trust Co. into removing the Stevens chairman from its board. Second, the union would block Senator John Chafee's re-election if the incumbent senator chose not to influence his second cousin, B&S Chairman Henry D. Sharpe, Jr., to settle. The strikers planned to canvass the state, each covering two hundred households.

Rogers gave the machinists good reasons to start campaigning. He explained that Hospital Trust held 17.5 percent of B&S's common stock, including Sharpe family, employee, and pension fund trusts; that the bank was B&S's prime creditor, lending over $3 million in 1981; and that the bank counted Donald Roach, B&S president and chief executive officer, among its directors. In addition, Rogers found that Hospital Trust "redlined" poor neighborhoods by providing fewer mortgages there than in wealthier areas. Union attorneys, noting the many strikers who lived in redlined neighborhoods, filed an objection with the Federal Bank of Boston.

The labor organizer used fliers and the machinists' newsletter, *The Triangle*, to launch and conduct the campaign. The fliers not only discussed interlocking directorates and genealogical

---

* This case was prepared by Paul A. Argenti, The Amos Tuck School, Dartmouth College. The case is intended for class discussion rather than to reflect either effective or ineffective handling of a management situation.

connections, but also indicated how to help the campaign (see Exhibit 1). *The Triangle* sought strikers' participation in scheduled pickets. The paper reported on picket plans and their outcomes and on campaign targets (see Exhibit 2).

CAMPAIGN IN ACTION

By July 1, strikers had set up informational pickets at Hospital Trust branches. They wore and carried picket signs, and told bank customers that they should bank elsewhere. During the next two months, strikers worked outside different branches up to five days per week.

Nearly every week the strikers participated in a mass rally. On July 13, two hundred machinists protested outside a Marriott hotel, waiting for B&S Chairman Sharpe's arrival to receive a Rotary "good citizen" award. Sharpe saw the commotion, drove to a rear parking lot, and slipped through a back door. The machinists then marched by Hospital Trust headquarters and City Hall en route to the State House. Nine days later, a similar contingent picketed at Hospital Trust headquarters. On this rainy Friday, the strikers marched around the banks, listened to speeches, and chanted their mantra: "Dump Roach!"

The July 28 rally was different. While some one hundred fifty strikers gathered outside a Hospital Trust branch, twenty bank customers -- machinists, families, and friends -- withdrew amounts ranging from $16.67 to $10,000. One sympathizer, a union local president at Corning Glass Works, withdrew $10,000.

MEDIA COVERAGE

Media provided frequent and widespread publicity that actually supported the campaign. Local media reported several times a week. Pickets and rallies provided visuals for television news, while the array of activity begged for written interpretations. Five local newspapers printed stories. The *Providence Journal-Bulletin* printed about fifteen stories or editorials during the eight-week campaign. National media also covered Rogers's campaign against B&S because the labor leader had past successes organizing J.P. Stevens unions and because the B&S strike had become the longest running in America. *Business Week*, the *Los Angeles Times*, the *New York Times*, and *The Wall Street Journal* chronicled the campaign.

When state political leaders reacted to the turmoil, labor organizer Rogers called it "a direct result of the corporate campaign." Senators John Chafee and Claiborne Pell and Governor J. Joseph Garrahy wrote the machinists and B&S management on June 22. They expressed their concern with the dispute and set up a July 26 meeting with a federal mediator (see Exhibit 3). At the July meeting, however, the stalemate remained unbroken.

B&S'S SILENCE

B&S executives decided to maintain a low profile. Dick Jocelyn, B&S manager of labor relations, said Rogers had not written any new testament. In Jocelyn's view, the union campaign was based on 1930s labor organizer Saul Alinsky's philosophies and sought results through enemy reactions. Thus B&S simply stayed silent, ceasing public communication and in-house newspaper publication. By ignoring strikers' accusations and demands, the executives avoided giving credence to the statements.

Many company employees did, however, communicate with the other besieged member of the business community -- Hospital Trust. B&S employees wrote to Hospital Trust Chairman Henry S. Woodbridge, Jr., indicating their support for the bank.

CAMPAIGN CLOSED

In August, Rogers's corporate campaign suddenly ended. The national machinist union, which provided 80 percent of the funding, decided not to renew Rogers's eight-week contract. Bob Thayer, District 64's business agent, said he believed Rogers had provided community support and had communicated issues to the strikers.

Rogers also felt he had helped the strikers and thus was shocked to learn his contract had not been renewed. He called the national's decision a "typical bureaucratic" error because the national administrators knew nothing about the campaign. According to organizer Rogers, leaving Rhode Island was one of the hardest things he had ever done.

When a *Providence Journal-Bulletin* reporter asked about Ray Rogers's departure, Director of Industrial Relations John Gordon only said "It is an interesting development." Yet B&S executives were relieved.

EXHIBIT 1

BEHIND THE SMILE IS A DIRECTOR OF RHODE ISLAND HOSPITAL TRUST NATIONAL BANK...

WHO IS ALSO DIRECTOR OF STRIKEBREAKING FOR BROWN & SHARPE

DONALD A. ROACH is a director of Rhode Island Hospital Trust National Bank. Maybe you've heard the bank's advertising slogan: "You feel better banking at Hospital Trust."

As for Mr. Roach, it seems **he** feels better busting unions, recruiting strikebreakers, wreaking havoc with the lives and livelihoods of 1,600 workers and seeking to substitute confrontation for the time-tested process of collective bargaining.

MR. ROACH is the President and Chief Executive Officer of Brown & Sharpe Manufacturing, one of Rhode Island's largest private employers. As such, he devised the strategy and set the policy that forced B & S employees—members of the International Assn. of Machinists—out on strike last October 19th. They are still on strike today.

Throughout this long dispute, wages have never been at issue. Concessions by the union covering 85% of the company's concerns have been repeatedly spurned by Mr. Roach and B & S Chairman Henry Sharpe Jr., who has termed the collective bargaining process itself "an extremely wasteful affair." B & S seeks to scuttle job security and impose a "rule-or-ruin" system of arbitrary reassignments in which the workers and their union would be totally excluded.

In February B & S announced it would retain the entire "replacement" work force of more than 500 strikebreakers and recall union workers only "as needed," even after a settlement. In April, underscoring his determination to break the union once and for all, Mr. Roach summarily rejected Gov. J. Joseph Garrahy's offer to set up a fact-finding panel to clarify and help resolve all outstanding issues.

BROWN & SHARPE is not a struggling, marginal enterprise: it is a robust and aggressive multinational giant whose net sales soared from $57.1 million in 1970 to $227.4 million in 1980, before sliding back to $205.3 million in the recession year of 1981. But rather than bargain in good faith with the workers, Mr. Roach has "repaid" their loyal service with indifference and disdain.

Rhode Island Hospital Trust National Bank, by sheltering and maintaining Mr. Roach on its Board of Directors, has aided and abetted his union-busting posture and, in the process, shattered the myth of its own constructive involvement in Rhode Island's economy. If his fellow directors cannot persuade him to resume good-faith bargaining and reach a reasonable settlement, they should remove him from their board.

YOU CAN HELP—please write to Henry S. Woodbridge Jr., Chairman, Rhode Island Hospital Trust National Bank, One Hospital Trust Plaza, Providence, R.I. 02903 (telephone 278-8000) or call your local branch and leave a message for Mr. Woodbridge to tell Mr. Roach: "Settle this dispute or get off our board."

I.A.M.A.W./CORPORATE CAMPAIGN
78 Kenwood St., Cranston, R.I. 02907

EXHIBIT 1 continued

HOW YOU CAN HELP:

- **PLEASE WRITE A LETTER** to Henry S. Woodbridge, Chairman, R.I. Hospital Trust National Bank, One Hospital Trust Plaza, Providence, R.I. 02903. Ask Mr. Woodbridge to tell Mr. Roach: "Settle this dispute or get off our board." If you don't have time to write a short letter, please take one of our pre-addressed postcards, sign it, and mail it to the bank.

- **IF YOU INTEND TO VOTE** In the Nov. 2nd election for U.S. Senator from Rhode Island, please write to the current senator—Sen. John Chafee, 5229 Dirksen Senate Office Bldg., Washington, D.C. 20510. Tell him if you're a registered Republican, Independent or Democrat—and let him know that if the strike isn't settled soon, the election results are sure to unsettle *him*. The striking Machinists would greatly appreciate copies of your letters to the bank and/or Sen. Chafee. Send to:

I.A.M.A.W./Corporate Campaign
78 Kenwood Street
Cranston, R.I. 02907

Corporate Campaign

AFL-CIO

The nation's longest strike—
WHY?

Three men and a bank:
Major obstacles to a settlement

1,600 Machinists Union members at Brown & Sharpe Manufacturing Co. in Rhode Island have been on strike since October 18, 1981. The company and the union agreed on a wage package even before the strike began, but for nearly a year management has persisted in demanding unjustified "givebacks" under the guise of "flexibility," prolonging what has become the longest strike now under way in the United States.

The company is seeking to impose an arbitrary reassignment system which would effectively exclude the workers and their union from having a voice in decisions affecting their lives. It wants to force the surrender of key job security provisions the union won in previous contracts negotiated since 1941, when the Machinists first organized B&S.

EXHIBIT 2

The Triangle

Machinists Newsletter

Local Lodges 1142, 1088 & 883
78 Kenwood Street
Cranston, R.I. 02907
(401) 944-4580

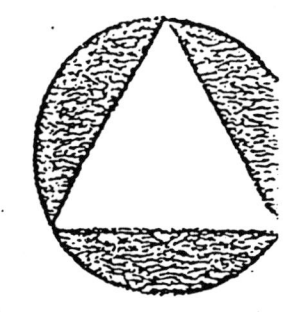

IAM Corporate Campaign No. 1

On the offensive

Corporate campaign launched

A new dimension has taken place in our struggle with the Brown & Sharpe Company. A new spirit has taken hold of our members, there's an electric-like feeling in the air, a sense of expectation that now we are in a position to put pressure on the Company and bring them back to the bargaining table.

Our members should be commended for their courage and determination during the past eight months. Facing the dull monotonous routine of going to the picket line every morning, the anger and frustration felt as we watch scabs drive in. The company that many of us have given most of our working lives to, now pits one worker against another to try and break our Union. For too long we have been on the defensive. Starting July 1st, the battle ground will change, the Machinists will be on the offensive.

This new feeling, this uplifting of spirit has been generated by a new development in the struggle between our Union and the Brown & Sharpe Company. Our International Union has brought in Ray Rogers, who received national acclaim for the corporate campaign he conducted against the J.P. Stevens Co. Ray and his staff from Corporate Campaign Inc. have developed a strategy to take the fight that has been fought on the doorsteps of our members for the past eight months and transfer it to the doorsteps of the power brokers and financial institutions that give credibility and support to the Brown & Sharpe Company.

The campaign will kick off July 1st with informational picket lines outside several branches of Rhode Island Hospital Trust National Bank and will escalate daily. The bank is a beneficial owner of 17½% of the common stock in B&S and is closely allied with B&S by virtue of the fact that the President of Brown & Sharpe, Donald Roach, is a director of Rhode Island Hospital Trust National Bank "which for many years has been one of the Company's primary lending banks, is Trustee under the Company's principal pension plan, and under the Company's Employee Stock Ownership Plan, and also provides other banking and trust company services to the Company."

Editor: John Coen

EXHIBIT 2 continued

ANTI-UNION

The anti-union, anti-worker policies now being practiced by Donald Roach and Brown & Sharpe against its workers seem pretty much in tune with some statements made by Henry S. Woodbridge, Jr., Chairman of the Board at Hospital Trust. To explain this a little more clearly, here are a couple of excerpts from Mr. Woodbridge's letter to shareholders in the Annual Report of Hospital Trust National Bank.

"We expect that the economy in Rhode Island will under-perform national and regional trends until such time as the negative influences producing high business costs in our State are reduced and/or eliminated. These negative factors include high energy costs, workers and unemployment compensation costs,"

"As such the State has ample strengths, such as: Competitive labor costs, with average hourly wages of manufacturing production workers at present well below the national average;"

Our campaign focusing on Donald Roach's position at Hospital Trust should accomplis one of the following: Force Mr. Roach to resign from the Board of Directors of Hospital Trust and/or convince Hospital Trust that it's in their best interest to use their considerable influence with Brown Sharpe to bring this labor dispute to a negotiated settlement.

WANTED

The International Union brought in Corporate Campaign Inc. to develop and implement a strategy. Ray Rogers is not the Messiah, he is not a miracle worker, he and his staff are organizers; we must provide the workforce. You now have an opportunity to put pressure on Brown & Sharpe like never before. There can be no holding back, we must give it everything we have and we will win. Your spouse can help, your kids can help, your parents can help. We need people to leaflet, canvass, make phonecalls, write letters. We need to know the organizations you belong too, church groups, religious groups, community, veterans etc. We want to hear any ideas you may have no matter how irrelevant you may think they might be, let Corporate Campaign be the judge. Call us at IAM Corporate Campaign HQ: 942-1122 or 942-1125 or stop in the office at 78 Kenwood Street, Cranston 02907.

EXHIBIT 3

JOHN H. CHAFEE
RHODE ISLAND

United States Senate
WASHINGTON, D.C. 20510

June 22, 1982

[Handwritten margin note: This letter is a direct result of the Corporate Campaign. In late July a letter signed by R.I.'s Governor & its 2 Senators & 2 Congress persons was sent to Moffett urging him to seize upon any opportunity to get the strike settled]

Mr. Robert V. Thayer
Business Agent
International Association of Machinists
District 64
78 Kenwood Street
Cranston, Rhode Island 02907

Dear Mr. Thayer:

With other Rhode Islanders, we are deeply concerned over the stalemate between District 64 of the International Association of Machinists and Brown & Sharpe.

While we would not presume to offer specific suggestions for a settlement, it is our hope that through our good offices, both sides would agree to resume bargaining under the auspices of the Federal Mediation and Conciliation Service.

The Director of the Federal Mediation and Conciliation Service, Kenneth Moffett, has agreed to meet with both sides in Washington in an effort to revive the negotiations.

A settlement of this dispute is clearly in the interest of Rhode Island, its business community and its workers. It is our hope that you, on behalf of District 64 of the International Association of Machinists, will accept Mr. Moffett's offer and agree to attend a meeting to be convened in Washington at the mutual convenience of both parties. Mr. Moffett will call you within a week to arrange this meeting.

An identical letter is being sent to Brown & Sharpe.

Your favorable consideration of this request would be appreciated.

Sincerely,

Claiborne Pell
United States Senator

John H. Chafee
United States Senator

J. Joseph Garrahy
Governor

Brown & Sharpe Teaching Notes

Brown & Sharpe

This case, like Hooker, is based on my own interviews with the people in the case and is one of the easiest to teach. You will find that the problems come out very easily and it allows you to also cover labor relations and the nature of unions in the United States at the same time you are trying to deal with the use of strategy.

A good primer before teaching this case would be Saul Alinsky's *Rules for Radicals*, Vintage Books, because it will give you insight into the possible strategies Rogers is likely to use against Gordon. In addition, you will be able to use lots of anecdotes while teaching the case to make students realize just how formidable an opponent Rogers could be.

What you need to do is get students to analyze the various constituencies that B&S must deal with. They are:

1. The media. They are a conduit for all other constituencies and can make a lot of B&S's pepper-fogging police force that is simply protecting the replacement workers. They will also be predisposed to Rogers because he is so experienced in manipulating the media and dealing with labor problems like this one.

2. The union. The union is really multi-layered. First you have the international headed at the time by William Wimpisinger, an avowed socialist. You also have to deal with the local and, in particular, the business agent, Thayer. Finally, you have to consider the needs of those union members who have crossed the picket lines. Is the union one constituency or many?

3. Other companies that Rogers might drag into the argument. Since Rogers works on interlocking directorates to pressure the company he is fighting, you can be sure that he is going to tap all of the obvious connections such as Sharpe's board membership at Brown University and the *Providence Journal* and Roach's connection to Hospital Trust. How strong are the company's relationships with these organizations?

4. Replacement workers/management. This group is what is keeping you going. How will they react to the intense scrutiny of Rogers media blitz? Without the support of the employees helping out, B&S is sunk.

5. The financial community. What effect will all of this have on shareholders, analysts, and bankers that you do business with?

6. <u>Customers.</u> Fortunately, B&S doesn't do business with the general public, but its industrial customers are likely to read about what is going on. How will they react?

7. <u>Suppliers.</u> Same as above.

8. <u>Families.</u> How will spouses react if the company is a pariah in what is a parochial community?

9. <u>The local and state community.</u> Rhode Island is a very catholic, family-oriented state, not a corporate-oriented state. How will this affect B&S?

Objectives

What does this company want to get out of all this? Do they simply want to get through Rogers? Can they deal with Rogers and make some kind of statement about their position on labor at the same time? Get students to focus intently on deciding what B&S wants to do in a larger sense. As a result of their communication strategy with each of the constituencies above, they are going to be perceived a certain way. How do they want to be perceived?

What resources are available. The company is weathering a strike, Rogers is coming for a specific amount of time, etc. How do you deal with these issues?

What is the organization's credibility with each constituency? It's pretty low with the union, probably okay with suppliers, etc.

Message

What should B&S do? They basically have the choice either to respond to the media and thus Rogers or they can do nothing. Make sure that the students lay out all of the pros and cons of each.

Respond. Engages Rogers who is much more eloquent, used to dealing with media. Exposes company to media scrutiny, reaches wider community, paints company as bad guy beating down workers.

Don't respond. Looks like B&S is guilty, not interested in what's going on, uncaring.

Brown & Sharpe (B) case

Fortunately, it is all laid out for you here. Read this carefully before teaching the case, and try not to signal the "answer" to your students.

One note of caution about this case. While it is an excellent example of how a company developed a strategy, stuck to it and basically succeeded, it also reinforces terrible stereotypes about closed-door policies that do not need any more support than they already have. What you are teaching them is that sometimes it's better to say nothing.

But the more important point is to think strategically about it so that you can get to the point where you know when you need to be proactive and when you need to keep your mouth shut. I like to teach this case after Coors (see chapter 6) because students get lulled into thinking that the open door is always best and here comes B&S with the best closed-door strategy I've ever seen. You need to think rather than follow blind rules.

You will really enjoy teaching this case. Allow 10-15 minutes to let students read B at the end of the class and to discuss it you will need another 15 minutes at least.

Chapter 9: Managing Government Affairs

This is the newest chapter in the book. I thought about adding chapters on a variety of subfunctions, but this one is by far the most important of those that I do not cover in this book. Over the next decade, my guess is that this will become more rather than less important as business gets bigger, technology gets more complex, and both the public and private sector start to realize how critical it is to work together in a global marketplace.

What I have tried to do here is give students a sense of why government affairs is important, how the function developed, and what the effects of government (e.g. regulation) can be on business. As with all of the chapters, you might want to look at what is current to elaborate on the material here. For example, Microsoft seems to be a potential target for government regulation. Get students to think about how their arrogance as a company will help or hurt them in the years ahead. Tobacco companies seem to be facing major problems as well. Have students pick up where I left off and evaluate how the government affairs functions have either helped or hurt big tobacco companies.

In the local communities where you live, how does government affect business? For example, if you have a manufacturing facility or a utility nearby, what does local government do that can either help or hurt the company? For companies like the hypothetical Dodds Paper Company, regulation for paper mills at the local level is a fact of life. Both the federal government, through the EPA, and the local government get involved in regulating such businesses.

You might also want to contact the government affairs office at both the local and national level for a major company near your school. You will get first hand information from people who are used to schmoozing to get their point across. You will find them extremely interested in helping you.

Overall, you should be able to put together a great class based on the information in the chapter, whatever you can glean from the local community, and the Dodds case. Let me offer some advice on how to approach Dodds.

<u>Dodds Paper Company</u>

As students look at the case, they will have a chance to explore the concepts covered in the chapter and to look at the specific problems in this company. I have disguised this case, but it is based on actual legislation that was proposed and was edited by someone who runs government affairs for one of the largest forest products companies in the US.

Possible Answers to Case Questions

Steps for addressing the proposed anti-chlorine legislation:

Step one: Brison should gather the facts about how the legislation specifically affects the company and analyze how the company might differ from the rest of the industry. Additionally, he should contact the company's environmental experts to determine if there are any technical changes to the legislation that would mitigate or eliminate the company's problem.

Step two: With the basic information in hand Brison can begin to develop the strategy for addressing the legislation. Based on the information in the case study, it appears that Dodds is basically in sync with the rest of the industry in opposition to the legislation. The two most likely strategy options are 1) "just say no" with reasons why the legislation is not needed, 2) oppose the current bill, but offer a compromise alternative that Dodds could support. (Outlined in step four.)

Step three: As part of the strategy determination, Brison will want to do an assessment of the anticipated course of action that other industry participants and environmental groups will take.

Other industry groups:

- will likely just say no on the grounds that legislation is not needed
- since it will cost the industry billions they can be expected to make defeat of the legislation a high priority, employing direct lobbying, grassroots and campaign contributions
- a fall back position of opposing the bill but offering an alternative the industry could support is unlikely because each manufacturing process is a little bit different and the only real common denominator is the chlorine based technology

Environmental groups:

- usually stick together, but occasionally one can be picked off
- will probably oppose any compromise because this issue is helpful in their fundraising efforts
- will extensively use grassroots and citizen "demonstrations" to gain media attention

Step four: Brison will want to develop the strategy options and arguments. Some things he may propose follow:

Option 1—"Just say no"

overall strategy: Join with industry association, suppliers of chlorine and customers of paper companies to try to defeat the legislation. Use tools of direct lobbying, grassroots/media and strategic campaign contributions to pro-business candidates to educate public policy makers.

arguments to be used:

- no need for the legislation
- the science on dioxin is an open question, not clear it is even a problem at current levels
- even if dioxin is a problem, the use of chlorine in the paper making process is not
- less than 1% of all dioxin today is created in pulp and papermaking
- even if the legislation is enacted, 99% of the "problem" will still be there
- the cost of the legislation is prohibitive for industry and will result in job loss
- imports will supply the U.S. paper market
- the legislation will support jobs overseas at the expense of U.S. workers
- several Scandinavian companies currently have a chlorine-free process, but their process results in different environmental problems that we don't have from using chlorine
- US customers want the product qualities of paper bleached with chlorine (i.e., brightness, etc.) that you don't get with other alternatives

Major advantage: It is usually easier to defeat something than to pass something. Therefore if the industry is united and they effectively communicate their side of the facts, it is more likely than not that they can preserve the use of chlorine and its various derivatives in the papermaking process. This strategy also does not preclude them from later coming back and offering a compromise proposal for 100 percent substitution of chlorine dioxide, although at that point they would be unlikely to get any environmental support for a compromise. It also gives Dodds the broadest level of flexibility in future technology advances. Since not all of Dodds mills have converted to OD 100 yet, they would have the flexibility to choose a different technology for the remaining mills, should something more beneficial become available.

Major disadvantage: It reinforces the industry's negative image of being more concerned about profits than human life and health. For Dodds it misses an opportunity to develop an identity as the environmental leader in the industry, and it misses the opportunity to protect its investment in OD 100 by forcing this technology to be set as the industry standard.

Option 2—Oppose current bill and offer a compromise alternative

overall strategy: try to partner with one "reasonable" environmental group on an alternative proposal that would eliminate the use of elemental chlorine in the papermaking process; build a coalition among "environmentally sensitive" customers (i.e., Time, National Geo.), other paper companies that currently use OD and/or ozone, and use basic direct lobbying, grassroots and strategic PAC giving to educate policy makers about the benefits of the compromise

Arguments that could be used:

- technology exists and is commercially available for bleaching pulp and paper without the use of elemental chlorine. In fact about 40% of U.S. produced pulp is made using OD 100 or ozone and this technology preserves the product qualities that US customers want
- the (OD 100) process provides additional environmental benefits other than just the reduction of chlororganics (i.e. color reduction)
- adopting this technology (OD 100) is an important prerequisite to a partially closed-loop mill (e.g. BFR technology) and, eventually to a closed-loop system which is where industry technology hopes to be able to go in the future. A closed-loop would essentially eliminate environmental problems in effluent
- the use of chlorine dioxide, combined with other steps such as oxygen delignification has eliminated detectable dioxin at most mills
- businesses that are concerned about the environment are working with environmentalists to ensure that there is a balance between economic growth and environmental protection through this compromise

Major advantage: Dodds could get very favorable press and build a reputation as a company that is concerned about the environment. This would help them with community relations, and could benefit them in selling paper to large customers that face pressure from environmentalists to purchase environmentally friendly paper. Additionally, they could get a competitive advantage over other industry competitors who do not have the OD 100 technology.

Major disadvantage: Dodds' CEO would *be persona non grata* among his peers in the industry association. The strategy may not work because they may not be able to persuade an environmental group or the other paper companies to join in the effort. Even if they are successful in the coalition stage, the compromise position still may not become law because of the strong opposition from the rest of the industry. Long-term, the industry association could be a less effective voice on public policy issues.

Tools to be used in both strategies:

Direct lobbying

- identify and meet with members and/or staff of the environment committee to gauge the level of interest by the committee, voice company position, and cultivate advocates on the committee
- ask local plant managers and public affairs staff to meet with Representatives in the district to let them know of the company's position and the direct impact of the legislation and/or compromise on the facility (Could be done as part of a plant tour or a meeting in representatives district office.)
- ask senior management officials to meet with the key (10 to 12) members of Congress who represent Dodds' facilities to advocate the company's views about the legislation and/or compromise

Grassroots

- cultivate credible third party spokespeople for the industry position such as scientists and or media types such as John Stoessel
- distribute to employees and/or suppliers and customers a white paper about the legislation and its impact on the company. The distribution should come from the person with the most credibility with the reader (i.e. CEO or direct supervisor to employees, purchasing manager to suppliers, sales manager to customers)
- enlist the help of Dodds public affairs/communications department to educate employees about the legislation (via company-wide publications) and ask them to help organize and implement a grassroots letter writing campaign at each Dodds location
- draft letters to the editor and op-ed pieces that public affairs staff could work to get placed in local newspapers
- help develop a plan for dealing with the media, including a proactive plan to get negative stories about the legislation placed
- enlist the help of Dodds' purchasing department in communicating with suppliers about the impact of the legislation on the company
- involve suppliers and customers in the grassroots letter writing campaign

Strategic Campaign Contributions

- since Brison knows that he has some time (i.e. expects legislation in the next year), he can identify the Members of Congress with whom he might need to cultivate a stronger relationship and begin attending fundraising events with those members. This will help Brison have better access to the policy makers and could aid him in arranging appointments for senior executive of the company. Of course, Brison will need to be sure that the targeted candidates share the basic philosophy of the company PAC and meet the criteria for contributions
- Brison could also use PAC contributions to support the campaigns of challengers to the Members of Congress who are the biggest problem for Dodds on this issue. For example, if there is a credible challenger to Congressman Kobel, Dodds should support him or her as long as their positions on issues are in sync with Dodds
- Dodds PAC could in the long-run help prevent this type of situation from recurring by supporting candidates that are more sympathetic to balancing the need for strong economic growth with environmental concerns. The more allies that Dodds and the industry have in Congress, the less likely it is that this type of threat will reemerge

How should Brison involve senior management?

- the most important thing Brison can do is bring senior management into the decision making process for Dodds strategy on the legislation. This way, senior management will have to buy into the process for managing the issue and will be part of the solution rather than just expecting Dodds to perform a miracle
- ideally, senior management should be willing to communicate with employees, with customers, and with suppliers as needed. Additionally, the CEO is often the best spokesperson for the company with Members of Congress and possibly key reporters. Others, such as the chief environmental officer of the company should be prepared with media training to talk to the press when needed

Other ideas for future:

- Dodds should work alone and through the industry association to develop sound environmental practices that can demonstrate to employees, press, and the public that the company and industry are committed to operating in a way that does not harm the environment. Examples of the paper industry doing this are the recycling goal (recover and reuse 50% of all used paper) which headed off mandated content legislation and virgin fiber taxes; also SFI for forestry

Chapter 10: Managing Communications in a Crisis

Crisis communication is extremely trendy right now. If you are interested in this area, I would urge you to read Laurence Barton's book, *Crisis Communication*, published in 1992 by Southwestern. It covers every aspect of the subject and is still by far the best book written on the subject to date.

Since crises are always happening, you can simply take a more recent example and collect materials about it to make this class more relevant and up to date. For example, when I first wrote this chapter, the world trade center explosion had taken place, but one could add the PepsiCola fiasco with syringes in cans, or the Michael Jackson allegations, which also affect Pepsi since he was their chief spokesperson, or more recently, the Texaco racial discrimination problems and Nike's sweat shops in Asia.

The Source Perrier case that I have placed in chapter 6 would also work here as a good experiential exercise. Depending on where you need more material, you can decide whether to use it as a media role play or give students a chance to evaluate and deal with the issue as a crisis. You might even want to combine the two chapters and use Perrier as the connection between them.

This chapter also reinforces lots of ideas that are covered earlier in the book. For example, the notion of credibility, introduced in chapter 2, as part of strategy is also a very important concept to cover with students here. As I discuss in the beginning of the chapter, its not just the crisis itself, but how the organization responds to it as well as how much credibility it has going into the crisis.

Barton's book also includes the matrix (included at the end of this note with OHTs), which he actually took from another source as well, that is very useful in evaluating crises.

What you decide to do with this chapter also depends to a certain extent on the level of students you are teaching. For example, if you are teaching executives, you should let them find out what the crisis communication plans are for their companies and make reports/evaluate them. If you are teaching MBAs, have them research a big company they are interested in and find out what plans they have. If you are working with undergraduates, have them research a crisis like Tylenol or Bhopal and evaluate it on the basis of the criteria that I include within.

Dow Corning

This case is a great one to end the course because it is very current, has strategic issues for you to focus on, and covers lots of different areas we talked about earlier in this book. For example, the immediate issue is media related (Chapter

6) but students need to think about employees (Chapter 8) and government relations (Chapter 9).

I have included a working paper that appeared in a shorter form in the *Corporate Reputation Review*. It gives a more complete overview of the case and would be a good place to start. I strongly urge you also to read John Byrne's *Informed Consent* and Marcia Angel's *Science on Trial*. Both are mentioned in the case and working paper. These books represent opposite positions very well articulated.

You should also contact Barie Carmichael at Dow Corning (517-496-6470) who is in charge of communications at Dow Corning; she will give you updates on the case and is sometimes willing to visit. On the opposite side, contact David Fenton of Fenton Communications (202-822-5200); he has a great tape and presentation offering the challenge to Dow Corning.

Begin the case in class, as always, with a thorough discussion of the problems. Here is what students are likely to come up with:

Problems

1. Breast implants represent only 1% of profit; why such a problem?

2. Company mismanaged its reputation.

3. Taking a fact-based, scientific approach against a very emotional set of opponents.

4. Company has an engineering and scientific mentality.

5. Company comes into the crisis with low credibility (it's unknown) and even lower credibility by association with Dow Chemical (which made Napalm and Agent Organge during the Vietnam War).

6. The scientific evidence is ultimately inconclusive. Nothing in journals to believe it's harmful, but a perception among constituents that scientists have been bought off.

7. Formidable opponents in O'Quinn (Plaintiffs lawyer) and Fenton (PR firm). Both more sophisticated than anyone at Dow Corning.

8. Problem likely to spread (and since case was written is has) to Dow Chemical itself. Presents managers with challenges here at home.

9. Swanson has high credibility given his background with the company, his ethical focus, and his wife.

10. Hazelton is not the most charismatic CEO in the world.

11. Oprah is very popular, but is it the right forum for this discussion?

Then get students focused on the questions at the end of the case.

1. <u>Go/no go on Oprah</u>: It's crazy for Hazelton to go on given the constituents he needs to deal with in this crisis. Students will, however, look at a proactive approach very actively given the Coors case in Chapter 6 and all I have said in the book about getting out in front of the media. Despite all that, no CEO has ever appeared on Oprah and Hazelton shouldn't be the first.

2. Looking at the material in Chapter 10 should get students focused on communications as discussed under "communicating during the crisis" (see pp. 229-31). Have them focus on each of the eight steps.

3. Dow Corning was initially unprepared, but they seemed to catch up very quickly as evidenced in Carmichael's promotions and their turnaround of the whole situation in favor of the company.

4. Use the corporate communications strategy model and the material in Chapter 2 to answer this question from both a go and no go decision. You might spend extra time on constituency analysis, in particular, to drive this decision.

5. Dow Corning should have seen this coming earlier. Many companies try to think about potential liabilities from both a financial and communications standpoint. The breast implant controversy would have appeared on any list of potential problems for this company. In addition, they could have done more to build credibility, tried to deal with Swanson more effectively, and focused on communications earlier.

Ask the PR people at Dow Corning if they have any visuals (videotapes) to share with you. It will make the case come alive.

<u>Exxon</u>

I have included this case, which appeared in the first edition, as a supplement to the chapter. I have also included the teaching note for you here.

Exxon U.S.A.

EXXON U.S.A.*

Frank Iarossi, a senior executive for Exxon, was sleeping soundly in his bed in a Houston suburb when the phone jarred him awake in the middle of the night on March 23, 1989. A frantic voice on the other end was the first he would hear about an oil spill that would become one of the worst crises in the history of American business.

"Mr. Iarossi, there's been an accident up in Alaska," said the voice on the other end. "Lots of oil was spilled over on Bligh Reef, clean up hasn't even started yet. Someone from Houston is going to have to get out here real fast."

As Iarossi put down the phone, a nauseous feeling began to rise up in his stomach. Just how bad was the spill? Who was responsible? And, most important of all, how should the company respond?

EXXON HISTORY

In the mid-1800's, a flood in the petroleum market sent the prices from $20 a barrel in 1859 to ten cents in 1861. John D. Rockefeller saw that the future of the industry depended on orderly production, transportation, and refining practices. Rockefeller started a small oil refinery in Cleveland in 1863, and seven years later formed the Standard Oil Company, incorporated in Ohio. The name Standard represented high, uniform quality. The company grew into a huge complex of refining, pipeline, and marketing organizations. Since states outlawed one company from owning shares of another, Rockefeller and his partners founded the Standard Oil Trust in 1882.

In that same year he formed the Standard Oil Company of New Jersey, a refining and marketing organization, as an operating arm of the trust. This company would bear the name Standard Oil (New Jersey) from 1892 to 1972. In 1911, a court ordered dissolution broke the oil trust into thirty four separate companies. Eight of these companies chose to keep the Standard Oil name. The negative public image of the Standard Oil monopoly remained with its name and Standard Oil (New Jersey) carried that burden as the largest of the eight companies.

For sixty years following the breakup, salesmen of the Standard Oil Company (NJ) sold their products under trademarks that included Esso, Enco, and Humble, but longed for a single name under which to market their product.

---

* This case was written by Professor Paul A. Argenti, The Amos Tuck School of Business Administration © 1992.

Standard Oil (NJ) and its affiliates took a momentous step in 1972 when they gave up their well known trademarks to become the Exxon Corporation. Although Exxon registered the name in countries across the globe, it continued to retain the Esso trademark outside of the United States because there was no compelling reason to abandon the well known Esso name abroad.

LEAVING THE PORT OF VALDEZ

As crewmen loaded the *Exxon Valdez* almost to capacity on the evening of March 23, 1989, the ship's captain, Joseph Hazelwood, went ashore with the chief engineer and radio electronics officer. The three men conducted some official business, ran personal errands, and met at a bar in the late afternoon. They played darts with local residents and each purchased one or more rounds of drinks. The radio electronics officer stated that he drank beer while Hazelwood consumed a "clear" beverage, and the chief engineer drank gin and tonic. The chief engineer said that he had three gin and tonics and did not recall how much Hazelwood had.

After about four hours at the bar, they ordered pizzas from a local pizza parlor and each had another drink. The radio electronics officer believes that Hazelwood drank a vodka while they waited for their pizza. The cab driver who drove the group back to the ship claims that no one seemed to be "under the influence of alcohol."

The state employs pilots to navigate vessels out of the Port of Valdez. The pilot who navigated the *Exxon Valdez* on the night of March 23rd stated that he smelled alcohol on the captain's breath upon his return from town, but his behavior and speech seemed unimpaired. The captain left the bridge soon after the ship began its journey and returned an hour and a half later when the pilot disembarked at Rocky Point. The pilot again smelled alcohol on Hazelwood's breath, but saw no signs of impairment.

There were heavy ice flows in both the inbound and outbound traffic lanes on the night of March 23, 1989 as the Exxon Valdez attempted to pass through the Valdez Arm. Hazelwood had two choices: he could slow down and navigate the ship through the ice field or navigate around the ice and pass within a half a mile of Bligh Reef. He decided to cross the traffic lanes and avoid the ice. Darkness posed difficulties for navigating through ice and passing near Bligh Reef only posed a hazard if there were either a propulsion or steering malfunction or a navigation error.

As the ship approached the waterway bordered by heavy ice on one side and Bligh Reef on the other side, Hazelwood asked the third mate if he felt comfortable navigating alone. Even though the third mate had performed excessive work and received little sleep in the past twenty-four hours, he felt comfortable navigating the ship around the ice. Hazelwood reportedly left the bridge to attend to administrative duties.

Hazelwood knew the area well and could have had an accurate mental picture that would have allowed him to visualize the vessel's movements around the reef. It would have taken him twenty minutes to maneuver the vessel safely around the reef, and he would have had two hours to finish his other duties before returning to port.

In addition, according to the Exxon Bridge Organization Manual, the captain or the chief mate was required to be on the bridge given the dangerous situation. Since the chief mate had worked long hours earlier, it was Hazelwood's obligation to be on the bridge. According to federal regulations, a Federal pilot had to be in charge of a vessel's navigation in those waters, and Hazelwood was the only officer on board who possessed the required Federal pilotage endorsement.

BACKGROUND ON JOSEPH HAZELWOOD

Hazelwood grew up on Long Island, drawn to the sea from an early age. As a teenage member of the Sea Scouts, he distinguished himself for calm and courage by climbing the 50 foot mast of a schooner to haul in a mainsail blown out by a violent storm. He attended New York's Maritime College, an elite and rigorous state school run in the Bronx. People remember him starting to drink there. Later he developed a reputation as a hard drinker among some of his fellow sailors, who also said that he always knew when to stop so his performance would not be seriously impaired.

He was one of a select group of his Maritime College classmates hired by Esso. His first commanding officer Steve Brelsford claimed Hazelwood had a sixth sense about seafaring that enabled him to smell a storm on the horizon, or watch the barometer and figure how to out maneuver it.

Exxon, however, issued a 1982-83 review of

officer performance on Hazelwood that recommended he be reassigned to shore duty. This appraisal was never signed or forwarded to Exxon headquarters for review.

In 1985 Hazelwood captained the Exxon Chester through a freak storm of thirty foot waves and fifty knot winds. The radar and electronics gear went out, and some of the crew were ready to abandon ship. Hazelwood calmed them, rigged a makeshift antenna, and guided the ship back to port.

He was arrested for drunk driving in 1984 in Huntington, NY. Hazelwood entered a rehabilitation program after that on the advice of his Exxon supervisor, Captain Mark Pierce. Hazelwood was put on 90 day leave after the arrest. Company records at Exxon show Hazelwood as "depressed and demoralized...that he had been drinking excessively and episodically resulting in familial and vocational dysfunction."

In May of 1985 Exxon administrative manager Ben Graves wrote a memo to Exxon's legal department reporting that Hazelwood had admitted returning to ships in port "in an intoxicated state on several occasions, and that shipmates...reported he had violated company alcohol policy on at least several occasions."

By 1988 Hazelwood had resumed heavy drinking and his 20 year marriage was on the rocks. Between 1984-1989, his driver's license was suspended three times for drunk driving violations. The Coast Guard renewed Hazelwood's shipmaster certification without checking his car driving record.

One crewman recalled that two months before the spill, Hazelwood invited him into his cabin "to destroy a bottle." "It's almost like Joe was trying to get caught," said a good friend of Hazelwood's. "He'd close his door, but everyone knew what went on. He would always say that everything was fine, but then why was he drinking? The guy was begging for help, but he kept it all inside."

THE SEVEN SISTERS

Seven giant corporations—Exxon, Shell, BP, Gulf, Texaco, Mobil and Socal (Chevron)—have had a strong hand in the control of the world's oil supply since the early 1900's. Like the classical sisters in ancient mythology, these Seven Sisters, as they were called as early as 1913, seemed to have achieved immortality. They were the first of the global giants. They had larger incomes than many of the small nations where they operated.

Exxon's 1973 annual report claimed, "Exxon was a multinational corporation at least fifty years before that term was commonly used." The Seven Sisters, led by the two largest, Exxon and Shell, strove to be self-sufficient oil companies whose oil could flow into their tankers through their refineries to their filling stations.

As the unopposed leaders of the oil trade through the 1960's, the Seven Sisters had an image of permanence and stability that "commanded the awe of governments and publics." The 1970's, however, saw a dramatic shift in the balance of power. Unlike the 1960's, demand began to meet and surpass supply. Oil had become the lifeblood of world energy and surpluses became a thing of the past. Free world petroleum demand rose from 19 million barrels a day in 1960 to more than 40 million barrels per day in 1970. Wells in the Middle East satisfied two thirds of this increased consumption and led to a dependence on Middle Eastern oil. In addition, the devaluation of the American dollar gave power to the sellers in the Middle East.

THE OIL CRISIS

The first challenge to the absolute power of the Seven Sisters came from Libya in 1969. At that time, Libya supplied one quarter of Western Europe's oil. As the cheapest oil to transport after the closing of the Suez Canal, Libyan oil was desirable to the profit hungry corporations. However, Libya received no extra concessions for their cheaper oil. When Colonel Qadaffi came to power in 1969, he threatened to cut back production if prices were not raised. The companies attempted to stand firm on their prices, but eventually Libya forced them to concede to a thirty-cent increase in the posted price and a hike in Libya's share of profit from 50 to 55 percent.

The Libyan crisis set off an avalanche among the oil producing countries and began to shift the balance of power from the buyers to the sellers. It began not only a retreat by the companies, but a seller's campaign to maintain sovereignty and control over their oil resources.

Earlier, in 1960, oil producing countries in the Middle East had formed the Organization of Petroleum Exporting Countries (OPEC) to help defend their oil interests. However, OPEC had little power in the 1960's with the oil surplus and dominance of the giant oil companies.

The Middle East was now, however, in a position to use their "oil weapon" to achieve both economic and political goals. Some politicians believed that they wanted to use oil to restrict American support of Israel. They also thought the middle eastern countries hoped to capture the "windfall profits" of the oil companies.

In 1973, war in the Middle East broke out and OPEC began demanding a 100 percent increase in the price of oil. The oil companies consulted with the governments of the major consuming nations and together rejected the demand as outrageous

THE OIL EMBARGO

OPEC's power rose in the 1970's, and in September 1973, the organization announced an oil embargo as a political move against Israel. Initially, OPEC's embargo cut back oil shipments by five percent every month. Only "friendly states" could maintain their levels of buying. After the United States announced a $2.2 billion military aid package for Israel, the Arab states declared an embargo on all oil shipments to the United States. The price of oil quadrupled in just two months and placed the oil trade in the hands of eleven countries, not seven companies.

The embargo put the Seven Sisters in a challenging position. They had to allocate their oil in a way that would not appear to defy the Arabs' boycott, yet would satisfy their customers throughout the world. And the American companies had to enforce an embargo of their own home country. As multinational corporations, some began to question the true loyalties of the companies.

The dramatic increase in the price of oil shocked the American public. Some people accused the companies of deliberately plotting the oil crisis and joining the Arab cartel to raise the price of oil. A public opinion poll showed that most people placed the blame for the energy crisis on the companies more than the Arabs. The companies seemed to buffer much of the anger that the public would have directed at the Middle East.

At the height of the oil shortage, Exxon announced record breaking profits. Profits were up 80 percent in 1973 to give Exxon profits that exceeded the profits of any other corporation up to that time: $2.5 billion. Exxon and other oil companies explained that profits had previously been too low because they needed the profits for the development of future energy resources. For example, Mobil advertised, "We're recycling the money he pays at the pump right back into oil-finding offshore, Alaska, anywhere." However, the companies could not convince the energy starved public so easily.

At the end of the embargo in 1974, Washington made many attempts to break the oil cartel and bring down the price of oil. The economy was in the midst of a recession and high inflation that could partially be attributed to high energy costs. By 1975, consumers had cut back enough so that supply began to exceed demand again and economists predicted the fall of OPEC. However, the Middle Eastern countries simply cut their production and maintained their fixed prices.

IRAN/IRAQ WAR

The outbreak of war between Iran and Iraq in the late 1970's brought further havoc to the oil industry. It initially removed eight percent of the free world demand for oil from the market and fear drove prices to an all time high. As prices and profits rose, oil companies sank large sums into new development. The frantic pace caused costs to rise out of control throughout the industry. Exxon spent over a billion dollars in 1980 on the Colony Shale Oil Project, which it had to abandon two years later due to the rising costs of the project and the falling price of oil.

High prices forced the public to make deeper cuts in consumption to lower their energy costs and lessen their dependence on the Middle East. Long lines at filling stations, fuel shortages, and angry consumers again plagued the oil industry. An agreement was reached in 1981 that brought prices down and ended the last large rise in oil prices of the 1980's as the laws of supply and demand gained control over prices.

OIL PRICES RETURN TO NORMAL

After 1983, the world saw a dramatic reduction in oil costs primarily due to reduced dependence on Middle Eastern oil. Development in other countries, including the U.S., flourished. Many turned to alternative, cheaper sources of energy. In addition, the industrialized nations moved toward conservation and higher efficiency. By 1985, the United States was 32 percent more oil efficient than it had been in 1973. These three trends reduced the demand on OPEC oil by 13 million barrels per day, a fall of 43 percent from 1979 levels.

OIL SHOCK

In late 1985, a third oil shock hit the world that reduced prices to as low as $6 per barrel from over $30 per barrel. The surplus in demand had created a war for market share among the oil producing countries. In late 1986, the leaders of OPEC ended the low prices. They established a price of $18 per barrel and instituted a quota system to support this price. Although prices fluctuated between $15-$18, this agreement remained solid through the 1980's. These prices reflected pre-1979 levels and therefore wiped out the increases of the early 80's.

DEVELOPMENT IN ALASKA

The interest in Alaskan oil began as early as 1923 when President Warren Harding set up a naval petroleum reserve on the Arctic coast of Alaska. Wildcatters poked around the region and big oil companies began to take a larger interest following the Suez Crisis in the mid-1950's. Many companies sought to relieve their dependence on Middle Eastern oil, but had to give up after drilling many expensive dry holes in the frigid climate of northern Alaska. Exxon began drilling in 1956, but suspended operations just three years later after drilling the most expensive dry hole ever drilled up to that time.

Richfield, a California independent, continued to investigate the Alaska region and Exxon became Richfield's partner through its Humble Oil subsidiary in 1964. Richfield merged with Atlantic refining to become Atlantic Richfield, or ARCO. ARCO and Humble continued to drill expensive dry holes in Alaska and their final, risky attempt was at Prudhoe Bay on the north coast in 1966. Many had their doubts and ARCO's head later stated, "It was more a decision not to cancel a well already scheduled than to go ahead." In 1967, they began drilling the Prudhoe Bay State well, which would be their last attempt in Alaska if it failed.

In December of 1967, they struck oil in the largest oil field ever discovered in North America. Prudhoe Bay would not destroy oil prices, but it would have the potential to slow American dependence on the Middle East and "reduce dramatically the tautness in the global oil balance."

The Big Three on the North Slope were ARCO, Exxon, and BP. Experts suggested that Prudhoe Bay could become the third-largest producing field in the world. The harsh physical environment of Alaska presented their only large obstacle. Technology had to be developed to drill and produce in such a frigid area with such extensive permafrost. The lack of roads and ice-filled waters also presented a transportation problem.

THE PIPELINE

After much debate, a pipeline seemed to be the best answer. One idea was an eight hundred mile pipeline south across Alaska to the port of Valdez where the oil could then be shipped through the Prince William Sound to markets in America or abroad. Many suggested building a pipeline across Canada into Chicago, but the idea was discarded for the "all-American route" which would be more secure and could add flexibility. In addition, the Canadian government frowned on the idea and such an extensive pipeline would take longer to build than a trans-Alaska pipeline.

In 1970, the major companies involved in the pipeline construction, including the Exxon Pipeline Company, incorporated the Alaska Pipeline Service after a joint venture the previous year. When the Exxon Valdez ran aground, British Petroleum owned fifty percent, Exxon and ARCO owned about twenty percent each, while Amerada Hess, Mobil, Phillips Petroleum, and Unocal all held smaller stakes.

However, the barriers to the trans-Alaskan pipeline were many. In addition to the technological building problems, the oil companies had to contend with Eskimos, Alaska natives, and environmentalists. The 1969 Santa Barbara oil spill energized environmentalists to win a federal court injunction in 1970 that blocked the building of the pipeline. They claimed that the companies were moving too quickly without sufficient understanding and caution.

The oil companies underestimated their opposition and spent $75 million on equipment to build the roads and lay the pipes. That equipment remained frozen on the banks of the Yukon River until the injunction was lifted five years later as an emergency measure after the oil embargo. By 1977, over a million barrels a day were flowing through the pipeline and over the following two years that amount grew to two million barrels, a quarter of America's total crude oil production. By 1977, the total cost of the pipeline system had reached $8 billion.

RUNNING AGROUND

According to the third mate, the following events led up to the grounding on Bligh Reef. As the ship approached the Busby Island Light, the third mate shifted the steering from automatic pilot to hand steering. He gave orders to the helmsman for a ten degree right turn of the rudder which would gradually turn the ship and return it to the traffic lane. He telephoned Hazelwood that the ship had begun to turn and the ship should pass safely through the ice.

After 1.5 minutes, he noticed that the ship had not turned and ordered a twenty degree right turn of the rudder. After another two minutes, he ordered a hard right turn, recognized that the vessel was in danger, and telephoned Hazelwood to say that they were in "serious trouble." At the end of the phone conversation, the third mate felt the vessel contact the bottom

THE ALCOHOL PROBLEM

The investigating officers who boarded the ship three hours after the accident detected a strong smell of "stale" alcohol on the captain's breath. When questioned about his drinking, Hazelwood responded that he drank two non-alcoholic beers while the vessel was at sea. The officers later found the two empty bottles in the captain's stateroom.

The investigating officers requested toxicological testing of the ship's personnel, but had trouble obtaining the proper equipment. When proper equipment was located aboard the ship ten hours after the accident, urine samples were taken from the third mate, helmsman, and lookout. The captain did not provide a urine sample because he was unable to urinate.

One half hour later, a medical technician boarded the ship to take blood samples. The captain provided the first blood sample and also gave a urine sample. Analysis of the samples found .06 percent ethanol in the captain's blood and .01 percent in the urine. No traces of alcohol were found in samples provided by other crew members.

Assuming that Hazelwood did not consume alcohol after the accident, calculations show that Hazelwood's blood alcohol concentration (BAC) level could have been around .27 percent at the time of the accident. This concentration is higher than when he was arrested for drunk driving in 1988 with a BAC of .19 percent. The arresting officer reported that he smelled strongly of alcohol, had difficulty getting his driver's license out of his wallet, and was unsteady on his feet. In most states, a driver is charged with drunk driving if his BAC is above .1 percent.

An Exxon policy dated March 1987 prohibited the use, possession, distribution, or sale of drugs and alcohol on company premises. Coast Guard regulation states that a person operating a vessel other than a recreational vessel is intoxicated when (1) the person has a BAC of .04 percent or (2) the person is operating any vessel and the effect of the intoxicant(s) on the person's manner, disposition, speech, muscular movement, general appearance, or behavior is apparent by observation. It also states that a crew member shall not perform or attempt to perform any scheduled duties within four hours of consuming any alcohol. The marine employer is responsible for ensuring compliance with this rule.

MEDIA COVERAGE OF THE OIL INDUSTRY

In the late 1970's, oil companies were heavy users of corporate advertising. They promoted their virtues with issue ads rather than their product. For example, Texaco ran environmental and energy crisis ads throughout the 1970's.

Only Mobil, however, maintained a steady commitment to issue advertising through the 1980's with their frequent advertisements in national magazines and the op-ed pages of major newspapers.

Despite these efforts, in the 1980's, many of the oil giants did not have a strong image with the American public. "Oil companies are held in remarkably low esteem," said James Foster, president and chief executive officer of Brouillard Communications in New York. "People don't know who they are or what they stand for. A shroud of mystery surrounds them, and it translates into a negative perception...Since the embargo days, the oil industry has gone into a shell and has not told their story very well. They consequently had very little reputation or equity to fall back on when they ran into problems. They've become invisible, and it's catching up to them."

COMMUNICATIONS AT EXXON

Although Exxon was one of the largest corporations in the world at the time of the spill, Exxon USA's office in Houston was only equipped with one man and an answering machine to respond to the crisis on March 23, 1989. Despite this, Frank Iarossi had to come up with a plan for dealing with the crisis in terms of the spill itself and how the company would communicate with several different constituencies.

Exxon U.S.A. Teaching Note

Exxon U.S.A.

This case includes only the accident itself and does not cover the aftermath. Therefore, you might want to read more about the incident in Davidson's, *In the Wake of the Exxon Valdez* (Sierra Club Books).

As for the case itself, get the students to focus on the following:

1. Who is really to blame?

2. How should the company handle the issue of alcoholism in the case of this captain?

3. What should they do about the way corporate communication is handled in the organization?

4. Use the matrix to decide what kind of crisis this is.

5. Develop a media plan. How should they organize this effort? Should they hire outside help? If so, who? If not, who would be best to do the job from within the company?

6. What should Exxon have done if it could turn back the clock?

7. How will the credibility of the organization, the industry, the pipeline itself affect this situation?

Solutions

What should Iarossi do? This is not an easy one to deal with but students come up with all kinds of creative ideas about how to deal with these sorts of crises.

For example:

1. Put the blame on the ship captain. This is probably not a good strategy given that the company knew about his alcoholism.

2. Be proactive. Exxon could apologize, take full responsibility, and pay for everything. Lawyers and engineers hate this approach, which is why Exxon didn't use it.

3. Shift the blame. This would have worked to some extent since many other organizations share the responsibility for allowing the environment to exist for a potential accident.

Use the material from Davidson's book to help develop these ideas further. A wonderful videotape was available from PBS called "Frontline: Anatomy of an Oil Spill." You can try to order it. It brings the case alive. In addition, a movie appeared on HBO and is now available in some video stores. It also adds another dimension to this case.

Appendix 1

Sample Midterm & Final

**Corporate Communication
Midterm Examination
Professor Argenti**

You have ninety minutes to complete this exam. Please do not handwrite responses. You may refer to any materials that you want. I will be grading responses based on content as well as macro and microwriting.

1. (a) Both Upton Sinclair, in *The Jungle*, and Tom Wolfe, in *The Bonfire of the Vanities*, contribute to the impressions that the general public has about business in the United States. Yet, Jurgis and Sherman are obviously very different characters from two different times in the 20th century. Contrast these two characters and their frustration with business. Then explain how such popular literature affects attitudes toward business. Use readings and class discussion to back up your assertions. (15 points)

   (b) Develop a corporate communications strategy for the new management at RJR to use in response to the HBO film, *Barbarians at the Gate*. Use readings to back up your assertions. (15 points)

2. Compare and contrast the two attached articles (one from 1985, the other from 1991, see Exhibits 1a and 1b) about P&G and its identity. Evaluate P&G's corporate image and identity strategy using readings, class discussions, and presentations to back up your arguments. (25 points)

3. Study the attached advertisements from the *New York Times* (Exhibit 2a) and *The New Republic* (Exhibit 2b) carefully. What kind of advertising is this? Who is/are the target audience(s) for these ads? What advice would David Kelley give to Mobil and Northrop? (25 points)

4. The attached article appeared in the *Wall Street Journal* on April 3, 1989 (Exhibit 3). Evaluate Exxon's crisis communication response at the time in light of our discussion and the readings. How would you evaluate their current strategy as portrayed in the CNN broadcast shown in class? (20 points)

5. Describe the ideal corporate communication function based on what you have read and heard in class. (20 points)

EXHIBIT 1a

Source: Eyes on Tomorrow by Oscar Schisgall ©1981, Doubleday

The New York Times / April 25, 1985

P.&G. Drops Logo From Its Packages

Satan Rumors Are Blamed

CINCINNATI, April 24 (AP) — The Procter & Gamble Company, which has fought nationwide rumors of a link between its moon-and-stars trademark and Satanism in recent years, announced yesterday that it is removing the logotype from its products.

The Cincinnati-based consumer products giant said that it would gradually eliminate the trademark as packages are redesigned. The trademark has been in use since 1850 and was patented in 1882.

P.&G. said it hoped that the move would help fight recurring rumors that the trademark is a symbol of Satanism.

What the logotype really shows, the company says, is the man in the moon, facing 13 stars that represent the 13 original colonies.

A spokesman for the company, Bill Dobson, said that more than 12,000 people have called the company in the last two months about the rumors.

"The bottom line is the move is being made because there appears to be little advantage to having the trademark on product packages," he said. "At the same time, it will remove one part of those false and malicious stories," he added.

P.&G. routinely redesigns packages and will eliminate the trademark as each package changes, he said.

Mr. Dobson stressed that the company, whose products include Ivory soap, Charmin bathroom tissue and Pampers disposable diapers, is not dropping the trademark entirely. Even after it is eliminated from packages, he said, it will still appear on corporate letterheads and publications.

"We are not abandoning the trademark in any way," Mr. Dobson said. "It will be used extensively in other places. We feel very strongly about that. This is a move that in the long term may remove one part of the confusion."

P.&G. set up a toll-free telephone number last week to answer questions about the Satanism rumors.

The rumors had reached a peak in 1982 and then died off, but Mr. Dobson said the rumors started spreading again earlier this year, fanned by the distribution of a one-page flier asserting the company is involved in Satanism.

Earlier this month, the company said that 60 percent of the calls it had received since the beginning of March had come from New York, New Jersey and Pennsylvania. At the time, P.&G. said, it had spent $100,000 fighting the Satanism rumor.

Callers said that they had heard that a P.&G. official appeared on a nationally televised talk show and discussed Satanism, and that the moon-and-stars logotype represents Satanism. In one version of the rumor, a P.&G. official is supposed to have said some of the company's profits supported a group called the Church of Satan.

P.&G. has responded that no one from the company has appeared on the talk show.

P.&G. also has hired two investigative agencies to try to track down the sources of the rumors. At one point the company went so far as to file five lawsuits against people — mostly

Continued on Page D8

Continued From First Business Page

door-to-door salesmen — who it said had spread the rumor. Those suits were settled out of court when the defendants stated publicly that the rumors were untrue.

Source of Rumors Unknown

The company has stated repeatedly that it does not know exactly what the Church of Satan is, or where and why the rumors began. "How it started originally we have no idea, and how it restarted we have no idea," Mr. Dobson said.

According to Mr. Dobson, research has found that customers generally did not notice the trademark on products and assigned little meaning to the logotype. Also, the trademark already has been reduced on some products for design purposes, making it barely recognizable. The trademark is only one-eighth of an inch in diameter on some packages.

"We'll simply take the trademark off the product packages as they undergo other package changes over the course of the next several years," Mr. Dobson said. "Each product package is changed on an average of at least once a year, for size or color or graphics or design or any number of reasons."

Mr. Dobson said that the decision to drop the logotypes would not involve any extra costs.

218

EXHIBIT 1b

P&G to Tout Name Behind the Brands

By ALECIA SWASY
Staff Reporter of THE WALL STREET JOURNAL

Procter & Gamble Co. is coming out of the closet.

After decades of keeping its name in the shadows, the consumer-products giant plans to market itself and various corporate projects along with such famous brands as Tide and Pampers. For instance, P&G will do more to advertise environmental efforts—such as recycling plastic detergent bottles and composting disposable diapers—when selling brands.

"Consumers now want to know about the company," not just the products, P&G Chairman and Chief Executive Edwin L. Artzt told Harvard Business School students recently. Keeping the P&G name separate from brands ignored "what the world would be like," he says.

Other companies, such as Toyota Motor Corp., Westinghouse Electric Corp. and Nestle S.A., have likewise recently launched campaigns to promote their names. Competitive pressures and growing consumer interest in issues behind brands make corporate identity more critical in marketing. "There's more parity" among products, says Laurel Cutler, vice chairman, FCB/Leber Katz Partners, a New York ad agency. So consumers often make purchases based on "do we feel good about a company?"

At P&G, one impetus for change was the company's experience in Japan. In that country, consumers scour packages and advertising for corporate names behind the brands. "Japanese companies learned a long time ago the importance of a strong company image," Mr. Artzt says. "So we adopted the philosophy of marketing the company as if it were a brand."

Besides, P&G has felt increasing pressure from various environmental groups that want to ban disposable diapers, such as its Pampers and Luvs brands. Eager to demonstrate its environmental efforts, P&G recently broke with tradition and put its name on ads that promote composting diapers as an alternative to burying them in landfills. Similarly, the P&G name has been used in Canadian commercials for concentrated detergents that use less plastic packaging.

P&G's specific plans are sketchy because the company has just begun considering how to expand its traditional marketing and public-relations strategies. Consumers are being polled about their attitudes toward the company, while the P&G magazine, Moonbeams, next month will introduce the notion to employees.

One option is to run ads similar to those in Canada that promote P&G's efforts to reduce packaging, Mr. Artzt says. But the Japanese approach of using the P&G name in all ads and packaging isn't likely to be copied here.

One thing Mr. Artzt wants to avoid is advertisements that merely hype P&G as being the parent of its brands. And he shuns the idea of suddenly calling brands like Tide, P&G's Tide. "My objective isn't to simply make it clearer that Jif peanut butter is made by P&G in the belief that it will make kids eat more peanut butter," Mr. Artzt says. "The role of the company is to stand behind brands on issues that can affect the brands."

Other companies that have tried to tie unrelated brands together have been lampooned. Beatrice Cos. was criticized for a corporate campaign in the mid-1980s that put Samsonite luggage and Tropicana orange juice in the same ad. "There was no consumer benefit in linking them together," says Ms. Cutler. At the time, the company maintained that the ads increased recognition of its name to 65% from 19% of consumers surveyed.

Gary Stibel, principal of New England Consulting Group, contends that most corporate advertising doesn't work because it doesn't get the same attention as brand advertising, which has been the more traditional way to build sales. "We don't force corporate advertising to meet the same quality standards," he says.

Corporate campaigns that work on public relations as well as advertising, however, can build good will among consumers. Toyota's campaign, "Investing in the Individual," promotes community service, not cars. One ad shows a South Carolina teen tasting sushi during her trip to Nagoya as a Toyota scholarship winner. "We wanted to attack the attitude that Toyota is something foreign," says Tim Andree, a Toyota spokesman.

Other campaigns aim to clarify a murky corporate identity. Westinghouse launched a three-year corporate campaign in 1989 after discovering that nearly half of its potential customers still thought the company made appliances. As a result of restructurings and acquisitions, Westinghouse now has interests ranging from broadcasting to waste management, but exited the appliance business 16 years ago. "People are beginning to change their perceptions of the company," says Albert R. Myers, Westinghouse director of communications programs.

Still, many consumers—and some of its own employees—don't yet know all parts of Westinghouse's eclectic mix, such as its role as syndicator of the Teenage Mutant Ninja Turtles television shows.

Traditionally, companies like P&G have avoided linking products with their corporate names, fearing that approach could backfire in bad times. Some worried that consumers would hold a grudge against an entire company and all of its products when annoyed with one brand. But Mr. Stibel contends that consumers are sharp enough to trace a product's heritage regardless of whether the parent's name is on the box or in ads.

Mr. Stibel, a former P&G brand manager, figures that a corporate campaign would have helped P&G limit the damage from perennial rumors that its man-in-the-moon logo is a satanic symbol. "If you maintain a low profile, you're vulnerable," he says.

Procter & Gamble and Nestle are among the companies that have launched campaigns to promote their corporate names, not just their brands.

EXHIBIT 2a

How profitable is our business?

Oil companies—especially the integrated "majors"—are big businesses. They take in a lot of money for the gasoline, diesel fuels, heating oil, and other petroleum products they make and sell. They also spend a lot for the goods and services they need to stay in business—the up-front money they pay for the right to drill on potential oil-bearing sites, money for pipelines, tankers, offshore platforms, refinery units, and all the other wares, both hard and soft, they need to conduct their daily operations.

And they earn a lot of money in the process.

But do they earn too much? Are their profits out of line?

At the outset, let's distinguish between profits and profitability. Profits, most simply, are what's left each year after a business pays all its expenses, from its operating costs through labor, interest expense, and taxes. As already noted, in the case of the oil industry, the amount is large. Profitability, on the other hand, is usually expressed as a rate of return—the percentage earned on the amount invested, for example.

If, for example, a business shows a profit of $100,000 at the end of the year, that may seem like a tidy sum—if you were in the business for a one-time killing. But if the proprietor has $2 million invested in that business, his rate of return—or profitability—is only five percent. And, he might do well to think of liquidating the business and putting the money into a U.S. Treasury bond yielding a higher return—headache-free.

Now let's relate these concepts to our business, the oil industry.

The Iraqi invasion of Kuwait made 1990 a year of volatile prices for crude oil, as were 1973-74 and 1979-80. In the previous crises years, oil industry profits and profitability jumped sharply. Those years were anomalies. In fact, for 12 of the 20 years from 1969 to 1989, the oil companies' rate of return on shareholders' equity trailed the average for nonpetroleum American manufacturing industries.

Over the years, such industries as broadcasting and motion pictures, pharmaceuticals, soaps and cosmetics, beverages, and tobacco—to name just a few—have been generally more profitable than the oil business.

Still another measure of profitability is the amount earned on each dollar of sales. For the oil industry, this generally amounts to just a few pennies. For the 20-year period mentioned earlier, we estimate we averaged just 3.0 cents profit on each gallon of petroleum products sold. To put these pennies in perspective, on gasoline sold in the U.S., the taxes paid to federal, state, and local governments averaged many times as much. Today, for example, the taxes on a gallon of gasoline are more than 10 times this 3-cent average, and are even higher in some places.

No matter how many pennies there are in our profit total—and, because of our size and sales volumes, there are a lot of them— bare numbers never tell the whole story.

Profitability is the crucial element if companies, ours included, are to attract the capital they need to stay in business.

Mobil°

EXHIBIT 2b

"Anywhere American pilots may have to go in the world, they'll face a network of deadly defenses. That's one reason why we've all worked to make every line of the B-2 so precise, every curve so carefully complex. Those intricate curves are part of the secret of Stealth. And Stealth is the secret of survival." — Claude Edington, Jesien engineer

NORTHROP
People making advanced technology work.

Engine inlet, B-2 Stealth bomber.

© 1991 Northrop Corporation.

EXHIBIT 3

AN OPEN LETTER TO THE PUBLIC

On March 24, in the early morning hours, a disastrous accident happened in the waters of Prince William Sound, Alaska. By now you all know that our tanker, the Exxon Valdez, hit a submerged reef and lost 240,000 barrels of oil into the waters of the Sound.

We believe that Exxon has moved swiftly and competently to minimize the effect this oil will have on the environment, fish and other wildlife. Further, I hope that you know we have already committed several hundred people to work on the cleanup. We also will meet our obligations to all those who have suffered damage from the spill.

Finally, and most importantly, I want to tell you how sorry I am that this accident took place. We at Exxon are especially sympathetic to the residents of Valdez and the people of the State of Alaska. We cannot, of course, undo what has been done. But I can assure you that since March 24, the accident has been receiving our full attention and will continue to do so.

L. G. Rawl

TO: Students in Corporate Communication

FROM: Professor Argenti

DATE:

SUBJECT: Final Exam

Although we did not spend a great deal of time in class on environmental issues, they will continue to grow in importance during your careers. The attached case on "McDonald's and the Environment" shows one major company struggling with environmental issues back in 1990.

Read and analyze the case thoroughly. Then respond to the questions raised at the end of the case in light of all that you have learned about corporate communication this term. As always, it helps to make explicit references to concepts and readings to back up your arguments.

You should be able to complete the exam in three hours, but feel free to take a bit more or less time depending on your skills as a typist. You may not discuss this exam with anyone before completing work on the test.

This final exam counts for 50% of your total grade. I will grade it on a 240 point scale. Your exams will be evaluated on both content and writing. Please use good macro and microwriting techniques.

Please turn exams into the box outside my door before 5:00 p.m. on Monday, May 31.

This exam is for use with McDonald's and the Environment case from Harvard Business School (#9-391-108).

APPENDIX 2

Overhead Transparencies for Each Chapter

Chapter 1 OHTs

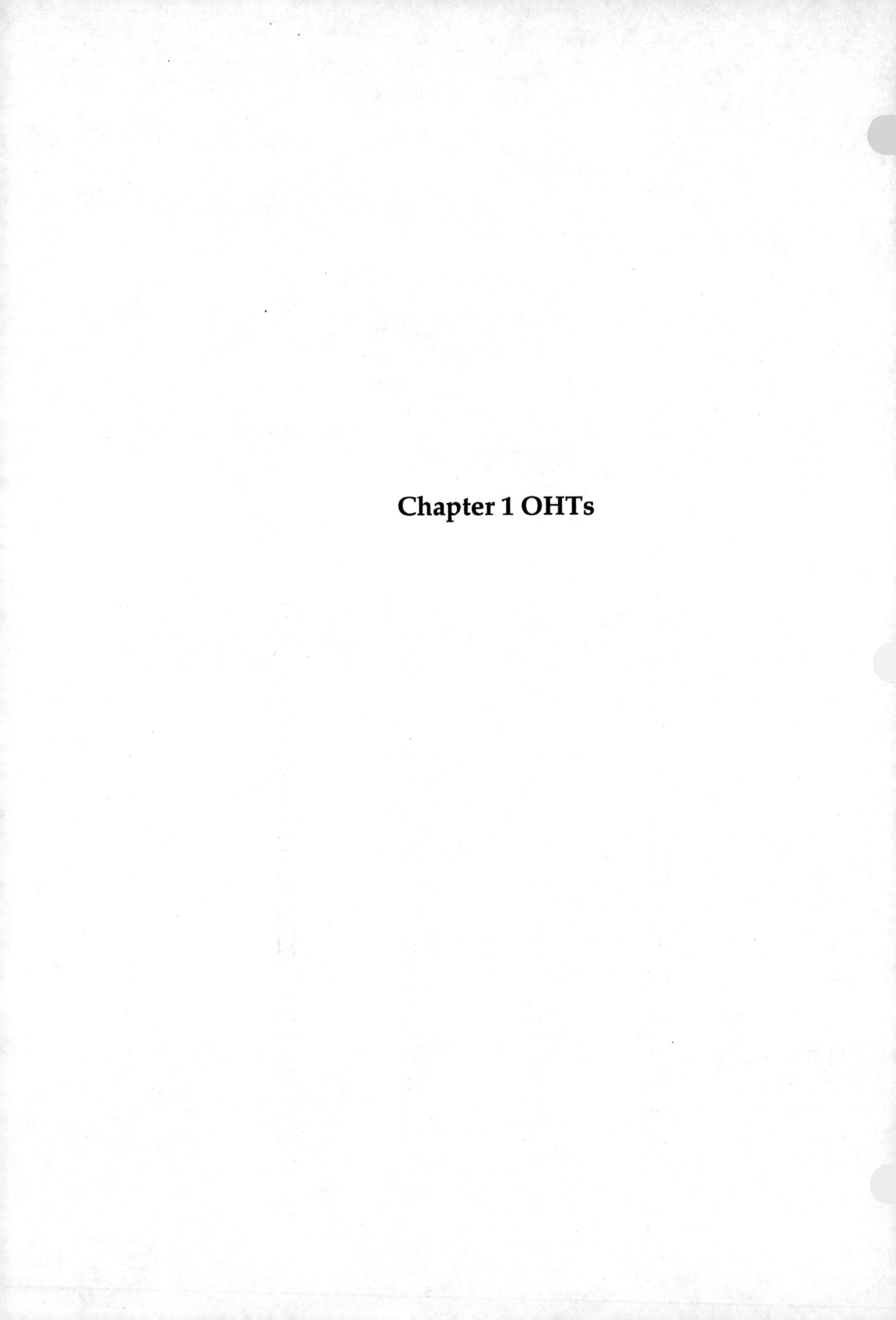

It's a New World

- Changing Attitude Toward American Business

- How Hollywood Hurts Main and Wall Streets

- The Borderless World

- How to Compete in a New World

Does Business Balance Profit and Public Interest?

	25%	50%	75%	100%
1968			70%	
1976	15%			
1984	30%			
1994	26%			

% "Yes"
YANKELOVICH

HOW MUCH CONFIDENCE IN THESE INSTITUTIONS?

	1966	1971	1989
Large companies	55%	27%	14%
U.S. Congress	42%	19%	10%
Executive Branch	41%	23%	27%
Supreme Court	51%	23%	26%

How to Compete in a New World

1. Recognize the new environment for business

2. Adapt without compromising principles

3. Keep communications on the cutting edge

4. Do not cut corners

5. Avoid the *gnat theory*

Execs Less Interested in Public

	Public Interest	Self Interest	D.K.
Federal Judges	54%	32%	15%
Cabinet Officers	37%	45%	17%
Labor Leaders	36%	50%	14%
Government Officials	34%	53%	13%
Senators	29%	60%	11%
Congressmen	29%	61%	10%
Execs of Large Corps.	18%	72%	10%

Rating of Ethical and Moral Practices of...

Alphabetical Order	Ranking Order
Congress	University Profs.
Corporate Execs.	Doctors
Doctors	President
Lawyers	Lawyers
President	Congress
University Profs.	Corporate Execs.

"Good" to "Excellent"
YANKELOVICH, 1994

Are Executives Overpaid?

Ken Griffey, Jr. $8,500,000

Andrew Lloyd Webber (playwright) $10,000,000

Arnold Schwarzenegger $15,000,000

Tom Clancy (author) $17,000,000

Oprah Winfrey $74,000,000

Steven Spielberg $165,000,000

Michael Eisner (CEO - Walt Disney) $203,011,000

Chapter 2 OHTs

Reinventing Communications

1. Ancient Roots of Communication Theory
2. Corporate Communication Strategies
   - Setting an effective organization strategy
   - Analyzing constituencies
   - Delivering messages appropriately
3. Corporate Communication Connection to Mission

Corporate Communication Strategy Model

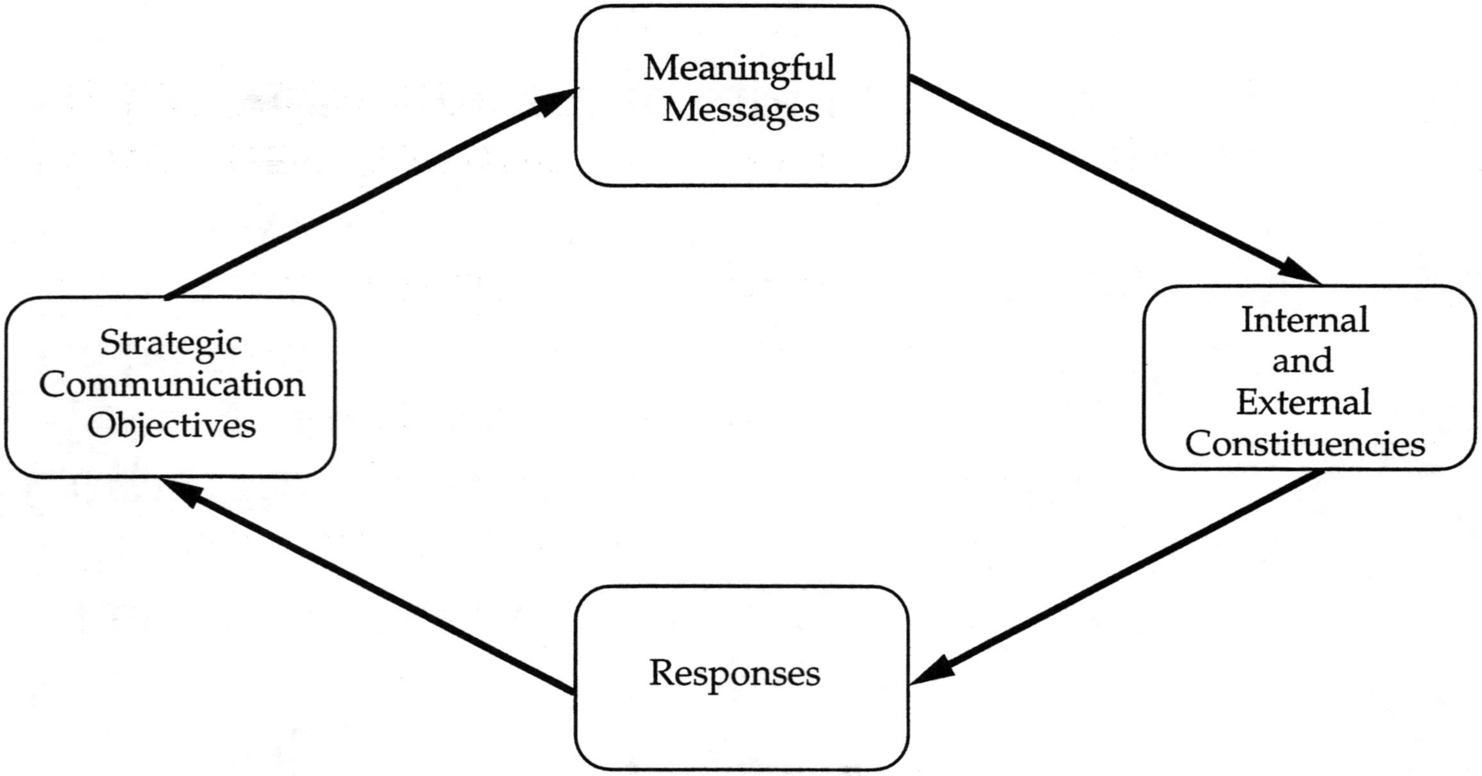

- Meaningful Messages
- Internal and External Constituencies
- Responses
- Strategic Communication Objectives

Using Corporate Communications Strategically*

- Why do companies need to rethink communications?

- How can they approach it strategically?

- What function does corporate communication serve?

- How does the function tie into the company's image and objectives?

*Use this OHT if you intend to cover environment, strategy, and function in a single lecture.

Choosing an Appropriate Style: Tannenbaum and Schmidt Model

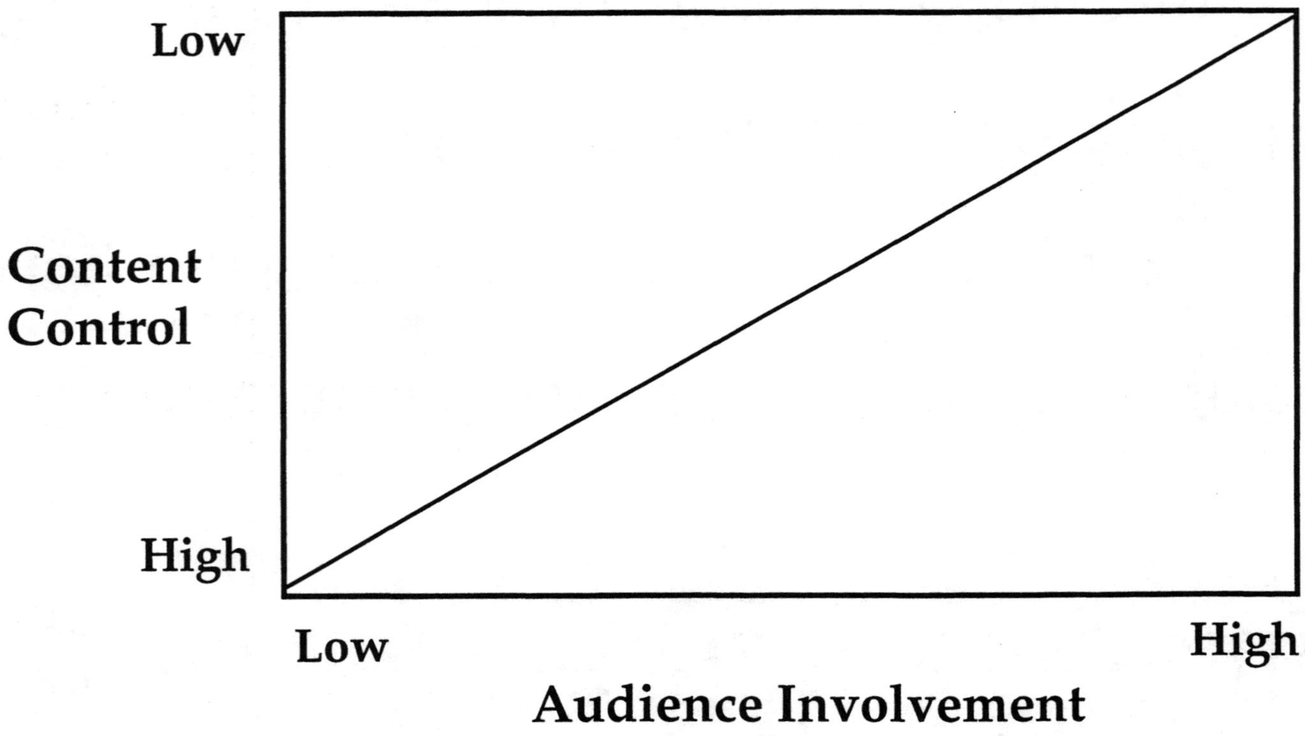

Content Control

Low

High

Audience Involvement

Low

High

Audience Memory Curve

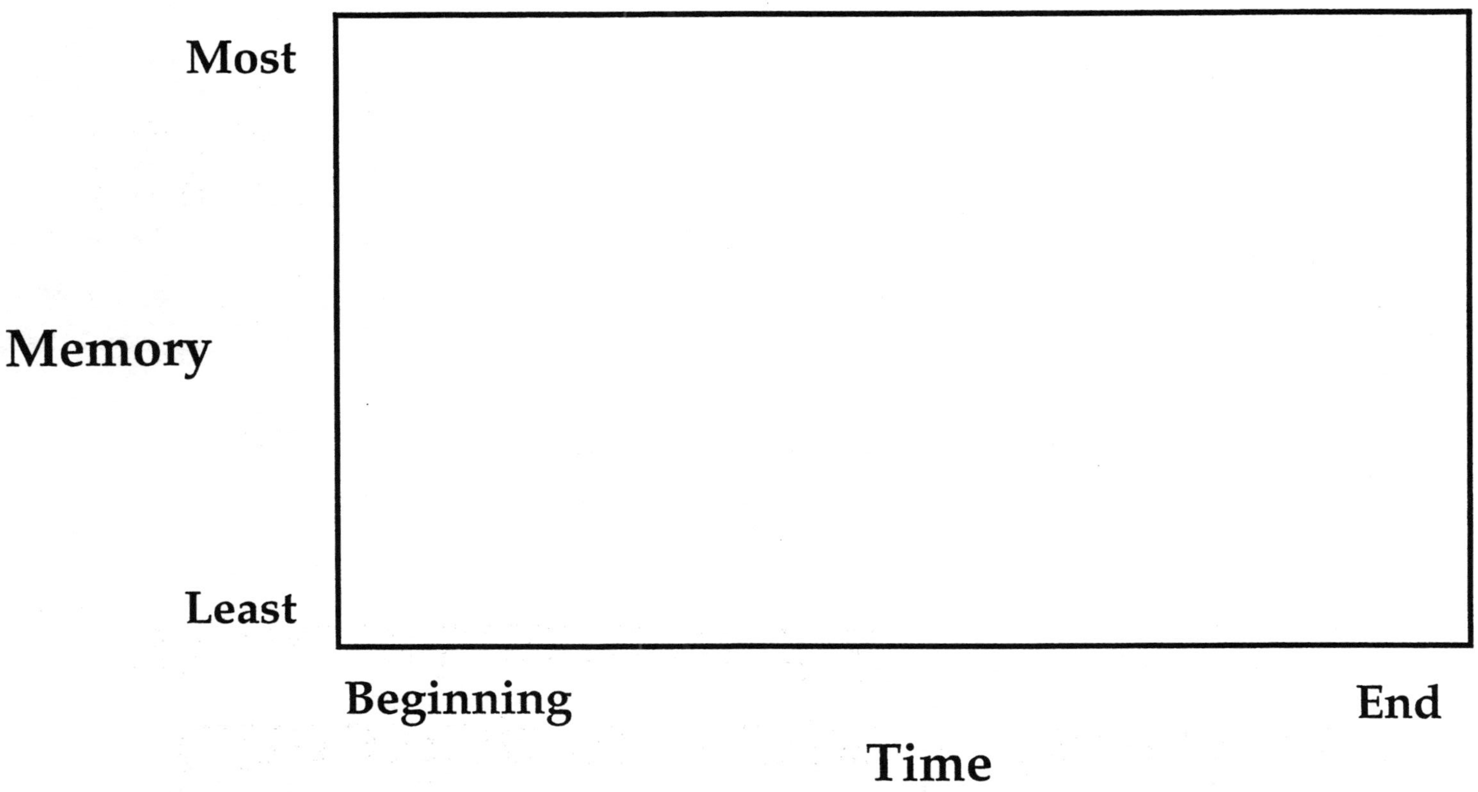

Memory
- Most
- Least

Time
- Beginning
- End

Corporate Communication Strategy Model

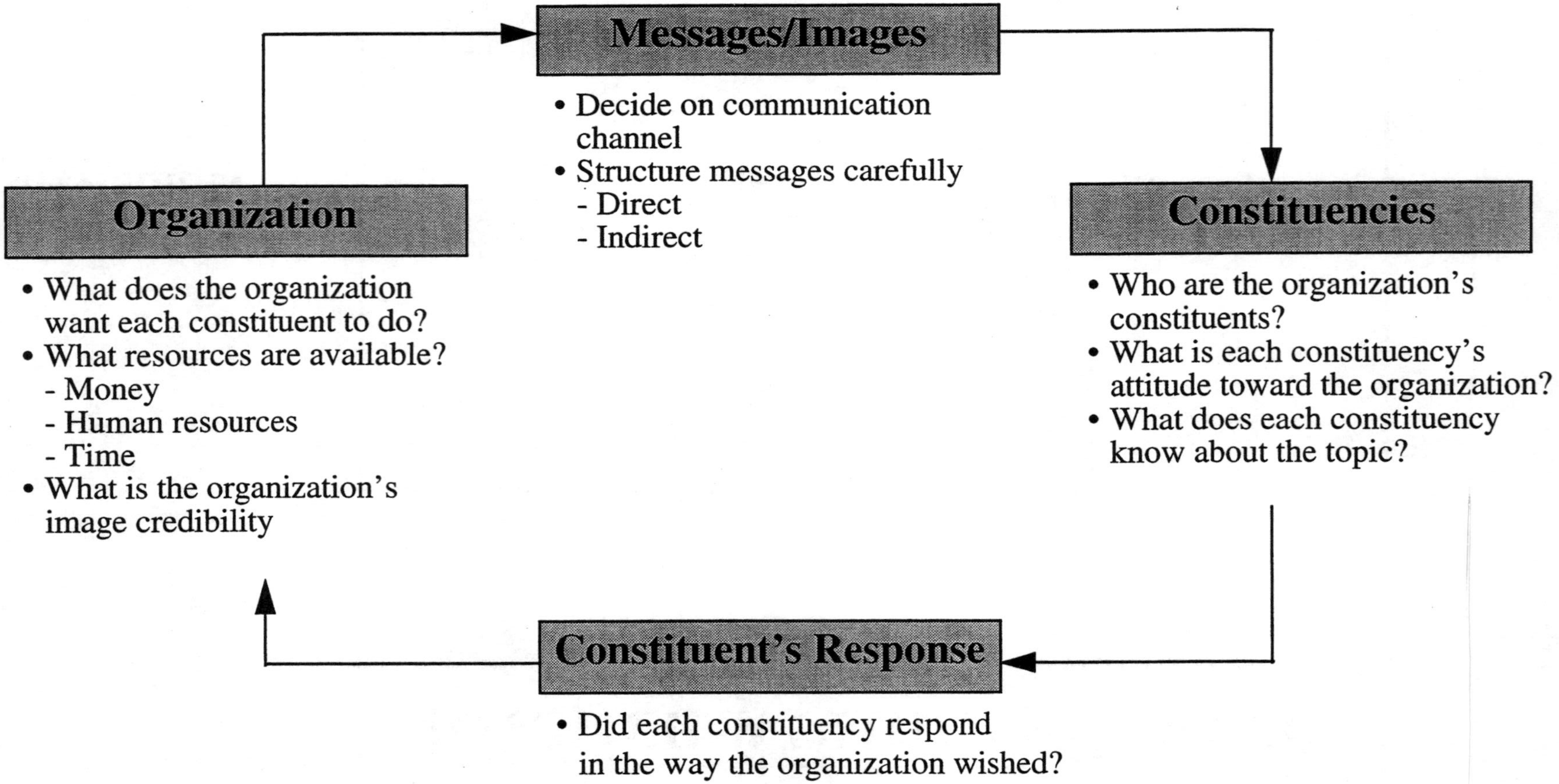

Organization
- What does the organization want each constituent to do?
- What resources are available?
  - Money
  - Human resources
  - Time
- What is the organization's image credibility

Messages/Images
- Decide on communication channel
- Structure messages carefully
  - Direct
  - Indirect

Constituencies
- Who are the organization's constituents?
- What is each constituency's attitude toward the organization?
- What does each constituency know about the topic?

Constituent's Response
- Did each constituency respond in the way the organization wished?

Chapter 3 OHTs

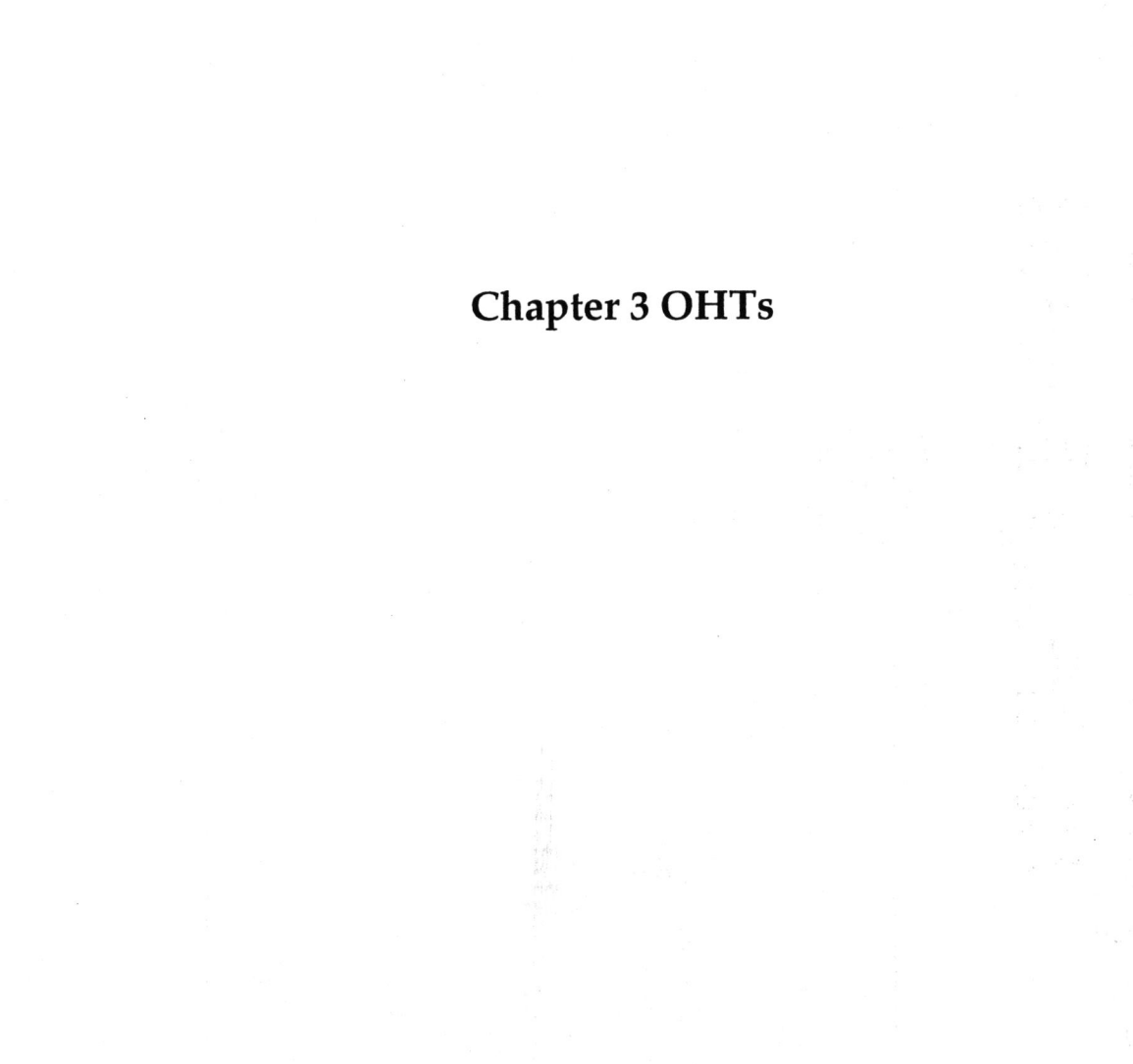

An Overview of the Corporate Communication Function

- From "PR" to "CorpComm"
- To Centralize or Decentralize Communications?
- Where Should the Function Report?
- The Functions Within the Function
- How to Integrate the Function

Ideal Structure for CorpComm Function

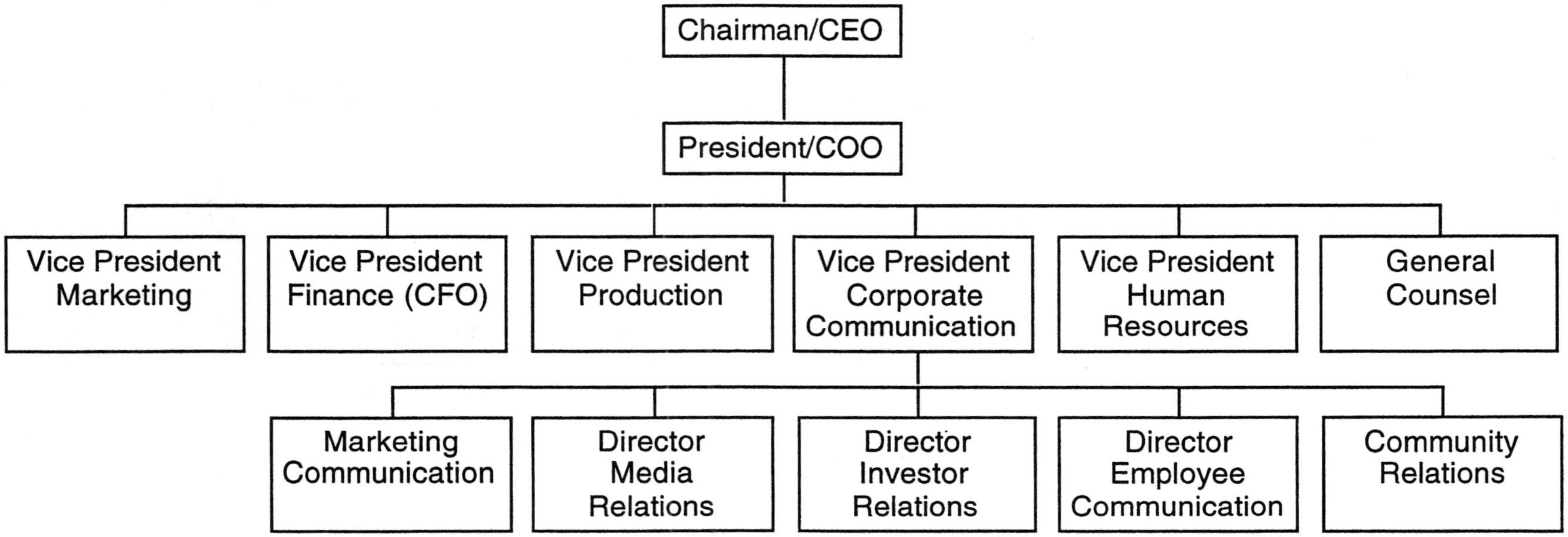

- Chairman/CEO
  - President/COO
    - Vice President Marketing
      - Marketing Communication
    - Vice President Finance (CFO)
    - Vice President Production
      - Director Media Relations
    - Vice President Corporate Communication
      - Director Investor Relations
    - Vice President Human Resources
      - Director Employee Communication
    - General Counsel
      - Community Relations

Functions Within the Function

Corporate image and identity
- corporate advertising
- corporate advocacy

Marketing communications

Media relations

Financial communications
- investor relations
- shareholder relations

Employee communications

Corporate philanthropy

Government relations
- lobbying

Community relations

Chapter 4 OHTs

Image and Identity

- What are image and identity?
- Building a solid reputation
- Is corporate identity a trend?
- How can you differentiate based on image and identity?
- How do you manage the unmanageable?

Managing the Unmanageable

Step 1: Conduct an identity audit

Step 2: Set identity objectives

Step 3: Develop designs and names

Step 4: Develop prototypes

Step 5: Launch and communicate

Step 6: Implement the program

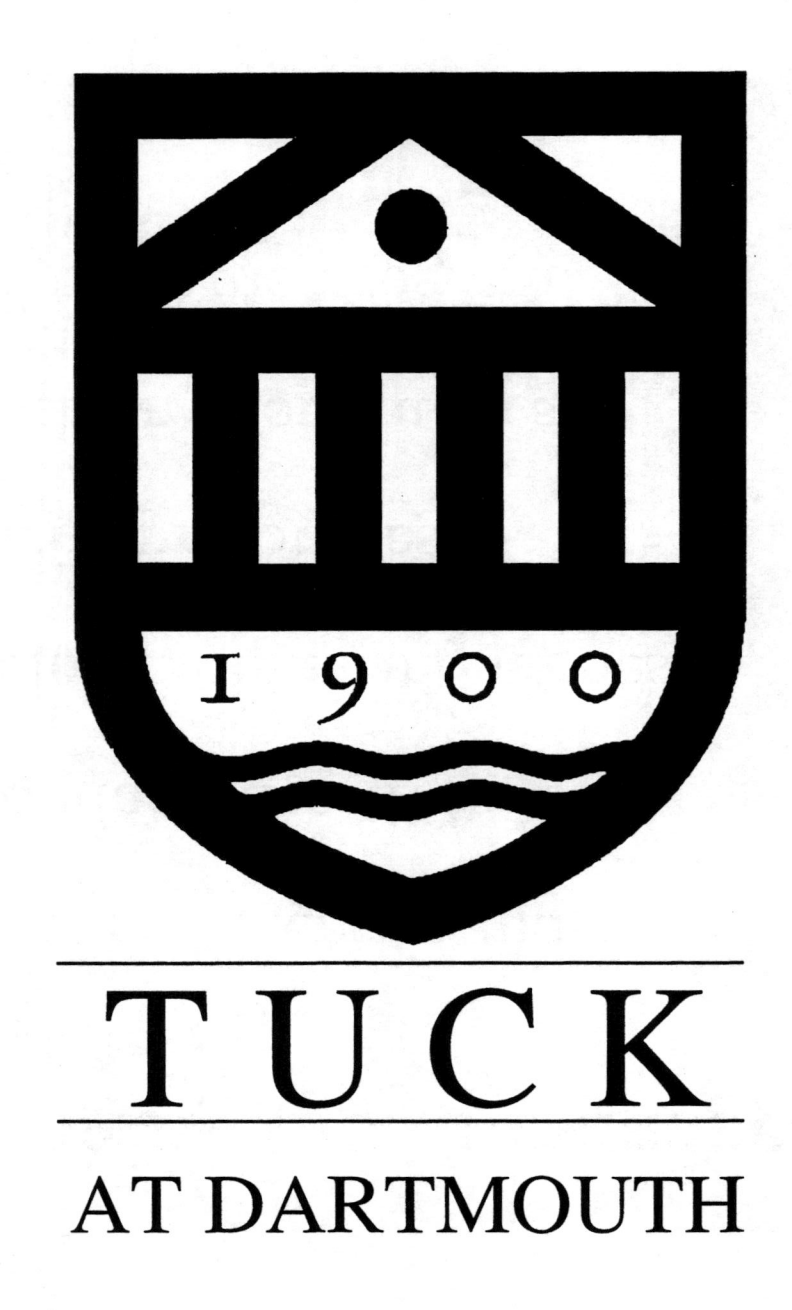

TUCK
AT DARTMOUTH

Chapter 5 OHTs

The Corporation is the Message

What is Corporate Advertising?

Where does it come from?

Who uses it and why?

Should all companies use corporate advertising?

Companies Use Corporate Advertising To:

1. Increase Sales

2. Create Goodwill

3. Retain and Recruit Employees

4. Enhance the Financial Effort

Chapter 6 OHTs

No More Press Releases

1. What are the news media?

2. How do you build better relations with the media?

3. How do you create a successful media relations program?

Building Better Media Relations

- Conduct research
- Respond to calls
- Prepare for interviews
- Maintain ongoing relationships

Creating a Successful Media Relations Programs

- Involve internal media relations personnel in strategy

- Develop in-house capabilities

Media Interview Tips

- Keep answers short
- Avoid "No comment!" response
- Listen to each question
- Use "bridging" to move closer to your objective
- Use anecdotes
- Keep body language in mind

Chapter 7 OHTs

A Random Walk Down Wall Street

1. The Evolution of IR as a Function

2. Environmental Changes Shaping IR

3. Developing an Investor Relations Program

Investor Relations Overview

1. Types of Investors

2. Angle of Presentation

3. Valuation Methods

4. The IR Team

Stock Marketing

1. Basic qualities of an IR program

2. Disclosure issues

3. Credibility issues

Chapter 8 OHTs

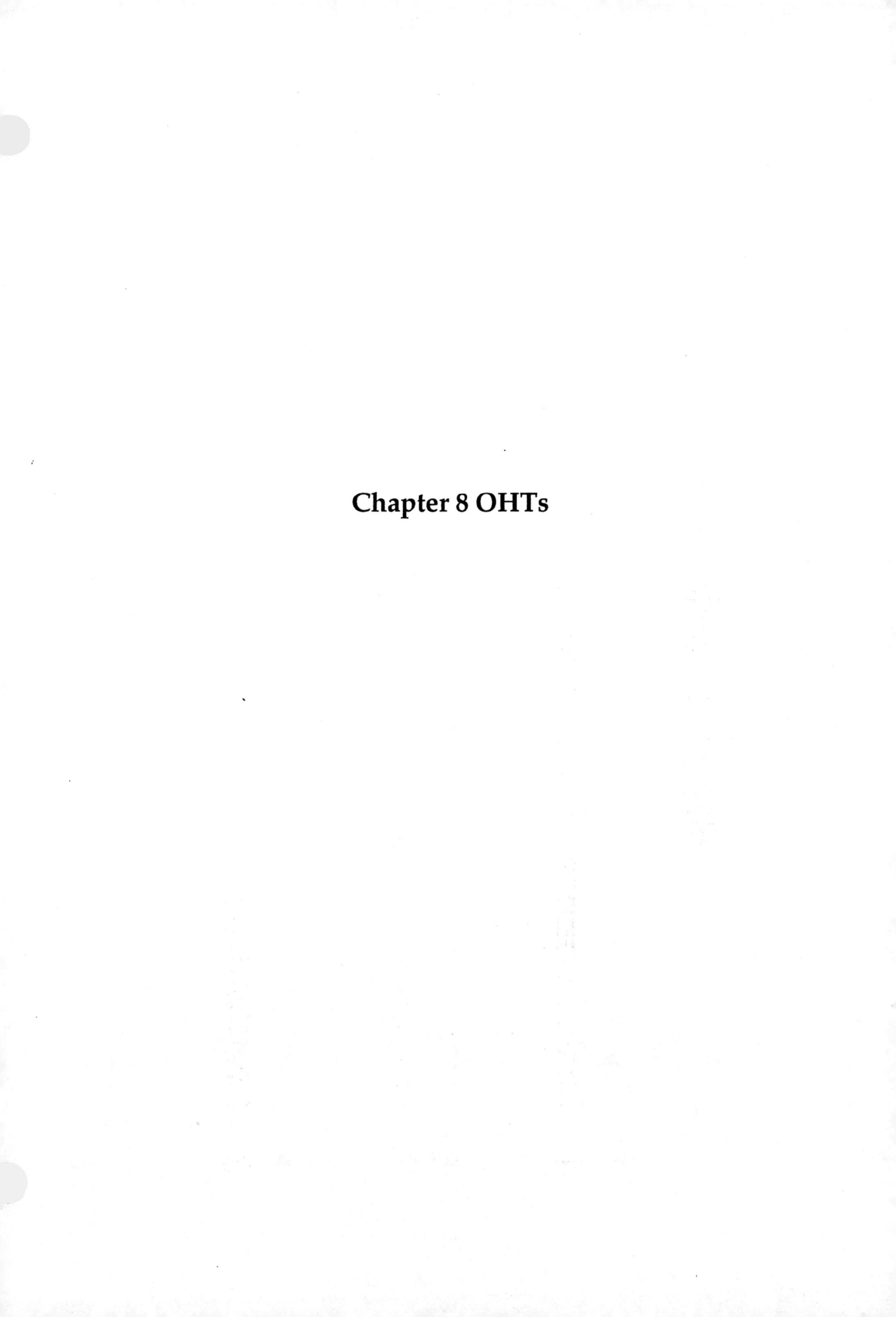

Communicating Internally

- Changes in the environment

- Organizing the internal effort

- Implementing an effective internal communications program

U.S. Workers Unhappy and Angry

25% are unhappy

25% are angry

CBS News Poll
Sept. 1996

Why Employees Take Jobs

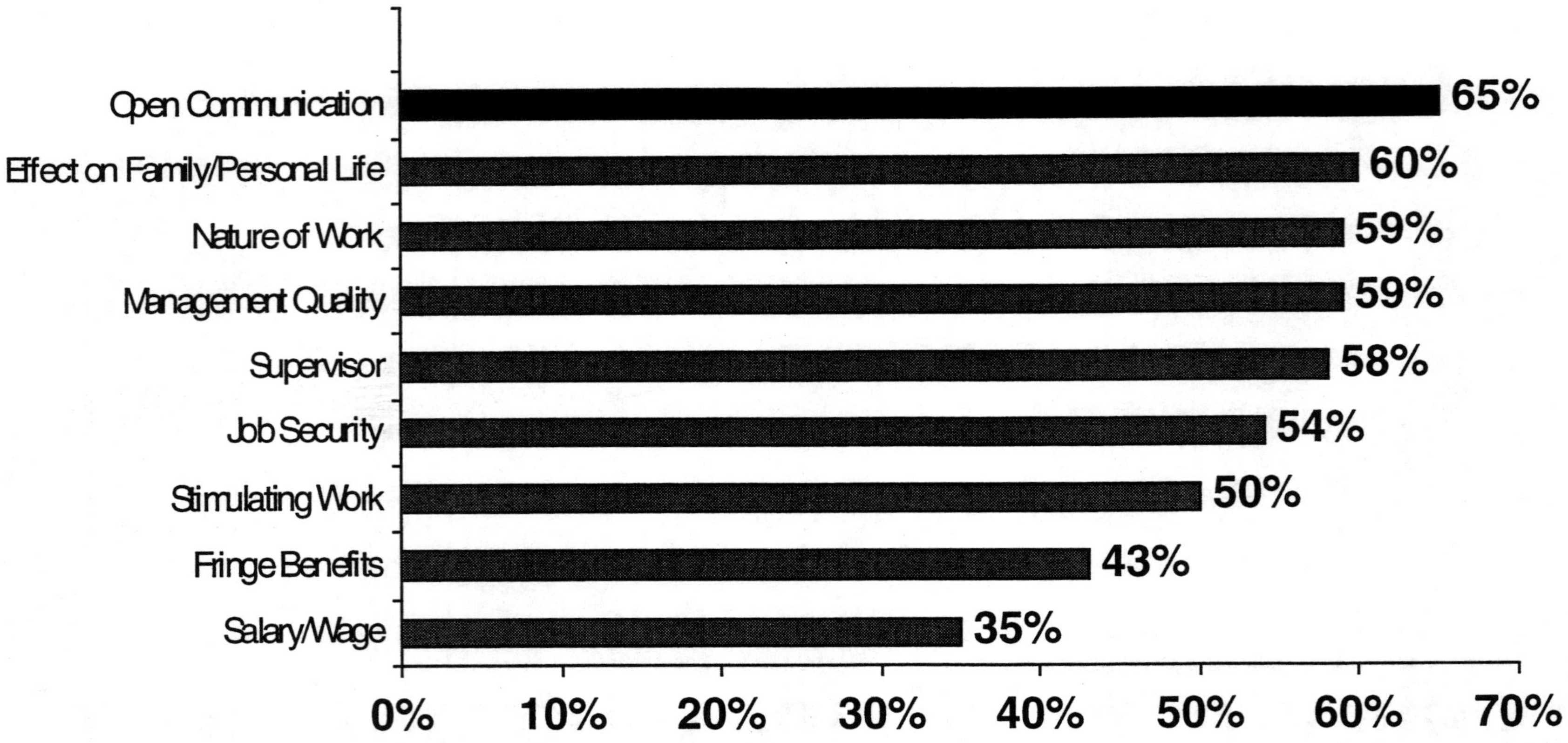

Factor	Percentage
Open Communication	65%
Effect on Family/Personal Life	60%
Nature of Work	59%
Management Quality	59%
Supervisor	58%
Job Security	54%
Stimulating Work	50%
Fringe Benefits	43%
Salary/Wage	35%

Source: National Study of the Changing Workforce, Families and Work Institute.

The wicked leader is he who people despise.

The good leader is he who the people revere.

The great leader is he who the people say,
"We did it ourselves."

— Lao Tsu

How to Succeeed with Employees

1. Create an atmosphere of respect.
2. Treat employees as insiders.
3. Build-up corporate loyalty: "Ambassadors of Commitment."
4. Capture more discretionary time.
5. Increase two-way communications.
6. Invest in decent publications.
7. Listen to and use the grapevine.

One-Way vs. Two-Way Communication

Figure 1

Elapsed Time	Perceived Accuracy	#	Actual Accuracy	#
	5 correct		5	
	4 correct		4	
	3 correct		3	
	2 correct		2	
	1 correct		1	

Figure 2

Elapsed Time	Perceived Accuracy	#	Actual Accuracy	#
	5 correct		5	
	4 correct		4	
	3 correct		3	
	2 correct		2	
	1 correct		1	

Chapter 9 OHTs

Managing Government Affairs

- The development of a regulator environment
- Effects of regulation on business
- Presidential involvement in business
- Business begins to manage government
- Modern government affairs offices

Companies Speak with One Voice

Management ⟶
Employees ⟶
Community ⟶
Government and Public Affairs ⟶

Message on Issues

Functions of DC Office

- Development of company position on issues
- Lobbying
- Administration of PACs
- Organize grassroots
- Education of employees

Legislative Issues

- Environment
- Forestry
- Tax & Trade
- Human Resources
- Energy, Transportation, etc.

Chapter 10 OHTs

What to Do When It Hits the Fan

1. What is a crisis?
   - crises in the 1980s and 1990s

2. How to prepare for crises

3. Communicating during the crisis

Communicating During the Crisis

Step 1: Get control

Step 2: Gather information

Step 3: Centralize communications

Step 4: Communicate early and often

Step 5: Remember that business must continue

Step 6: Make plans to avoid the next crisis

Dimension Control Matrix

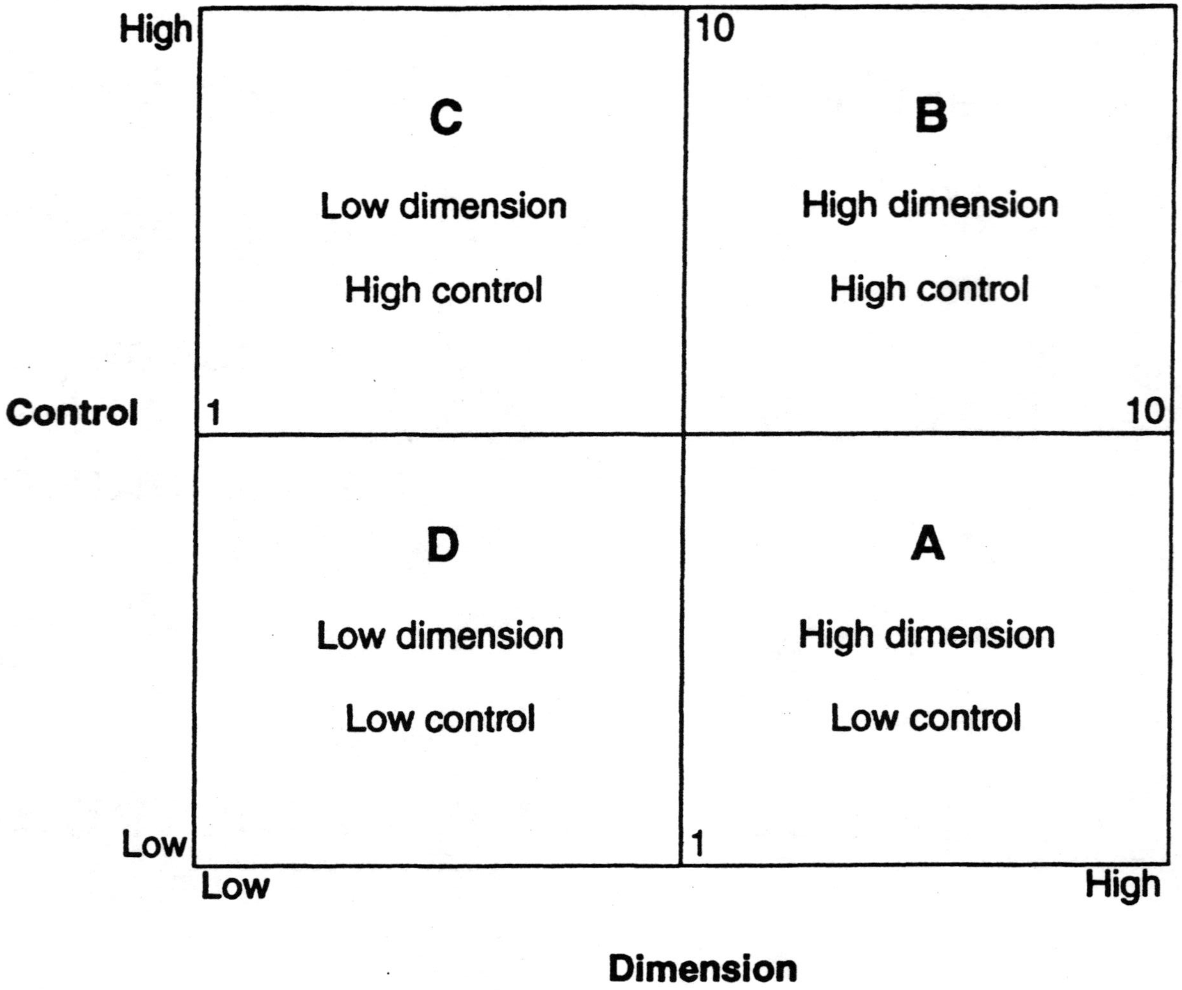

High	**C** Low dimension High control	**B** High dimension High control
Control		
Low	**D** Low dimension Low control	**A** High dimension Low control
	Low	High
		Dimension

APPENDIX 3

Additional Bibliography

Additional Readings for IM

Chapter 1: The Changing Business Environment

Abend, Jules. *Levi's, Claiborne, Kmart: Getting Refocused. The changing retail environment discussed at American Apparel Manufacturers Association's 1996 Outlook.* Bobbin, February 1997, p. 20

Cooper, Robert W. "The ethical environment facing the profession of purchasing and materials management," *International Journal of Purchasing and Materials Management*, Spring 1997, p. 2-11.

Hart, Stuart L. "Beyond greening: Strategies for a sustainable world," *Harvard Business Review*, January/February 1997, p. 66-76.

Krohe, James, Jr. "Ethics are nice, but business is business," *Across the Board*, April 1997, p. 16-22.

Luthar, Harsh K. "Perception of what the ethical climate is and what it should be: The role of gender, academic status, and ethical education," *Journal of Business Ethics*, February 1997, p. 205-17.

Chapter 2: Communicating Strategically

Munter, Mary. *Guide to Managerial Communication: Effective business writing and speaking.* 4th edition. Upper Saddle River, NJ: Prentice Hall, 1997.

Tucker, Mary L. "Organizational Communication: Development of internal strategic competitive advantage," *Journal of Business Communication*, January 1996 p. 51-69.

Chapter 3: Overview of the Corporate Communications Function

Argenti, Paul A. *The Fast Forward MBA Pocket Reference.* New York: Wiley, 1997.

Caywood, Clarke L. (ed.). *The Handbook of Strategic Public Relations and Integrated Communications.* New York: McGraw Hill, 1997.

Powers, Vicki J. "Internal Communications as a strategic function," *Strategy and Leadership*, March/April 1997, p. 44.

Chapter 4: Image and Identity

Haig, William and Laurel Haper. *The Power of Logos: How to Create Effective Company Logos*. New York: Van Nostrand Reinhold, 1997.

Landry, John T. "Corporate identity: Seek substance over style," *Harvard Business Review*, May/June 1997, p. 12-13.

Leuthesser, Lance. "Corporate identity: The role of mission statements," *Business Horizons*, May/June 1997, p. 59-66.

McCarthy, Michael. "Jaguar asks Ogilvy & Mather to create a 'common language': Global corporate identity assignment," *Adweek* (Eastern Edition), June 2, 1997, p. 5.

Rogers, Stuart C. "How to create a graphic identity for your practice," *The CPA Journal*, February 1997, p. 42-5.

Schmitt, Bernd H. *Marketing Aesthetics: The strategic management of brands, identity and image.* Free Press, 1997.

Chapter 5: Managing Corporate Advertising

Abugel, Jeff. "Ad Bust: Slowpoke marketers lose billions," *Business Marketing*, May 1997, p. 1.

Chapman, Lisbeth Wiley "A media-smart marketing strategy: Developing story ideas," *Journal of Financial Planning*, June 1997, p. 91-3

Freeman, Laurie. "1996 Business-to-business Agency of the Year: NKH&W wins award for its dedication to great creative, integrated marketing," *Business Marketing*, April 1997, p. 41-2.

Thurow, Roger. "In the global drive, Nike finds its brash ways don't always pay off," *Wall Street Journal*, May 5, 1997, p. A1.

Chapter 6: Managing Media Relations

Wolf, Allison Wheeler. *Making the Most of Media Mayhem*. Bobbin, February 1997, p. 74-5.

Chapter 7: Investor Relations

Courtis, John K. "Corporate annual report graphical communication in Hong Kong: Effective or misleading?" *Journal of Business Communication*, July 1997, p. 269-88.

Morrow, Edwin P. "Simplifying investment communication," *Journal of Financial Planning*, June 1997, p. 97.

Sosnoff, Martin. "Symbolism in financial reports," *Forbes*, May 19, 1997, p. 283.

Thomas, Jane. "Discourse in the marketplace: The making of meaning in annual reports," *Journal of Business Communication*, January 1997, p. 47-66.

Toth, Debora. "The art of business," *Graphic Arts Monthly*, Febrary 1997, p. 95.

Wildstrom, Stephen H. "Surfing for annual reports," *Business Week*, April 14, 1997, p. 22.

Chapter 8: Employee Communications

Bachman, Karen. "Does anybody do it better? Honeywell's internal communication program; speech adaptation," *Across the Board*, January 1997 p. 55.

Bonvillian, Gary. "Managing the messages of change: Lessons from the field," *Industrial Management*, January/Febrary 1997, p. 20-5

Crowley, Ginger. "Dialoging: Transmitting the right message," *Employment Relations Today*, Winter 1997, p. 11-20.

Mariotti, John. "Stealth Management: How do you respond to 'clueless' commands?" *IW: The Management Magazine*, Febrary 17, 1997, p. 38

Milburn, Trudy. "Bridging cultural gaps; communication aspects," *Management Review*, January 1997, p. 26-9

Milligan, Patricia A. "Are you sending a one-sided message? From the new deal in employee relationships," *Across the Board*, Febrary 1997, p. 57.

Pettit, John D., Jr. "An examination of organizational communication as a moderator of the relationship between job performance and job satisfaction," *Journal of Business Communication*, January 1997 p. 81-98.

Robbins, Alan. "E-mail: Lean, mean and making its mark," *New York Times* (Late New York Edition), May 11, 1997, section 3 p. 13.

Sheikh, Fawzia. "Something lost in the translation: Companies that go global can run into big problems just communicating with their own employees," *Marketing* (Maclean Hunter), February 24, 1997, p. 14.

Waddell, Janet R. "Communication styles: Are we overstating things just a tad?" *Supervision*, January 1997, p. 11

Wainwright, Arthur D. "People-first strategies get implemented," *Strategy and Leadership*, January/ February 1997, p. 13-17

Weiss, Donald. *Saying the wrong things at the wrong time.* Getting Results—for the Hands-on Manager, v. 42, p. 2.

Chapter 9: Government Affairs

Boege, Robert S. "ASAE Government Affairs: Issues and Actions," *Association Management*, January 1996, Suppliment Leadership, p. L82-L84.

Wilson, Caroline. "Charter issues, credit unions drive debate at America's Community Bankers' Government Affairs Conference, Washington, D.C.," *America's Community Banker*, v. 6 (Apr. 1997) p. 8-9.

Chapter 10: Managing Communications in a Crisis

Albrecht, Steven. *Crisis Management for Corporate Self-Defense: How to protect your organization in a crisis—how to stop a crisis before it starts.* New York: American Management Association, 1996.

Benoit, William L. "Image repair discourse and crisis communication," *Public Relations Review*, Summer 1997, p. 177-86

Footlick, Jerrold K. *Truth and Consequences: How colleges and universities meet public crises.* Phoenix: Oryx Press, 1997.

Noecker, Stephanie. "Forging ahead: Foseco capitalizes on steel exports and turns the crisis to its advantage," *Business Mexico*, v. 6/7 Special Issue 1997, p. 26-8.

Sutter, Mary. "Leaving the crisis behind: IBM readies itself for the recovery," *Business Mexico*, v. 6/7 Special Issue 1997, p. 30-2